THE
HOMEFRONT

THE
HOMEFRONT

AMERICA DURING WORLD WAR II

Mark Jonathan Harris
Franklin D. Mitchell
Steven J. Schechter

G. P. PUTNAM'S SONS
New York

The authors gratefully acknowledge the following sources for permission to
quote from material in its control:

The University of Southern California for excerpts of the oral history
interviews in this book. The University of Southern California retains
exclusive ownership of all copyrights to the interviews.

Irving Berlin Music Corporation for an excerpt from "This Is the Army,
Mr. Jones!" by Irving Berlin at page 46. © Copyright 1942, Irving Berlin;
© Copyright renewed 1970, Irving Berlin; © Copyright assigned to Mrs.
Ralph J. Bunche, Joe DiMaggio and Theodore R. Jackson as Trustees of
God Bless America Fund. Reprinted by permission of Irving Berlin Music
Corporation.

Library of Congress Cataloging in Publication Data

Main entry under title: The Homefront

1. United States—History—1933–1945—Addresses, essays, lectures. 2.
World War, 1939–1945—United States—Addresses, essays, lectures. 3.
United States—Biography—Addresses, essays, lectures. 4. United States—
Social conditions—1933–1945—Addresses, essays, lectures. I. Harris,
Mark Jonathan, date. II. Mitchell, Franklin D. III. Schechter, Steven J.
E806.H64   1984   973.917   83-16088
ISBN 0-399-12899-9

Designed by Richard Oriolo

Printed in the United States of America

ACKNOWLEDGMENTS

For their generous support of the research for this book, we thank the National Endowment for the Humanities, the California Council for the Humanities, and the University of Southern California.

We also want to thank Pamela Cedar for organizing the photographs and Joyce Compton, Carol Denker, Shirley Green, Nancy Rosenblum, Judith Skeldon, and Mark Suffrin for their diligent archival research. Ellen Baskin, Karen Croner, Rene Kirby, and Paul Mindrup were extremely helpful in conducting preliminary interviews; and Ben Shedd helped enrich this book by directing many of the interviews for the Homefront film.

Our special appreciation goes to the thirty-seven persons whose memories and reflections of life on the homefront appear in this book.

*For the many people who graciously shared their
World War II experiences with us*

CONTENTS

INTRODUCTION
by Studs Terkel

Aside from the Civil War, the two most traumatic epochs in American history were the Great Depression and World War II. The face of our country—indeed, of the world—was inexorably changed. For better and for worse. What is even more singular is that the end of one, the Depression, came with the beginning of the other, the German invasion of Poland; 1939 was the end and the beginning.

True, the New Deal created jobs and restored self-esteem for millions of Americans. Still, there were ten million walking the streets, riding the rods, up against it, despairing. All this changed under the lowering sky of World War II. What had been a country psychically as well as geographically isolated became, with the suddenness of a thunderclap, a society engaged with distant troubles.

Our huge industrial machine shifted gears, as it were: ploughshares were beaten into swords (or their twentieth-century equivalents, tanks, mortars, planes, bombs). In the words of President Franklin D. Roosevelt, Dr. New Deal was replaced by Dr. Win the War.

As millions of young men, from farms, small towns and big cities, became instant warriors in alien lands, the women back home left home, for at least eight hours a day (or night), to do what hitherto had been exclusively men's work. The great many of them "manned" defense plants. For the first time in their lives, they brought home a paycheck. Though at war's end these newborn working women were urged, as their patriotic duty, to go back home "where they naturally belonged" and give their jobs back to the boys who did their patriotic duty Over

There, the taste for independence was never really lost. Like Wrigley's Chewing Gum, its flavor was longer lasting, no matter what the official edict. Millions of these women were forever changed by their work experiences during World War II. As a matter of course, family life was never to be the same. For millions, their home would never again be a Doll's House.

War's harsh necessities affected another group as well: the blacks. Though the armed services were segregated and black GI's, with rare exceptions, were restricted to labor batallions, at home it was somewhat different. As with women, their muscles and skills were needed in the defense plants. The perverse imperatives of war brought about relatively well-paying jobs for black men and women, who would otherwise have been regarded with less than benign neglect. Still, even this might not have come about were it not for constant pressure from black organizations and labor leaders.

Wartime "prosperity" extended into a period of postwar prosperity, with America becoming the most powerful industrial as well as military power in the world. Its exports were now truly worldwide as well as its politics. The GI Bill, the emergence of the Consumer, the springing up of a new kind of housing development—the blue-collar suburb—inalterably changed conditions in life as well as attitudes. Despite the valleys of poverty that still existed in Appalachia and the dark ghettoes of the cities and among the neglected old, an air of self-satisfaction and righteousness pervaded until, at least, our misadventure in Vietnam. For though we were profoundly affected by World War II, the great many of us never understood its horrendous nature. The obscenity of war itself had never really been visited upon us.

True, 300,000 young Americans were killed and countless millions maimed in this epochal victory over fascism; and an inconsolable grief possessed their families; and parks, squares and streets were named after these heroes, sung and unsung. Yet, most of us were unwounded and untouched.

Ours was the only combatant country that was not invaded; ours were the only cities that were not bombed and made into rubble. The Soviet Union, our ally in World War II, lost twenty million. (Harrison Salisbury figures it was closer to thirty million.) Not a family was untouched. Britain was blitzed, and air raid shelters became as familiar as the tea break. German cities were fire-bombed. Need we mention Hiroshima and Nagasaki?

With the power of a thousand suns lighting up the two Japanese cities, World War II has left us—the U.S., the U.S.S.R. and a fast-growing company of other nuclear-possessed nations—with a new kind of legacy: the capacity to blow up the planet and write finis to the history of our species.

In the pages that follow are the testaments of American homefront survivors of World War II: their remembrances of what it was like in the States from 1941 to 1945, of lessons learned and lessons yet to be learned. In some cases, these were the best years of their lives; in others, the worst. In all instances, it was a time indelibly remembered.

THE
HOMEFRONT

·1·

PEARL HARBOR:
A DAY TO REMEMBER

Yesterday, December 7, 1941—a day that will live in
infamy—the United States of America was suddenly and
deliberately attacked by naval and air forces of the Empire of
Japan.

—President Franklin D. Roosevelt,
Address to Congress, December 8, 1941

I knew that this was a turning point, that our lives would
never be the same again.

—Edward Osberg

During the 1930s, the powerful forces of isolationism and pacifism combined to keep the United States at peace. Reflecting the popular mood, Congress enacted neutrality laws and appropriated little money for the Army and the Navy. In 1939, the U.S. Army ranked thirty-ninth in the world, had a cavalry force of fifty thousand, and still used horses to pull its artillery. The U.S. Navy, with two oceans to patrol, lacked parity with Japan in the Pacific.

American policies, however, began to change with the outbreak of war in Europe in September 1939 and the drive by Japan to establish a Greater East Asia Co-Prosperity Sphere. Congress, at the urging of President Franklin D. Roosevelt, revised the existing neutrality legislation to permit the Western democracies and China to obtain

National Archives

war supplies on a "cash and carry" basis. Hitler's conquests in 1940 and the threat Nazi Germany posed to Great Britain led Roosevelt to provide the British with fifty destroyers in exchange for bases in the Western Hemisphere. At the same time, Congress sharply increased appropriations for the national defense and provided for the drafting of men into the Army. In March 1941, Congress passed the Lend-Lease Act, which in the course of the war would provide more than $50 billion of economic and military aid to our beleaguered allies. The shipment of vital supplies to Europe invited attack from Hitler's submarine fleet and provided the occasion for war between the United States and Germany. A state of quasiwar actually existed between the two countries in the Atlantic after July 1941. Yet Hitler, wisely showing restraint, did not declare war against the United States. He did not take that step until December 11, 1941, a few days after the U.S. was attacked by Japan.

Similarly, Japan was bent upon the establishment of an Asian empire that she deemed appropriate for a modern industrial nation, and she did not want war with the United States, either. The Japanese government hoped that diplomacy would secure American acceptance of its new order in Asia. The United States, however, fashioned diplomatic and economic weapons against Japan, starting with a policy of nonrecognition of the Japanese conquest of Manchuria in the early 1930s. Japan's war on the mainland of China after 1937 and its designs on Southeast Asia after 1940 challenged American economic interests. The U.S. responded by abrogating a commercial treaty with Japan, imposing an embargo on scrap iron and oil, and freezing Japanese assets in the United States in 1941. These acts, coupled with Japan's determination to establish its empire, led the two into a diplomatic impasse that would only be resolved by war.

In the last few days of peace, official Washington and informed Americans who had followed the news of the deteriorating relations between the United States and Japan realized that war was imminent. The Japanese strike would come, it was believed, on British or Dutch territory or a neutral Southeast Asian nation. A war-alert message was transmitted from Washington to Hawaii on December 6, 1941, but no American official from President Roosevelt on down believed that a Japanese strike on Pearl Harbor was within the realm of possibility.

Thus the Japanese attack on Pearl Harbor on Sunday, December 7, 1941, came as a stunning surprise. The assault force of torpedo planes and bombers that were launched from Japanese carriers about three hundred miles from Hawaii swept in shortly after dawn, sinking or damaging eight battleships, three destroyers and three cruisers. The extent of the damage and the loss of more than 2,300 lives compounded the country's shock and incredulity and provoked indignation, fear and an intense desire for revenge. Isolationism and pacifism died practically overnight.

Americans of all ages who were living on that Sunday knew intuitively that the nation had come to a turning point in its history. They knew that the war would alter the course of both their lives and the life of the nation.

This book recounts the triumphs and tragedies of the war years through the recollections of a cross section of ordinary Americans from all parts of the nation. In editing the oral interviews for this book we have retained the flavor of spoken rather than written English. The interviews, together with the photographs and posters of that period, chronicle an era of extraordinary events that many Americans still regard as the most significant of their lives.

MARJORIE CARTWRIGHT

I graduated from high school in 1941 and started to look for work, but there were no jobs of any kind to be had. I lived in Clarksburg, West Virginia, a small town—around forty thousand people. The factories were working with skeleton crews, and no one was hiring. If a person wanted to go to Pittsburgh or Baltimore or Philadelphia or some of the larger cities and take a job, they could generally find something there. My boyfriend had already left Clarksburg to join the Navy, but I was seventeen and I didn't want to leave my hometown. My parents didn't approve of my leaving, either. They preferred that I try to find something around home, but it was very difficult.

Finally, I got so discouraged I went to see a psychic who lived in Clarksburg, to find out when the Depression would end, when I would be able to find a job. She said to me, "Something terrible is going to happen to this country before the leaves are green again. Your boyfriend is going to be involved in this tragedy. Something terrible is going to happen to him, but he will come through it. Go home and tell his mother that something will happen to him, but not to worry about her son. She will hear from him in a few months.

"Also be sure to send him the Ninety-first Psalm* to say every day and night.

---

*"He that dwelleth in the secret place of the Most High shall abide under the shadow of the Almighty . . . A thousand shall fall at thy side, and ten thousand at thy right hand, but it shall not come nigh thee."—PSALMS 91:1,7.

Pearl Harbor: A Day to Remember • 21

Tell him to memorize that and don't forget to say it."

She told me, "This is going to be one of the worst tragedies that will ever befall our country, but don't worry, our country is going to be victorious."

At the time I didn't know what she was talking about. It was all a mystery to me. Several months later, of course, Pearl Harbor was bombed and I understood. My boyfriend's ship had been at sea and had come into Pearl the night before the Japanese attacked. He was on a heavy cruiser, and the larger cruisers were anchored in the outlying part of the harbor. When the Japanese struck, naturally they bombed the interior of the harbor and all the installations. While the bombing was going on, the ships on the outside of the harbor got up steam and set out in search of the Japanese Navy. They were at sea a month before anyone heard from him. We contacted the Red Cross, but they were unable to find him, either. Because of what the psychic had said, though, I never lost hope that he was alive.

JOHN GROVE

On Saturday, December 6, 1941, my sister and I were visiting my mother and four younger brothers at their little farm home near Sebastopol in California's Russian River country. All evening we sat around an ancient radio, listening to news reports of Japanese naval activity between the Hawaiian Islands, Guam and the Philippines. There was a steady stream of these reports coming in, but officials seemed to be regarding them as inconsequential. As our family talked about it, we could see a parallel with the reports from Western Europe that had flooded the newspapers a week before the German invasion of Russia that June. Moscow had denied then that anything warlike was going on. They kept saying, "We have a treaty with Germany, and nothing's going to happen." After a week of these denials, the Nazi blitz-

krieg was launched against an unprepared U.S.S.R. Now we were hearing the same kind of reports over the radio.

About midnight we all concluded, "Within twenty-four hours the Japanese are going to attack us. Maybe Honolulu, possibly the Philippines, maybe Guam, maybe all three places, but somewhere. That's all that the imminence of this warlike activity can mean.

The next day around noon, I was driving through Vallejo on my way back to Berkeley. My route passed right by Mare Island Navy Yard, and I was stunned when I saw uniformed men and vehicles scrambling in mass confusion on the waterfront facing the island. Hundreds of military personnel were just milling aimlessly around. Others were streaming on board little ferries over to the island. I knew something was very wrong, and I turned on my car radio and, of course, learned the terrible news. It didn't take very long before I also realized that it came as a complete surprise to the military. To this day it's something I haven't gotten over. How could we, just dumb civilians, figure this one out, and yet the military be asleep?

Only later, much later, did it become known that American military commanders and the President's aides had been unbelievably negligent. I think there may be another partial explanation: We Americans were basically racist in our attitudes toward the Japanese. Because most prewar Japanese exports of manufactured goods to this country were shoddy imitations of quality U.S. or European articles, it was not surprising that Americans felt that "Jap" ships, planes, tanks and guns were of poor quality and that, by extension, the American fighting men were also superior. An all-too-common American expression in 1941 was, "We can beat those Japs with one hand tied behind our backs." The racism was even worse than the grammar. Another example was an article in a respected U.S. aviation magazine in the summer of 1941 which declared that Japanese military pilots would have no chance against our pilots because all Japanese had poor eyesight. I read that stupid article.

EDWARD OSBERG

That Sunday my wife and I were having dinner at my father and mother's home in Chicago. My sister, who had just recently been married, and her husband were also there. I turned on the radio about one-thirty in the afternoon, just as Mother called us to come to the dining room to have dinner.

I got so excited when the announcer broke through that we delayed our dinner for half an hour. We ate in a state of shock. I was an avid reader of the newspapers and had seen the portents that something was going to explode somewhere, but I didn't know how or when, and, of course, I didn't expect Pearl Harbor. When it came, it was a tremendous shock.

I knew that this was a turning point, that our lives would never be the same again.

BARBARA NOREK

Every Sunday our family went to the movies, the matinee. Abbott and Costello was my father's favorite. I never could stand them, but nevertheless we would all go. On December 7 my mother and father and my two younger sisters and I were all in the car on the way to the movies when the announcement came over the radio that Pearl Harbor had been bombed.

"Oh, my God, we've got to go home," my dad says.

Of course in the back seat there was this uproar from the kids. "We want to see Abbott and Costello."

"We can't," my father says. "Pearl Harbor has been bombed."

"What's a Pearl Harbor?" we all wanted to know.

"When I get home I'll get out the

Buildings are sandbagged against the threat of bombing.

Wide World Photos

atlas and see if I can tell you about it."

Actually I don't ever remember him telling us where it was. The only thing I recall was that I didn't go to the movies that day. The following week they closed down the schools in Berkeley, and everybody rushed around and bought blackout paper to glue over the windows to keep the light from showing. It was all very exciting because it was something different than what had been a sort of dull existence. Suddenly things were happening. People were panicking, my mother was crying that the end of the world was coming. It was exhilarating.

BARBARA DE NIKE

My husband and I spent that Sunday at the Cloisters, an art museum in New York. On the way back to our apartment in the Bronx, we stopped at an ice-cream store that he had gone to as a boy and wanted me to see. That's when we heard the news.

The owner of the ice-cream parlor was a German who had been in World War I, and he was extremely distraught. There were young people forming little lines and marching in and out of the ice-cream store, singing in almost a tone of celebration. I remember the owner standing there saying, "They just don't know what they're doing." It really was very striking.

I hadn't been married terribly long and was pregnant, so I was very upset. My first thought was what was it going to do to us as a family.

RACHEL WRAY

In August 1941 I had come out to Whittier, California, from Oklahoma to join my boyfriend, who was in the Navy. George came home in September, but the news was a little bit touchy with Japan, so he was called back after a week. In December he was going to take a thirty-day leave and we were going to make arrangements to get married. The day that he left San Francisco to hitchhike down to Whittier, Pearl Harbor was attacked. When he and his buddy arrived at seven o'clock that night, there was a telegram waiting for them at George's mother's house asking them to come back. They left at seven the next morning. I saw him again for three days in June when the ship took on provisions in San Diego, then I didn't see him until June of 1944.

DON JOHNSON

The day of Pearl Harbor my wife and I were away for a Sunday trip, about forty miles from our home in Flint, Michigan. There was an immediate concern—uncertainty, panic, a feeling that you needed somehow to seek a place where you'd be protected. We got in our car and quickly started that forty-mile trip back home, knowing that was the best thing to do, to get home where you felt safe, where you'd have proper communications. I remember our feelings on the trip back. First it was indignation, then it turned to anger, and by the time one went to work the following morning it was determination: "They can't do that to us."

MARGARET TAKAHASHI

It was Sunday morning in Los Angeles when we heard the news. We were too shocked to go to mass. At first we just didn't believe it. It was one of those things that are beyond belief. Then when people started calling, and we were pretty sure it was true, we were upset and angry and outraged.

Later we started to worry and become uneasy, but I thought the war would be over in a couple of weeks and everything would be all right again. I just couldn't believe it when it kept dragging on. In fact, Japan seemed to be winning, and that was hard to believe. We had this feeling that America was so invincible. Compared to the United States, Japan was like an appendix, and suddenly it had burst.

HENRY MURAKAMI

On December 7 I was umpiring a baseball game for the younger boys on the playground on Terminal Island, and we got through late. We were the last boat to go out fishing that afternoon. When we reached the lighthouse on San Pedro, all of a sudden we met the Coast Guard. They came up to us and said,

"Go back to the port and stay there until further notice."

We didn't know what was happening. We hadn't done anything wrong. But they wouldn't tell us anything. So we came back to the fish harbor. It wasn't until we got off the dock and heard all the radios that we understood why the Coast Guard had sent us back.

DELLIE HAHNE

At the time of Pearl Harbor I was twenty-one, a music major at Santa Barbara State College. That Sunday I was having breakfast with friends. Somebody turned on the radio and flipped through the dial. We didn't catch the actual words that the announcer said, but the voice was so tense, so full of emotion, that we all froze.

I was absolutely stunned. My mother had told me how she had felt when war was declared in 1917. I thought, My God, it's happening to me. Then came the hideous fear that the bombers would come and we'd all be killed. It was a horrible moment.

In an incredibly short time—it seemed to be almost a matter of moments—a wave of patriotism swept the country. As we drove home we felt, This is our country, and we're going to fight to defend it. When we got home that evening we were glued to the radio. "The Star-Spangled Banner" was played, and everyone in the room automatically rose. And we were disillusioned college students—the 1940s version of the 1960s kids. The outward show of patriotism was something that I had always sneered at, but we all stood and we all tingled. So the fervor started right off the bat. It was like a disease, and we all caught it.

The next day we all returned to classes, but there was a Japanese student in my art class who stayed in her room and was afraid to leave because of the attack. The art teacher mentioned this to us, and we all thought, Well, she should. We had no understanding, no pity, no tolerance. She was a Jap and that was that.

WILLIAM PEFLEY

I was working in the navy yard in Portsmouth, Virginia, when Pearl Harbor was bombed. We were in the office that Sunday where we always caught the news on the radio about what was going on in Europe. And when we heard about the bombing, we immediately went out of the shop and told the others, and everybody said, "Let's get to work and get these damn ships out and get them Japs."

Overnight there was a complete change in attitude. We weren't just helping England anymore; we were helping ourselves. Now it was our war.

So everybody decided, "No matter what the hours may be, let's get the ships out. Whatever we can do to help this war effort, we are going to do." And from that point on, we started working ten, twelve, sixteen hours at a stretch.

HENRY FIERING

It was about two-thirty in the afternoon. I was home reading in my living room when the news came over the radio. I'm sure my reaction wasn't any different from millions of Americans. I was stunned. I felt hopelessness, anger, uncertainty. I had been in the midst of organizing a shop in Cleveland, and I was due down there the next morning, but I took no union leaflets and had no intention of organizing. I'll never forget the somber mood of the workers as they came in. The only thing on anybody's mind was the war, the possible war.

· 2 ·

A NATION ON THE MOVE

"Go west," that was the theme. "Everything is great in California, all doors are open, no prejudice, good jobs, plenty of money."

—SYBIL LEWIS

When Germany plunged Europe into war in September 1939, America was still struggling to overcome the ravages of the Great Depression. Although the United States was no longer on the verge of social collapse, for many people life was still overwhelmingly bleak. More than seventeen percent of the labor force—almost ten million people—remained unemployed. Countless others had long since given up even the pretense of looking for work. Few who had suffered the despair and deprivation of the thirties could feel optimistic about the future.

The fall of France in 1940 spurred the United States to begin a modest defense effort. Despite America's reluctance to become involved in the European war, the country welcomed the boost that defense spending gave to the economy. People began to migrate to defense sites in search of jobs.

After Pearl Harbor, the government launched a massive spending campaign to convert to a full-scale war economy. Suddenly work was available for almost anyone who sought it. For millions who had suffered the unemployment and underemployment of the Depression,

the war was a time of opportunity. It has been estimated that as many as twenty million Americans—about 15 percent of the population—left their homes to find employment. From the mill towns of New England to the hollows of Appalachia, from the scrub land of Texas to the shantytowns of Atlanta, Americans embarked on a mass migration for jobs. Hill folks from Tennessee learned to forge steel in the giant mills of Indiana; Midwestern farm girls discovered how to rivet in the burgeoning aircraft factories of Los Angeles; sharecroppers from rural Georgia found themselves wielding acetylene torches in the vast shipyards of Mobile, Alabama.

Military service also uprooted millions of men and women. As they left the farms and the cities and crowded into military posts, naval bases and air stations, they strained the capacity of the civilian sector of the economy. Their numbers swelled when wives and children joined uniformed husbands and fathers and took up residences close to military centers.

Wherever a defense plant or a new military base was erected, the town, especially if it was small, was almost immediately overwhelmed. In 1942 more than 80,000 new workers invaded Mobile. On the West Coast 126,000 flooded San Diego, doubling its

population within three years. Within a few months the backwater town of Seneca, Illinois, quintupled its population of 1,200.

Most cities were unable to cope with the massive influx of people. Schools, transportation and public-health facilities were all overburdened. Housing was particularly scarce, and rents climbed sharply until the Office of Price Administration imposed a ceiling on rental housing. In the first year of the war local residents turned garages into apartments, warehouses into dormitories, their homes into rooming houses. In some towns beds were in such short supply that they were rented out three shifts a day. In many communities shantytowns sprang up outside city limits. These squalid camps of trailers and temporary shelters had no sanitation and waste disposal and became breeding grounds for disease.

The federal government attacked these problems by building low-cost public housing for defense workers and attempting to provide other help for besieged communities, but the government's efforts could not keep pace with the mushrooming growth of defense centers. Although hardships, shortages and crowded conditions were a fact of life throughout the war years, most people took them in stride and good humor. Complainers were met with the universal retort "Don't you know there's a war going on?"

LAURA BRIGGS

I was born in 1930 and grew up on a 120-acre farm just outside of Jerome, Idaho. Prior to the war we lived pretty much as people had since 1900. Farmers still relied heavily on horses. In fact, I can still hear my father out in his fields screaming at his team. In 1937 we finally got electricity and a refrigerator, but we had no indoor plumbing.

When I was growing up, it was very much depression times. My father was working fourteen hours a day and he wasn't really making any progress economically. He couldn't even make the payments on the farm. There was just no money anywhere.

In August of 1940 my mother was expecting a baby, but because we had no money my parents decided they couldn't afford a hospital. The baby was born at home and didn't survive because there were birth complications. It could have easily survived with competent medical care in a hospital. This shook my parents very much, and they got discouraged and depressed.

My mother's brother, a rather adventuresome type, had been having struggles on the farm, so he went to California. He heard of big money—the defense plants opening up. That's all people talked about. Then Pearl

Harbor happened, and there seemed like an immediate upgrading of energy in the country. Before this you couldn't really see yourself in a different area, in a different situation. Now you could see something else—hey, we can go out to California and get some big money no matter what. Neither my father nor my mother had ever been off the farm before, but they decided to sell as much as they could, pack up the rest and move to California.

We had a farm sale and sold everything, the old threadworn carpets off the floor, even the linoleum—it was scarce and brought a big price, cracked and broken as it was. We made enough for my father to pay off his land. He rented the farm to his brother, and with the few dollars we had left we started for California.

We had a '41 Chevy, a black five-passenger coupe, two-door. There was my mother and father, myself, my eight-and-a-half-year-old brother, and my baby brother who had just been born. My father found an old homemade-type trailer that we loaded to the gills with the necessities, clothes and bedding. That was it. We were on the road for a couple of days, and I think my baby brother screamed all the way from Idaho to California. He wasn't very excited about this, but we were. We were on our way to the golden land. I can just see us standing up and fighting and driving my mother crazy with "When are we going to be there? What's it going to be like? Can we stop?" It was traumatic for my parents, but we thought it was marvelous. We thought we were going to Paradise.

We crossed the desert into California, and finally we saw some palm trees and some orange trees—which was pretty exciting. Then we hit the Los Angeles traffic, and my father completely panicked. He said, "No white man in the world can live in a place like this!"

We arrived at my uncle's house in Long Beach, California, and my daddy started looking for work. Daddy was very intelligent and a good farm manager, but he didn't have a formal education. He didn't even know how to fill out a job application. I remember he went to one of the plants, and this personnel manager got rather exasperated because Daddy just seemed so out of place there. Daddy said, "I can't answer all these questions, I haven't done any of this stuff, I don't even know what this means. What's a degree?" We didn't think of ourselves as *Grapes of Wrath*. We thought of ourselves as first class anywhere. We still do. Finally the manager said, "Well, Mr. Hansen, just what can you do? I'm willing to help you out. We need men." My dad says, "I can dig the best goddamn ditch you'll ever see in your life." So they liked him and put him to work as a laborer.

After we moved to Long Beach I was enrolled in school, and I took note the first day that things were going to be pretty different. It really was something of a culture shock. There were a lot of farm people there like us who had come from Texas and Oklahoma and Arkansas and suddenly had money they had never had before. And these twelve-year-old girls were wearing black crepe dresses, high heels, silk stockings, their hair piled high, and lots of makeup like the movie stars they had seen. That was their ideal.

So I had a problem. First of all, I didn't have shoes. We got only two shoe-ration coupons a year, and I had spent mine on the farm on cowboy boots and ice skates and I promised I wouldn't complain about not having shoes. My brother donated his black high-top basketball shoes, and I had to wear them. They looked really great along with my chickenfeed-sack dresses (which were common on the farm) and my country braids and no makeup. I realized right away at school that I was not going to be a social success.

I remember I was trying to make friends with one girl who seemed a little bit open and who walked the same route to school that I did. She seemed friendly enough so that I finally wangled my way into her house. But one day I was in the rest room in one of the stalls and I overheard her talking to another girl about what a little slob I was and how ashamed she was to have me around her. I remember freezing and waiting until she left, then I walked on home. I made a point never to be around her, or anyone, again. I was isolated, and yet I wasn't that unhappy: I accepted it and found other things to make me happy.

I loved the curriculum, I loved the new worlds of music and art I was discovering. I was a good student, and the teachers were kind to me. It was exciting listening to their new ideas and hearing the children talk in class. It was all fascinating to me.

My mom and dad did not feel the same way. I remember them sitting at the table there in the kitchen in Long Beach and looking out the window and commenting how it just didn't seem the same as Idaho. Having houses in rows and no space in between was somewhat uncivilized from their point of view. Dad said, "How in the heck can you go outside and even take a pee without some neighbor watching you?" And yet as close as the houses were, the neighbors weren't friendly. In the morning they'd walk right by you— "Walk right by you!" my dad said— and not even say hello, not even acknowledge you were there. My mother hated it; she hated shopping; she hated going downtown. She was afraid of traffic and afraid of the buses. She had my baby brother in a stroller at that time, and she was afraid someone would kidnap him. She didn't have any friends, she didn't have her farm women's club, and she couldn't buzz down to the store and talk to people on Saturday about what was going on.

We lived in Long Beach for about three months, but apparently it kept getting worse for my mother. She was miserable and cried every day. One night Dad came home from work and she had the car and trailer packed, everything out of the house. She said, "We are going back to Idaho, *tonight!*" Somehow he knew that there was no point in arguing, so we went.

Our stay in California was only a few months, but it was probably one of the momentous times of my life. I felt it shaped my personality by showing me there were other worlds out there, other possibilities. In my childish thinking then, I didn't like my mother very well for her small-town feelings and her inability to adapt. I didn't like my father for not standing up to her and saying, "You're being silly about this. Let's adjust and make the best of it." He was a strong man, too, but I suppose he had ambivalent feelings. I didn't. I loved California and didn't want to go back to Idaho. I didn't throw a tantrum and say I wouldn't go, because you just didn't do those things, but in my mind I knew that someday I would return.

FRANKIE COOPER

I grew up in central Kentucky, on a farm outside a small town called Richmond. It was a pre–Civil War farm with a pre–Civil War house. We didn't have electricity, we didn't have indoor plumbing, and we didn't have a telephone. The closest thing we had to a modern convenience was a gasoline-driven-motor washing machine. We were real proud of that because we were the only ones in the community who had one.

We had plenty of food from the farm, so we didn't consider ourselves poor. We raised chickens, and from the chickens we got not only meat but also clothing from the sacks their feed came in. The sacks were pretty and we made dresses out of them. We starched and ironed them and that was it. When my daughter was born I even made her underwear out of sacks.

We were isolated, though. We didn't understand that there was another type of world, because we didn't see it. We had a battery-operated radio and used to listen to Amos and Andy. Then we turned it off to save the batteries for the next night.

I went to high school in central Kentucky, and I met my first husband there. In 1939 we were married. My husband was from Illinois and he didn't like Kentucky so well. There were no job opportunities for young people. In the spring of 1942, after the war had been going a little while, we decided to move. My girl at this time was about two years old, and I thought it was time I did something toward the war effort. In order for my husband and I both to have jobs we had to go to an industrial section of the nation, so we moved to East St. Louis, Illinois.

I was twenty-one years old and had never worked before. My first job was at the American Steel foundry, in Granite City, Illinois, right outside St.

Louis. I worked as a molder's helper, the dirtiest job that anyone can imagine. The only thing I could compare it to would be the coal mines, and that's the way I looked when I came off the job.

It was real scary at first. I caught the bus before dawn with a lot of people, and with my Southern accent I could hardly understand a lot of what was said. In an area like East St. Louis there were a lot of different accents, like Swedish, Norwegian, German and Polish, and it was almost like a foreign language to me. My mind couldn't keep up with the speed of their conversation. When I was thinking one sentence they were already talking another. And a lot of things I didn't understand because their vocabulary was so different. That was a real problem. My foreman used to get irritated with me because I was a little slower in understanding. I guess I was one of those country gals that had a hard time getting used to the city.

But I wanted to learn and found that people were pretty patient and generous with me. They'd try to get me to talk, because they liked to hear my accent. Everybody would say, "Hi, Kentucky, how're you doing? Is the grass really blue in Kentucky?"

Another problem we had was housing. Housing was difficult to find in East St. Louis, because there were so many people. One lady turned a five-car garage into five apartments. This is what people began to do, fix up their garages so they could rent them. Store fronts too. Sheets were put up to divide storefronts. We got a house for a while, but we couldn't live there because it was only partially finished and it was cold and it was in a section where there were enormous rats. But we didn't have it too hard. Finally we found a two-room apartment.

It was a great change from Richmond. I had electricity and indoor plumbing. I just walked across the street to the grocery store. I had money to buy any kind of food I wanted. We had a secondhand car, so we didn't have to walk anymore. We went to the movies occasionally. We even went out to eat, which was brand-new to me. I had never

done that. Never. Just the little things that we would call little simple things now were a new experience to me. I could go in a butcher shop and buy corned beef, which I had never seen before. Outside of my speech, which was an impediment for me, I enjoyed everything.

Meeting people from different places made me see that I actually didn't know about anything else but the little community I was raised in. The stories that people would tell, just their way of life, all of it was new to me. I was fascinated. I wanted to learn everything, to take in as much as I could.

SYBIL LEWIS

I grew up in Sapulpa, Oklahoma, a small town about fifteen miles from Tulsa, population around ten thousand. It was a very poor town and very segregated. All the blacks lived on the north side of town, across the railroad tracks, and the whites lived in the south part of town. Our parents made it very clear that we stayed on our side of the railroad tracks. You only crossed them if you had some business to go to in town, then you came right back.

All the schools, naturally, were segregated, and all restaurants, movies, and entertainment of any kind was on a segregated basis. The blacks would enter the movie theater through the alley and sit in the balcony. Segregation was the way of life. As a young child I was just told what to do, but as I grew older I began to wonder why I couldn't go in restaurants downtown and couldn't go to the public parks and playgrounds on the other side of the tracks. I was curious about these things and had difficulty accepting them, because even at an early age I could see that there was more to get out of life. But my parents explained to me that there were limits—in other words, blacks had a place and they had to stay in it.

While I was attending school I worked for white families in Sapulpa. I did the everyday work, the washing, the ironing, cooking and cleaning house. I was paid three dollars and fifty cents a week and I needed the money because my family could not afford to give me the things I wanted. It was hard work for a fourteen-year-old, washing and ironing, mainly white shirts starched very stiff, but that was the way of life in Sapulpa.

The woman I worked for was very wealthy and had everything in the way of material things that a woman could want. I would look at the three-fifty a week that I was getting, and then I would look at all her shoes and clothes and gloves and purses, and I said to myself, One day I'm going to work where I can have some of these nice things.

I had always been told that California was a liberal state and there was no segregation there. "Go west," that was the theme. "Everything is great in California, all doors are open, no prejudice, good jobs, plenty of money." My sister had a girlfriend who moved from Oklahoma to Los Angeles, and she sent us her yearbook from Jefferson High School. I saw photographs of blacks, Mexicans and whites and Orientals all together, and I just wanted to come to a place like that. My sister came before I did, and she encouraged me to come, too, so that made it easier for me. Finally I came out to Los Angeles. When I arrived, though, I found it wasn't quite the way I had imagined.

There were opportunities in California, but you had to be pretty persistent, because there was a lot of prejudice and discrimination too. The Californians resented you coming in, getting good jobs. And the Southern whites who migrated to California were always dropping the "nigger bit" to remind you they'd brought their prejudices with them.

A lot of the people came from Oklahoma, Texas, Arkansas. They had come out here just as I had, looking for a job to make big money. We had all been reared in segregated towns and states. They had never been around Negroes. I had never been closely associated with whites. So, as we worked together, we began to experience some of the same things I left in Sapulpa. You'd find "Go back to Arkie" or "Go back to Oklahoma" written in the rest rooms. And you would see signs, "We'll win the war without you, Ni—," and you knew what "Ni—" meant. In talking with some of the white girls at work, though, I found that to say "nigger" was just a way of life. Many of them had never been near, let alone touched, a Negro. So slowly we learned to work together, but in many ways California was no different from Oklahoma or the South, because people brought their feelings with them.

WILLIAM PEFLEY

During the Depression my family had a very tough time. My father had a thriving Studebaker agency and garage in Greencastle, Pennsylvania, but he lost everything in '29 and '30. A friend of his, a doctor, had talked him into putting all his money in stocks. When the stock market broke, all the stocks he'd invested in went clear under. We lost the garage, the agency, everything but our home. The crash laid us flat, and we had a tough time for years.

In '36 the machine shop in the next town hired my father because he was such a good mechanic. And my father asked them if they wouldn't hire me too, because we really needed the money. So they took me on as well. I worked there for six months and I was laid off for six months. Then they'd call us back because they had a little more work, then they'd lay us off again. You were never sure if you were going back or not. You couldn't plan anything, you couldn't buy an automobile, you couldn't buy clothes, because you never knew how long you were going to be working.

Finally, in 1939, my father went to work in the navy yard in Portsmouth, Virginia. They were converting destroyers from coal to oil to send to England, and they needed men to do it. My father told me about it, and I put in an application. In the latter part of 1939 they called me, and I went down there as a third-class machinist.

I had never seen a battleship or destroyer before in my life. When I saw my first battleship I couldn't believe there was such a thing in the world. And to see the ocean too. That was the first time I had ever seen the ocean.

Going to work in the navy yard after coming out of the machine shops in Pennsylvania, I felt like something had come down from heaven. I went from forty cents an hour to a dollar an hour. We had all the overtime we wanted, and I felt like at last I'm getting up in the world. I was able to buy some

working clothes for a change, buy a suit—I didn't have to depend on somebody's hand-me-downs anymore. It just made a different man out of me.

After Pearl Harbor they asked everybody working the yard if they knew of a friend or relative, man or woman, anybody they could get to come to work there, that we must have more workers or we were not going to win this war. Of course all of us tried to get anybody we knew who was able. Then the government ran ads in the paper and magazines—big ads—trying to recruit people from other states. So we had people coming from all over the coun-try. I was amazed how people would find out, clear out in Arizona, Wyoming, Florida. Many times we would be eating our lunch in the engine room and somebody would say, "Where are you from?" I'd say, "Pennsylvania." "Oh, heck, I'm from South Carolina." Somebody else would say Ohio, or Kansas. They were coming in there from everywhere.

Up to Pearl Harbor, Portsmouth was sort of a dead town; there was little going on. But once we entered the war, the navy yard went from 4,500 people to 48,000. When the new workers started to arrive, there was just nowhere for them to live. Wealthy people with big, sixteen-room homes were turning them into rooming houses, there just wasn't anywhere else to put people. So the government started to build cheap houses and apartments. They had to get them up overnight so the new recruits had a place to live. They built and built and built and still hardly had enough for the people.

Portsmouth couldn't keep up with all the people coming in. It had been such a lazy town that they weren't prepared for this. The grocery stores didn't have enough to sell people. There wasn't enough police force, or fire protection, there wasn't enough hospitals. As far as getting any medical care, it almost couldn't be done. All the young doctors were recruited into the service, and all that was left were a few elderly ones. If you had a broken arm

you had to sit for hours before someone would even come to tend you. One time it got so bad the government had to bring in a hospital ship full of doctors and nurses to take care of the civilian workers.

The buses were so crowded that you were lucky to get on one. The navy yard was running three shifts, and, of course, the buses were, too. The government didn't allow the bus company to buy any new ones, because the automobile companies were making tanks instead. So a lot of times we'd wait for hours to get a bus. The bus would come and it would pass right by because it was too full. Then the next bus would come along, you'd get on and go a few blocks, then the bus would break down, and everybody would have to get off and start walking. This went on during the whole war.

ELSIE ROSSIO

Before the war Seneca, Illinois, was a very small, very quiet farming community. The ladies used to stand in the middle of the street and visit, and if a car came along it either went around you or you moved quietly to the side. The population of the town was registered at 1,235 and there was only one big industry, the Du Pont Company's dynamite plant, where my husband worked.

In early 1942 we began hearing ru-

mors that a shipyard was coming to Seneca, but many of us did not really believe it until one morning we were awakened in the wee hours by the sound of huge trucks moving down Main Street. Just a few days later, the sound of jackhammers and the *rat-a-tat-tat* of carpenters' hammers began echoing day and night.

The site of the shipyards and dock was at the southeast corner of town on the banks of the Illinois River, but you

TIME IS SHORT ← OUR FIGHTING FORCES NEED SHIPS NOW → STAY ON THE JOB

could hear the jackhammers everywhere. Even the dogs realized it. They used to cross the streets so easily, but all of a sudden they disappeared, because there was just too much commotion.

I don't know how the word got around, but people came from everywhere, from all states of the union. Within a few months the population rose to 6,500. At the peak there were more than 27,000 people employed at the shipyards. They were people from all walks of life. Some professional men quit jobs teaching, or closed their businesses, or continued in them and took

shift work at the yards. Eventually my own son went to work there on the afternoon and evening shift as a sort of office boy, and he wasn't even sixteen yet.

At first the shock of all these people was numbing. Cars were just rolling into town, and there wasn't anyplace for them to stay except a few that got hotel and motel rooms in the neighboring towns, but they came with little tents and sleeping rolls. Some slept on porches, under trees, in their cars, just anywhere.

Being an old-fashioned patriotic citizenry, we all pitched in to do our part and open our homes to roomers and boarders where possible. My husband and I were just ordinary people of modest means, but we had an extra bedroom and found two carpenters who had come together from Indiana and were willing to sleep in the same room. They took the upstairs bedroom, and we took the downstairs one and moved our boy down on the couch.

I got up at four-thirty in the morning to make the carpenters' lunches and fix breakfast for them, as they had to be at work by five-thirty. My own husband left for work at the Du Pont plant at six-thirty, so he was the next breakfast, and then my little son followed about seven. However, I loved to cook and really felt good about helping out my country.

Later during the war I went to work in a doctor's office. One of the town's two family doctors was called into the service, and for a time we had only one doctor, who did a heroic job of working day and night to care for people. Then a dedicated young man, Dr. Meyer Silverman, arrived to fill in. He came to my door one morning and asked me if I might not like to work in the office. They were trying to get help with everything, so many of us who had no actual training took the jobs. At first the work frightened me. I thought I couldn't do anything like that, but I gave it a try and I learned quickly. I did the bookkeeping, which was very simple in those days.

The thing I remember most is trying to make room on the schedule for all the people needing attention. The doctor's office was upstairs, along with the dentist's office, and they shared a small waiting room, which could not begin to hold the overflow. Many of our patients were from the shipyards—they came with small injuries like eye burns from welding torches, cuts, fractures, things like that. The men would sit lined up down the stairs until I could get them in. I remember one man who had fractured his arm badly and had to be in a cast. In spite of the doctor's cautioning to keep it dry, he would get it wet and need a new cast about every few days. He was a big lovable roughneck and would not stay home from work, but he tried the doctor's patience with his endless changing of casts.

To handle the influx of workers, the government eventually built three housing areas, totaling 1,467 family units, plus a dormitory for three hundred men. For a short time we lived in one of the war apartments, when the house we were renting was sold. That was an education in itself. The walls were paper thin, and the bedrooms were on either side of that thin wall. You could almost hear your neighbor breathe. The first night we slept there, I was awakened at midnight by a man who had just come off the night shift. He dropped his shoes as he took them off, and I thought it was in our bedroom. I shook my husband and whispered someone was in our room. He turned on the light and then we realized it was next door.

There was little privacy, and one had to be careful of conversation in the bedroom. I remember one night when one of the men brought a prostitute home with him about midnight, when his wife was in another state visiting her parents. He was in a most jovial mood after an evening in the tavern and anticipating his exciting night ahead. I could hear every word. He showed the lady his wife's dresses in the closet and told her she could pick out a couple of things and model them for him. Also, she kept begging him to say he loved her, and he evaded that neatly. I went out on the couch to sleep, as my husband was on the night shift, and tried to shut out the party next door.

In the morning I was awakened about five by voices in the next apartment. He was trying to evict the lady before the neighbors were up, and she was trying to take the dresses he had promised her the night before. He spoke so harshly to her and called her a tramp and said she wasn't fit to touch his wife's things, and he finally pushed her out the door. I couldn't help but feel a twinge of pity for her as she walked away with her red wrinkled coat clutched around her. I recognized her as a woman who had come to town with the boom and searched out alone and lonely men. But I can still hear her saying, "Please say you love me!" Even in her wretched profession, she looked for a word of love.

After the war Seneca once again became a small, quiet town, but I think the shipyard days lighted a spark that left us never quite the same—more open to strangers and to progress. I'm glad I knew those times!

DON JOHNSON

I was working at AC Spark Plug Division of General Motors in Flint, Michigan, when the war began. My responsibility was for manufacturing planning, and right after Pearl Harbor we got the signal that we should put our total efforts into conversion to war production.

I was called, along with many others, to a meeting in the auditorium of the plant. When I arrived there, I discovered people in military uniforms and the top officials of our company, including our general manager. The topic was a new product that we were going to build, a navigational computer bomb sight, a product we had never heard of before. By the time I left that meeting I discovered that I was team leader of a small group of six, and I had a stack of prints that I could just barely get my chin over. I headed back to my own desk to call those people together to do the process planning and estimating of the labor standards for a product we had never seen. We had to produce that product to those standards within ninety days, and we had one whole week to work out the plan.

The conversion from producing conventional products to war goods was a large-scale, complicated effort. Before

SURE— I'M WORKING HARDER

COME ON, GANG! WE'RE BUILDING ARMS FOR VICTORY!

National Archives

the war we were producing accessories for automobiles, from air cleaners to spark plugs. With the advent of the war we started producing Browning automatic machine guns, navigational computers and bomb sights. The new products required that we gut and strip the plant of the equipment we were used to operating, put that equipment outside for storage, and replace it with new equipment for war production. In fact, we jokingly said, and it was often true, that you went through a door in the morning that wasn't even there in the afternoon. All of this required intense effort. We all had to put in extra hours a day and extra days in the week to get the job done. The company went to a three-shift operation, twenty-four hours a day, seven days a week.

After Pearl Harbor there was an immediate change in people's attitude toward their work—their sense of urgency, their dedication, their team work. When the chips were down, people dealt with it like survival. Things that might have taken days longer were done to meet a target so you didn't hold somebody else up—even if it meant putting in extra hours and extra effort. It ended up being a period in which you got very exhausted, but there was a determination, and there was a lot of satisfaction in being able to make that contribution.

Long after the war I found out in a conversation that when we submitted our plan for the navigational bomb sight the parent company came to look us over and concluded that we didn't have the capability to produce it. We were never told that, though, we just went ahead and did it. There was never any doubt on our part that we would do what we'd committed ourselves to do. We just did not accept "Can't do."

·3·

THIS IS THE ARMY, MR. JONES!

This is the Army, Mr. Jones!
No private rooms or telephones!
You had your breakfast in bed before,
But you won't have it there anymore!

—"This Is the Army, Mr. Jones!"
Lyrics and music by Irving Berlin, 1942

Nazi conquest in Europe in the spring and summer of 1940, as well as the nation's deteriorating relations with Japan, prompted Congress to enact a peacetime conscription law, the first in American history. Passed in September 1940, the draft, as it was popularly known, required all males between the ages of twenty-one and thirty-six to register with local boards of the Selective Service System. After the United States became a full-fledged belligerent, the draft laws lowered the entrance age to eighteen and eventually reduced the age limit to thirty-five. In all, more than 31 million men registered for the draft and more than 15 million men and women served in one of the branches of the armed services from 1940 to 1945, either as draftees or as volunteers.

The shared experiences of the soldiers, sailors and marines during World War II represents one of the greatest social experiments in collective group living in American history. While each individual was subject to the demands of military discipline and barracks life,

the armed forces did not attempt to alter the prevailing social conventions. Consequently, the services segregated blacks from whites and permitted discrimination and racial prohibitions to flourish on and off base. Official government policy declared that mixing races "would produce situations destructive to morale and detrimental to the preparation for national defense."

Still, the Army promoted a broad social democracy among soldiers drawn from every level of society and every ethnic and religious background. The collective living experience threw college graduates together with illiterates, Christians with Jews, Catholics with Protestants, Yankees with Southerners, and farm youth with street-wise young men from the cities. The Army conducted classes in reading for the illiterates, introduced elementary hygiene to those ignorant of these basic needs, and provided a well-balanced diet for all. Provincialism and regionalism were broken down by the uprooting and mixing of millions of Americans who otherwise might never have traveled beyond their native region.

Men of draft age who were not in uniform during World War II may have owed their exemption from the military services to various

This Is the Army, Mr. Jones!   •   47

reasons: able-bodied men required for vital industries and agriculture could be granted immunity from the draft; an astonishing 6.5 million were found either physically, mentally or emotionally unsuitable and were classified 4-F. Approximately 42,000 men—about one tenth of a percent of draft-age men—registered their opposition to the war and military service as conscientious objectors. Depending on how authorities ruled on their classification, the CO's spent the war either in a civilian public service camp or in prison.

The legacy of the World War II servicemen and -women—approximately 240,000 women served in the military—is mixed. On the one hand the GI's (named after their Government Issue uniforms) were members of the largest fraternity in the nation. Friendships—indeed, relationships as close as any formed among brothers and sisters in the same family—were forged and remain strong even today. Many veterans regarded their military experience (but not the experience of combat) positively, especially when coupled with the GI Bill that helped them secure a college education after the war and a low-cost home loan. Others viewed the time spent in the service as years of lost opportunity, indeed as a hiatus from life itself. However servicemen and -women viewed their military experience, the intermingling of people from different cultural, social and economic backgrounds had a lasting impact on both the veterans and the country that they served.

ELLIOT JOHNSON

On December 7, 1941, three of my friends and I were eating in a Chinese restaurant in downtown Portland, Oregon. Suddenly the door of the kitchen burst open and the Chinese owner came running out, gesturing wildly and talking almost incoherently. That roused our curiosity, and we went into the kitchen, got his radio and came back. Of course, it was being announced that the Japanese had bombed Pearl Harbor.

There wasn't any doubt in our minds of the seriousness of this thing. We got up and went directly to Marine headquarters enlisting station. There was already a line several blocks long.

When we finally got to the entrance to the building there was a card table set up and a man sitting there with a phone headset. I gave him my name and address and he told me to step out of line. I said, "Why?" He said, "You've already got a letter in the mail." And, sure enough, the next morning I got a letter from the President of the United

Library of Congress

States. "Greetings," it said, and on January 12, 1942, I was in the Army.

The same day I was inducted, I was sent to Fort Lewis, Washington. They unloaded us about two-thirty in the morning. It was snowing. And that night I had my first introduction to army discipline, which is one of the greatest things that I got out of the Army. We had to learn to make our bed that night and make it right. You didn't go to bed until you did it right.

The next day we were issued clothing, and I found out that there were some very enterprising people in the world. One of the men who had been drafted had set himself up as a tailor. The pants I was issued dragged at least a foot beyond my shoes onto the sidewalk, and for fifty cents that enterprising young man altered my pants and made them fit.

Within three days we had boarded a train and set off for Fort Knox, Kentucky. I had never been out of my little backyard before, and suddenly I'm seeing the great United States, the plains of the Midwest, and the red earth and the mountains of Kentucky.

We arrived at Fort Knox and there was a whole mixture of people I had never been exposed to. Northerners,

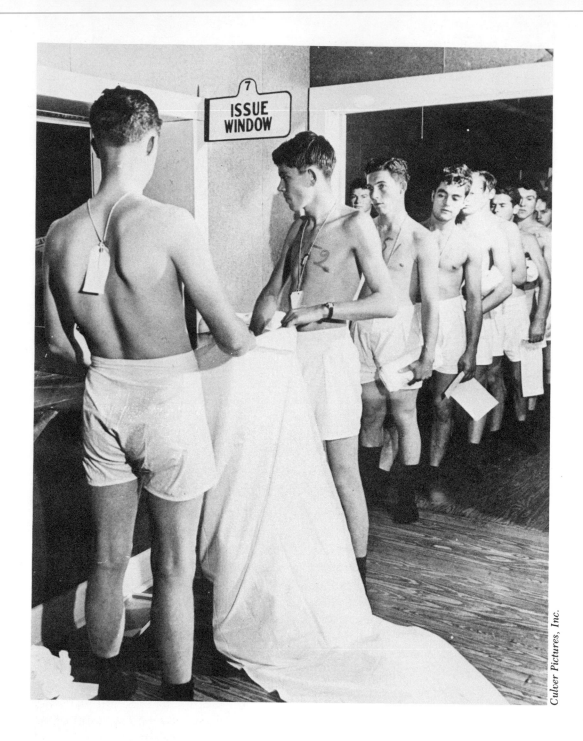

50 • THE HOMEFRONT

Southerners, Midwesterners, and each of us, I found, was entirely different and even had different dialects in those days. I met people from Oklahoma, Okies we'd call them, and people from the hills of Tennessee and Kentucky. As we began to get acquainted, I discovered to my surprise that many of them could not read or write their own names. I began writing a lot of letters for these men, and I did it all through the service. And they would get replies from people who also couldn't read and had someone else write their letters for them.

But I also learned that people who couldn't read or write could be pretty damn smart. They could take a rifle apart in the dark and put it back together just as fast. They had their own music and musical instruments. They wrote their own songs, and it was beautiful music.

Since I had graduated from college, after basic training I was immediately shipped to officer candidate school at Fort Sill in Lawton, Oklahoma. Then I was assigned to the Fourth Infantry Division in Augusta, Georgia. This was my first real taste of the South. I remember when I reported to the battery commander. It was a hot afternoon and I walked in and threw him my best highball: "Lieutenant Johnson report-ing for duty as ordered, sir!" And he just put his hands in back of his head and rocked back in his chair and stared at me. I was at rigid attention and had to hold my salute until he returned it. I can remember the fly on the end of my nose and the sweat rolling down my forehead, and I could feel my eyes crossing, and still that man didn't return my salute. Finally, after a very long time, he asked, "Northerner or Southerner?" I said, "I'm a Westerner, sir." And he threw me a salute and said, "Relax, you'll do."

The South was also my first exposure to bigotry. I remember the shock I had at the Southern attitude toward Negroes. I went to a crowded restaurant once and one of the fellows that was with me was this true, dyed-in-the-wool Southerner. The waitress took us over to a booth, which four young black men had just vacated. My friend stood back by the door. "I'm not going to sit there." I asked why not, and he said, "Sit where those niggers have been sitting? Not a chance." So they found another booth for us and we sat down. The waitress wasn't upset by it at all, but it was quite a shock to me because in Oregon there had been only one black in my high-school class, and we were good friends.

DON CONDREN

I grew up in Amarillo, Texas. My parents were very, very poor. My father worked at a smelter until he was laid off in the early thirties, and until the war started I don't recall that he ever had a steady job. I had eight brothers and sisters, and we lived in a house that had two rooms, no running water inside, no indoor plumbing. We were relatively well fed—I don't remember ever going hungry or worrying about it too much—but we weren't well clothed. When I was a kid we wore bib overalls and went barefoot in the summer. In the winter we wore lace-up boots, and it was snowy and cold. Necessity created a lot of closeness in our family, though. We were a very close-knit group.

I was drafted into the Army in 1942, when I was twenty years old. I'd never been out of that part of Texas before. It was a real learning experience—learning to not have my family around me all the time. Our family had always been very supportive of each other.

In Amarillo the community was strictly Anglo. You had Southern Baptists, Methodists, a few Presbyterians—very few Catholics, and no Jews. I have never known a Jew personally. I didn't know what being a Jew meant in terms of religion or culture.

When I first got in the Army, I ran into a lot of people from New York. Their speech grated on me, let me tell you. I also ran into a lot of Italians, and they had manners that were somewhat different than mine. I came from a community where one would say "You first" and not crowd in at the front of the line. And I ran into a lot of pushing and shoving and crowding in the Army. In the South we also have a lot of formalities—you say "Mr." and "Mrs." and "Thank you"—and I found those things lacking. I didn't dislike these people, mind you, it was just that their mannerisms were so different than what I was accustomed to.

I was first sent to Wichita Falls, Texas, which is much like Amarillo, only hotter and less comfortable. Then I was sent to aircraft-mechanic school in Burbank, California, which was very good. I really enjoyed southern California. There was a whole opening up of things, lots of stimulation. Part of it was just my age, but part of it was seeing new things. I liked the visual beauty and the good weather. And people were especially friendly. On weekends I used to hitchhike all over southern California, just taking it all in.

LARRY MANTELL

I was a poor Jewish kid who lived way out of town, on Ninety-eighth and Normandie, in Los Angeles. I lived in a very low-middle-class neighborhood. I had no ambition, zero, about going to college. I got out of high school and three days later I was in boot camp in San Diego.

At the San Diego Training Center I went into culture shock. I was an only child, two months away from being eighteen, and very naïve, very unso-

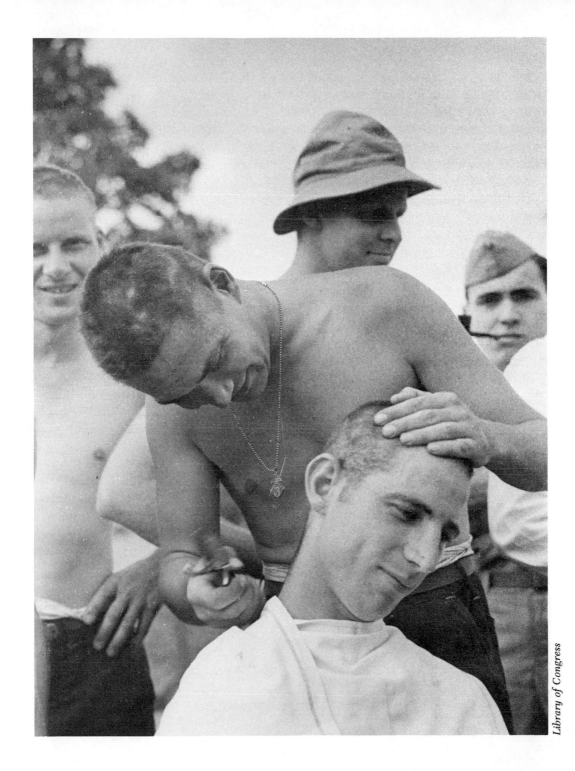

This Is the Army, Mr. Jones!   • 53

phisticated, sheltered. Suddenly I'm thrown in with people from Oklahoma, Texas and the Southeast. Some of them had never used a toilet facility, never brushed their teeth. Some of their hygiene was totally out of touch with what I had grown up with.

I met guys who had never seen a Jew. They would look upon me as almost an ogre, because they'd only heard about Jews. This was a jolt. I think that was a good part of the growing up that happened to me in the service.

I remember the World Series came along and I got suckered into some sort of a bet and I lost my whole month's paycheck, and I went into the latrine and cried. I couldn't believe anything like this could happen.

When I got out of boot camp I had pneumonia, so instead of going to aviation gunnery school I ended up in a naval hospital. Before I was discharged from the hospital, I was brought before a board of inquiry. There was some feeling that I had incurred some lung damage. I thought they were going to discharge me, so I went before the board and pleaded not to be discharged. I could have been out of the service three months after I joined and been earning a lot of money in those inflated wartimes, but I begged to stay. It would have been totally socially unacceptable not to be in the service.

As it turned out, the board was right. When I was on shipboard, we got hit twice by kamikazes and I suffered smoke inhalation, which did create some permanent damage to one of my lungs.

WILLIAM MULCAHY

I was one of the early draft numbers that came up. I was examined four separate times, and I tried to enlist twice in the Signal Corps. All six times I was rejected because of bad eyesight. At that time I was the originator of the joke when the doctor said, "Do you see the chart on the wall?" And I said, "What wall?" And it was true. I am legally blind today. Finally the colonel in charge of the top military medical team for Philadelphia said to me, "Stop coming back, son, you're just taking our time." Even with a waiver of insurance, there was no way that they would accept me with the eyesight I had.

So I felt considerably left out and like most 4-Fs at that time, a little bit of a freak. It was a rather lonesome feeling. But I had done what I could. That kept me from feeling as I might have if I were merely working in a war plant in order to avoid military service.

JOHN ABBOTT

I spent much of my youth in Scarborough, New York, a private community twenty-nine miles north of New York City, right on the Hudson River. It was a very affluent society of private schools, servants, cars. I was a young, handsome rich man's son. The world was my apple.

Ever since I was about ten or eleven, though, I knew I was not going to have anything to do with war or killing. One experience I had at that age particularly affected me. From early childhood, I did not get along with my brother Donald, who was two years older than I. Since he was bigger, I wanted to do something that would make me bigger, too. So I took his .22 rifle and went out into the woods with the intention of shooting something. I saw this bird silhouetted in a tree, just sitting there, innocently singing. I raised the rifle and squeezed the trigger and the bird plummeted down. I ran up to the tree, and here was the bird laying there. My stomach just dropped. I felt sick all over. I didn't feel like I was big at all. I felt like I was some real monster, taking that little bird's life, ending its song. That was really important to me, knowing that I had no right to take another life. I had no right to use violence against others, even birds or animals.

Another experience that affected how I felt was reading the medical books of my boyfriend's father. His father was a doctor and had a library of thick volumes. I used to spend a lot of time looking in these books. Some of them were pictorial histories on the treatment of men wounded in World War I. It started with some kind of mess that didn't look anything like a human being. Then on each succeeding page you'd see them add a little more skin, or a foot, or part of a head or face, or put an ear back until this blob resembled a human being at the end. And I thought, why do people have to do this to each other? I knew there was nothing that could get me to join that kind of effort or help in any way.

Still, when I went to college and my teacher handed out a questionnaire to all the males in class to fill out for the draft, I was stunned. The teacher passed them around as casually as if they were questions for an exam. I filled out the form with great fear and trepidation, stating that I would not be able to participate in any form of war. My local draft board sent me back a second questionnaire for those claiming conscientious-objector status. I did not claim that I was one or seek that classification. In fact, the questions in the CO form gave me a great deal of trouble. "Do you believe in a Supreme Being?" "What is your religious training and beliefs?" I felt these questions had little or no meaning for drafting

John Abbott in 1941. *Courtesy of John Abbott*

than I had ever been. I knew I had to be especially sure about how I felt and acted. My strength was in the feelings I had held for so long, and that I believed I must live with myself in spite of a world which was turning its back on what I was taught were basic truths.

People you knew all your life, family friends that you called uncle or aunt, heard you were a C.O. and all of a sudden they wouldn't talk to you anymore. My sister's girlfriend lived not too far from us and was in our house all the time. When it became known that I had taken a stand against the war, her father called up and said, "Don't ever come here again. Don't ever speak to my daughter again. We don't want to see you anymore." It was a real shock to me that people whom I had thought of as not only my friends, but even family, would say something like that.

Even though my dad told me that he loved me and would do anything to help me, he thought I was really crazy and knocking my head against a stone wall. And my mother went absolutely insane. She was very upset about my being a conscientious objector and how it would spoil the image she had of herself and her family. She asked me, "Who told you to tell the draft board all those crazy things?" Out of just plain hurt and anger, because she's always been the authority figure in my life, I said, "God told me to say that." She went upstairs, and my dad told me she was in bed for three days.

me, but I recognized that I must do well with the answers.

It was at this time that I began to realize the world I was in was in great trouble, and that the pressure was on to see that every able-bodied man be pushed into service for "our just and right cause against the enemy." I soon realized that my choices (if you want to call them that) were few: either comply or be punished for not going along. The pressure on me was tremendous. I felt it was totally unfair to ask eighteen-year-olds to make such judgments while still green behind the ears. I couldn't understand how there could be a law telling us that killing was wrong and yet my own government was asking me to kill others whom I didn't know, fear or hate. It made no more sense to me than killing the bird did when I was a child. I felt the lines of battle between myself and Selective Service were drawn and a long struggle was coming in which I had to be stronger

But as isolated, as alone as I felt, I knew I had to reject any effort to be sucked into this maelstrom, this big dark, black hole of the war effort.

DELLIE HAHNE

My brother was two years younger than I, and we were very close. He and his friends could see the war coming, and I would listen to their talk. They were unanimous: they all agreed they'd have absolutely nothing to do with the war. "Somebody else can get their heads shot off, not me," they'd say. If a war broke out they decided they would get bottled water and supplies and provisions and go into the Glendale hills and hide. When the war started, the entire group, my brother and all his friends, enlisted. Some enlisted the following day, and some took a little longer, but they all did a complete about-face.

My brother could have gotten out of the service, too. My father was in a vital business. He was supplying wholesale produce to the battleships in the armed services, and my brother was his assistant. My sister said, "You don't have to join up, because you're an important part of Pop's business." But my brother refused the exemption. His wife backed him up in his refusal. She said, "I'd rather have a dead hero than a live coward for a husband."

So he enlisted in the air force.* He wanted to be a flyboy.

SHIRLEY HACKETT

The war turned the whole world upside down. Everything changed immediately, from the food you put on your table to your relationship with your boyfriend. Suddenly he had to make plans about going into the sevice. He knew the draft was coming, and he wanted to have a choice of which branch of the service he would enter. So many man enlisted on their own. There was a tremendous feeling that "I've got to get in this and end it so we can get

back to living again."

My boyfriend tried several places and he almost didn't get in—he had very poor eyesight—but they relaxed the qualifications for a lot of men who would ordinarily have been considered 4-F, and they accepted him. I saw men accepted who, physically, I often wondered how they got in.

We had a circle of friends in Wallingford, Connecticut, all young men about the same age who played ball

---

*In June 1941 the Air Corps became the Army Air Force. It remained that until September 18, 1947, when it became the U.S. Air Force, as now.

together, who were all in the National Guard. I don't recall exactly, but it seemed like it was less than two months that they were all called up. And immediately all the young men started to pressure the girls to have sex because they wanted to get close and they didn't know if they'd be seeing each other again. A lot of the girls were put on the spot because they loved the guys, and God knows what was going to happen. But in those days premarital sex was such a taboo thing that most of the girls said it was either marriage or nothing. Marriages happened so fast that I can remember one month where I attended four weddings. Right after they were married the men were shipped out. Some of the couples didn't even have time to go away on a honeymoon. Their unit was sent off to New

Guinea, and they didn't come home for several years, if they did come home.

The men seemed to put on a very brave front, almost a happy front. They acted very proud to go, and there was a great deal of laughing and joking on the surface about where they might be sent and the exotic girls they might meet, but every so often it would become awfully quiet, and we realized there was no joke anymore. They were going to war.

When the gals would meet we would discuss among ourselves how fearful we were. Maybe the men discussed it with each other, but they certainly didn't discuss it very much in front of us. Looking back, I'd say there definitely was a certain amount of fear among the men, but they weren't allowed to express it in those days. You had to be a

(NY15) NEW YORK, Oct. 23--GRIEF EN MASSE AS GUARDSMEN LEAVE--These grieving women were in the crowd that gathered at Grand Central Terminal today to bid farewell to relatives and sweethearts among the New York National Guardsmen who left for a year's training at Fort McClellan, Anniston, Ala. Mass hysteria at one time sent hundreds of the women crashing through police lines onto the tracks. (AP WIREPHOTO)

big strong hero. My own boyfriend would express some things to me, but nowhere near the way young people do today.

The only time I saw the men crack was the wedding of the last couple. They had no time for a honeymoon; they didn't even have time for a reception. They had to say their goodbyes to each other right there at the church. Some of the men were in uniform already, and their wives were there with them. All of a sudden, maybe because we couldn't have a celebration, it dawned on us all what was happening, and for the first time I saw the men really cry. They realized, we all realized, that this was probably the last time that we were going to be together for a long, long time. And for a few moments it hit us all, just as if a cloud had come over the whole scene, and we knew things were not going to be the same ever again.

·4·

AMERICA CALLING: TAKE YOUR PLACE IN CIVIL DEFENSE

The first year of the war was very scary . . .
Nobody knew what was going to happen, and there was
always this fear of attack.

—JAMES COVERT

It was very easy to get people to volunteer to help toward the
war effort, because that was the main effort in all our lives, to
end the war before it reached our shores.

—ESTHER BURGARD

You don't know what this country can do when people are
pulling together, breaking their necks to do what they can.

—SHIRLEY HACKETT

The Japanese attack on Pearl Harbor shattered America's belief in the inviolability of its shores. Pearl Harbor powerfully demonstrated that planes launched from carriers could strike devastating blows thousands of miles away from their home base. In the Atlantic, German submarines lurked off the East Coast and, for a time, sank American transport vessels at twice the rate they could be replaced. Japanese submarines operated for a few years off the West Coast and shelled an oil refinery outside Santa Barbara, California, on

WE MUST NOT FAIL THEM

National Archives

February 24, 1942. At his February 17, 1942, press conference, a reporter asked President Roosevelt about the possibility of an enemy attack by sea or by air. The enemy, Roosevelt replied "can come in and shell New York tomorrow night, under certain conditions. They can probably . . . drop bombs on Detroit tomorrow night, under certain conditions."

Fear of an enemy attack on the American mainland prompted millions to volunteer to assist their communities in civil-defense efforts. By serving as air raid wardens, fire fighters, plane spotters, shipyard security guards, or in myriad other positions, many on the homefront were able to achieve a sense of participation in the war.

Civil-defense efforts also served to instill a sense of mutual cooperation among Americans. Scrap drives were launched throughout the country to make up for shortages of critical material like tin and rubber. The iron in one old shovel, Americans were told, could be recycled to make four hand grenades. The patriotic

housewife was urged to separate and save her garbage, especially tin cans and fat. One pound of fat, it was pointed out, contained enough glycerin to make one pound of black powder.

Most popular of all civilian war efforts were "victory gardens," which sprang up everywhere in backyards, gas stations, rooftops, even parking lots. In 1943 Americans planted 20.5 million victory gardens, which produced at least a third of all the vegetables eaten in the U.S. that year.

Although most Americans freely donated what they no longer wanted or needed for the war, the government asked them to make even greater sacrifices. To pay for the enormous cost of the war— nearly $200 billion—the federal government imposed a five percent surcharge, or "Victory Tax," on all income taxes. In January 1942 the U.S. also established the Office of Price Administration to ration scarce items and stave off inflation by controlling prices.

Rationing was probably the most controversial part of the government's civilian-defense program. The OPA rationed twenty essential items during the war, from sugar to gasoline. Red-point coupons were issued for meat, butter and fats, blue points for canned and processed foods. Gas restrictions were even more elaborate. Motorists were assigned either A, B, C or E (emergency vehicle) priority and were issued gas coupons accordingly. The government also imposed a nationwide thirty-five-mile-per-hour speed limit and a ban on pleasure driving in order to conserve both rubber and gasoline.

Although there was much grumbling about rationing—especially gasoline—most Americans accepted the system as fair. In fact, the majority of people ate better under rationing than they did during the Depression. For those who could not tolerate the restrictions, it was always possible to purchase scarce items on the black market, if you were willing to pay the price. Buying restricted items from "Mr. Black," as illegal entrepreneurs were called, carried a social stigma, but was not uncommon. One of every four respondents to a wartime Gallup poll said they considered at least occasional patronage of Mr. B. justifiable.

Voluntary and compulsory civil-defense efforts promoted both the war and the country's feeling of national solidarity. War bonds, scrap drives, rationing, victory gardens gave the country a sense of common purpose and an opportunity for all its citizens to participate vicariously in the battle overseas.

THOMAS A. SCOTT

I was classified 4-F because of a circulatory condition in my legs. Because I was 4-F I couldn't be a general and I couldn't work down to a private, so I figured what else can I do? Anybody who was rejected for the service was conscious of the fact that he wasn't doing what other guys his age were doing. Going around in civilian clothes wasn't exactly a comfortable feeling. And since I felt I had a duty and a responsibility towards the war effort, I went into civilian defense as an air raid warden.

Our mission was to protect the homefront. If it hadn't been for air raid wardens in Britain they would have been in a hell of a way. Right? We didn't know whether the Germans would come over here. Their newer planes had the capability to do it. In World War I the United States didn't have to worry about that. All they had to worry about was submarines. In World War II, we had to worry about airplanes coming into Philadelphia.

One of our responsibilities as an air raid warden was to make sure everybody had their lights turned out at night and that people weren't wandering around without any place to go. After dark, to make certain there were no lights burning anywhere, we used to climb onto the roofs to see if there were any skylights illuminated. A lot of people would leave the light on in the bathroom instead of anywhere else in the house. That was the worst thing you could let happen, because often there was a skylight in the bathroom. One time we ran into a very suspicious incident when we caught three skylights, one right in our post, one up at the western end of Overbrook, and one up in North Philadelphia, which made a direct arrow to the navy yard. Well, we jumped quickly on that and got the civilian-defense people to take a plane and check it out.

Another of our duties was to have one or two wardens on alert at all times to watch for anything that might happen in the neighborhood—like suspicious strangers wandering around. In

Library of Congress

TELEPHONISTS

addition to that, of course, we had other responsibilities in the event of an air raid.

Our post organized the first full-scale mock air raid in the area. It covered roughly a two-block-square neighborhood in which we had approximately eleven hundred residents. In April of '42 we had a full-scale demonstration, showing what air raid wardens actually did. We had trucks running around throwing Fourth of July flares to imitate magnesium bombs. Then we had people pretend that they were hurt and faint. It was up to us to take care of them until a medic came along. Sev-

eral thousand spectators lined the porches all around the area to watch. People from all over Philadelphia came.

Everybody participated, tailors and grocers and druggists, people in all kinds of occupations, because it was a mixed area. There was a job for everybody from ten years old on up. We had air raid wardens and volunteer police and volunteer firemen. We even set up a messenger service for the kids. So everyone felt they were actively participating in the war effort. We had over a hundred persons out of eleven hundred who were actively involved.

During the war I was also involved

with the Volunteer Port Security Force, which was organized to man the port of Philadelphia with volunteers to relieve the military of that responsibility. There were over seven thousand volunteers, from all walks of life, lawyers, cabdrivers, stockbrokers, which I was at the time, anyone who had flexible hours. We served eight hours a day, every sixth day, around the clock. We would alternate from the A to the B to the C watch. Our job was to board the ships in port and patrol them. We had to buy our own uniforms and report an hour before our shift to headquarters to get our guns and equipment. The force was so successful that we reduced the accident and pilferage rate in the port below the peacetime rate, which was amazing. Service was later extended to other ports across the country.

As the war went on and more and more men were called into the service, our ranks began to thin. So I suggested that we set up recruiting headquarters for the Port Security Force in the army induction center at Thirty-second and Lancaster where all the draftees were taken for examination. The result was that anybody who was rejected was automatically sent over to us. We told them, "You're lucky. You don't have to go into active service. You can join the 4-F's and other rejectees." We got a hell of a lot of recruits that way.

I also became involved in the Civil Air Raid Warning Service through a partner in one of the stock exchange firms who learned I was interested in civilian defense of all kinds. He asked me to head up the Civil Air Raid Warn-

ing Service for the First Air and Third Service Command, which covered practically the Eastern seaboard as far as Ohio. We worked four-hour shifts, one day a week, all around the clock. There was always a Philadelphia policeman, one of our people, and an air force officer on duty at all times. It was our responsibility, anytime a threat appeared, like an unidentified airplane, to send out the air raid warning signals—yellow, blue or red, as the case indicated—all the way out to Ohio, up to New York, and down to North Carolina. As the war progressed, and more people were drained off into defense work or the service, we had to recruit more volunteers here too, and I organized another successful recruiting campaign among the graduating classes of the Philadelphia-area high schools.

I was also one of the top speakers for the War Finance Committee in every one of its drives. During the war we all had a common objective. It gave us the impetus to work together and show we were all on the same team. When President Roosevelt was reelected to his fourth term and they asked me again to speak for the War Finance Drive, I said I'd come but only on one condition, that I work with a union organizer, because "these damn union people, they've put Roosevelt in, let them pay for it." So I got tied up with one of the union leaders, and we went out to the factories to sell bonds together. They would introduce him, and they'd all give him a big hand. He'd say, "Now, he's a stockbroker. We don't like each other, but doggone it, he's got a message for you, too." Then he'd

FOR ALL WE HOLD DEAR

Buy WAR BONDS

introduce me, and then I'd come back and say, "I don't like him either, but doggone it, we're in this together and both sides are fighting: capital is fighting, labor is fighting, we're all fighting on the same team. Now let's see how much money we can raise." And it worked out beautifully. The union organizer and I became good friends and we conducted a very successful campaign.

During the war I saw that in a crisis you could get everybody to work together. I think that's one of the things that we learned during the Depression, and it was borne out again in World War II. When people are up against it, they have a tendency to be more tolerant and to help each other. When you get into a crisis the humanity comes out in most of us. During the war we had a specific objective. Everybody had certain obligations, and doggone it, they fulfilled them. But the minute the war was over and that objective disappeared, of course, it all fell apart.

SHERIL JANKOVSKY CUNNING

As a child growing up during the war in Long Beach, California, I lived constantly with the fear we might be invaded or bombed. We lived only three blocks from the beach, and before the war started we would walk down there with our mother and play in the waves and sand. But during the war the whole coast was blocked off from civilian use. All along the bluffs, they set up giant antiaircraft artillery and camouflage netting which to a small child appeared to be several stories high. You couldn't see the ocean anymore. All you could see was the guns and camouflage.

We also had air raid alerts which made the possibility of invasion seem very real. Because Pearl Harbor had been bombed and California was on the Pacific and close to the Japanese, we felt we could have a surprise air attack at any minute.

My father was the block air raid warden. I'll never forget the fear I felt as he went out during air raid alerts and left the family huddled in the hallway. The sirens would go off, the searchlights would sweep the sky, and Daddy would don his gas mask and his big hard hat and goggles and go out to protect the neighborhood.

Although we had blackout curtains, my parents didn't really trust them not to leak light. So we sat in a hall closet with all the doors closed in order to be able to have the lights on. We had a wind-up Victrola which we'd take in there with us. My mother would sing to us to keep up our spirits. But we couldn't help being afraid for our father. And afraid for ourselves. Our prime protector was out protecting someone else. It gave us the feeling of being abandoned. The searchlights and sirens struck great fear in our hearts and yet it was exciting.

Many of our games involved war themes. We made hideouts and plans (and alternate plans) in the event Long Beach would be invaded or bombed. My sister and I planned for situations in which we might be like the poor, starving children of Europe we saw in the newsreels, living without parents, in rags, in bombed-out buildings. We were convinced that if attacked only children would survive and all adults would be killed.

We had a back closet that we figured was the safest place in the house to hide in case of invasion. My mother stored all her old clothes in there in big rubber garment bags. We figured that nobody would find us behind those bags. But just in case they did, we kept a bottle of ketchup in the closet. We were going to douse ourselves with it and lie there as if we had already been bloodied and killed, so that they would walk away and not stick their bayonets into us.

What was funny is we always thought

it would be the Germans who would invade. Although Japan was on the other side of that ocean out there in our front yard, we had very strong visions of storm troopers in big boots invading our shores. The Japanese were going to bomb us, but it was the Nazis who were going to open that closet door and see two little dead girls. I'm sure that came from the newsreels and *Life* magazine. *Life* came every week to deliver the war to our doorstep and replenish our fear.

The war also brought my first experience of death. I remember the day that we got the news that my cousin was killed when his troopship was torpedoed. Yet there were so many stories and movies around about someone coming back after being declared dead that I thought, Well, maybe they'll discover Jimmy alive someday. My mother tried to make me realize. "No, Jimmy is really dead. He was in the middle of the ocean. There isn't going to be any finding Jimmy." And I remember her crying, saying things like "He was so young, he never hurt anybody, and he never had a chance to grow up and be a man." It was a long time after the war before I gave up my hope that he would return.

Besides the fear, the war also created a sense of distrust. I can remember posters everywhere with Uncle Sam holding a finger up to his lips. "SHHH." Don't give away secrets. "Loose lips sink ships." You weren't supposed to trust anyone. You heard it on the radio, saw it in the movies. They'd tell you even the nicest person could turn out to be a spy.

Yet, at the same time, there were also a lot of positive things about the war, a kind of game atmosphere and team spirit. I remember all the neighborhood women sitting around the kitchen table pooling and trading ration coupons. My grandmother raised chickens so we often didn't need our meat coupons. And we made our own butter. So one month we might trade our meat or dairy coupons for sugar. The next month we might trade our sugar for steak or nylons. I know rationing was sometimes a hardship to my mother, but as a child seeing all these coupons trading back and forth, it was like watching a big Monopoly game.

Then everybody grew a victory garden. We had the most miserable, hard-as-cement, three-by-five-foot plot of ground, and grew radishes and carrots as our contribution to the war. But radishes weren't anybody's mainstay, and our carrots never got bigger than an inch. Yet we all wanted to do our part for the war. You got caught up in the mesmerizing spirit of patriotism.

There was a huge neighborhood lot on our block where many people grew things. You could hardly walk in that plot. There were a dozen different kinds of squash, corn everywhere, beans growing on poles taller than my head. As a child it seemed like the Garden of Eden. Community spirit always ran high. Everybody grew something different and traded around.

My grandmother belonged to a sewing circle at the church, and she would take my sister and me with her. All the little girls were taken. We tore up sheets

Educational Audio Visual, Inc.

America Calling: Take Your Place in Civil Defense • 71

and we rolled bandages for the soldiers. And we made up little bags with shaving articles and cigarettes and chocolate bars which they sent to the hospitals.

Then on Thanksgiving my grandmother would always call the USO and invite soldiers, total strangers, to come for dinner. We thought that was just great, having these handsome young men at our dinner table, people from areas of the country that we'd hardly ever heard of. We were very impressed.

The war pervaded every aspect of our lives. Even the Christmas parade. The tanks would go down Pine Avenue, great hulking machines, then Santa Claus would come. And we cheered for the tanks as much as we cheered for Santa Claus.

I remember the war bond rally at Bixby Park. It was one of the most memorable events of my life. The war made me special. I got to be on stage.

My costume was American-beauty-rose satin and it had a big white lapel that went from my shoulders down to my abdomen and formed a ∨ for Victory. I remember my mother sewing it, and I remember actually doing this tap dance on the stage in Bixby Park. Arm in arm, like the Rockettes, we formed a big ∨, and all the audience out in the park was cheering us on.

It was a time of many dichotomies. We were taught patriotism on the one hand, distrust on the other. Although there was great fear, there was also a good feeling, a believing in our country and our government, a sense of us all pulling together.

The imprint of those times still remains. The sight of searchlights (now used as advertising spots) continues to produce terror in me, a run-and-hide, cover-the-head response. But I also long for the feeling of patriotism and the community spirit of those years.

JAMES COVERT

When the war started, both my father and my brother enlisted. My father went into the Navy, and my brother went into the Army Air Forces. I was nine years old and all of a sudden I was the man of the family. I was at home with my mother and I would have to take care of her.

My mother managed a little grocery store, and I did errands for her, delivered groceries and so forth. I hung around the store a lot and heard all the adult talk and absorbed all the adult feelings. To me World War II was like a gigantic stage production. It was as if I was a character actor on a global stage, watching this huge drama unfold around me. It was a tremendously exciting time.

The first year of the war was very scary, though. We lived in Portland, Oregon, and there was this feeling that

I gained really from the adults that the Japanese were actually going to go beyond the Hawaiian Islands and attack the mainland. Nobody knew what was going to happen, and there was always this fear of attack. All the neighborhoods had their air raid wardens and their buckets of sand and arm patches and whistles. Every night you went to bed and wondered if there was going to be an air raid. I remember one time we went to the beach for a little vacation, and the Shore Patrol, who patrolled the beach with their dogs, came up to our cabin and asked us to close the blind. There was a little sliver of light showing through and there might be a Japanese submarine out there in the Pacific that would see it. That really made quite an impression on me.

At school we used to memorize the silhouettes of Japanese Zeros because we didn't know whether they were going to attack or not. We used to have air raid drills too. We'd climb under our desks and practice what to do if we were attacked. There was this sense of apprehension that it could occur. The sirens would go off and you wondered if this was the real thing. It was frightening.

Once the Battle of Midway had taken place, and after Guadalcanal, the fear of invasion, even with the Japanese in the Aleutians, declined. In the later part of the war I don't recall people taking the blackouts seriously. Once 1942 was over, there was a feeling that we were going to win. It was just a matter of how long and whether personal tragedies would strike our family

or not. After that it was like a marvelous experience. To be honest, I wouldn't have missed World War II for a minute.

I vividly recall the Doolittle raid on Tokyo in April 1942. It was perhaps the first really uplifting moment for Americans after the start of the war. We heard the news about seven o'clock in the evening, and we decided to have a family party, the three of us—it was just before my brother enlisted. We broke out the Double Cola, and I stood on a chair with a sheet wrapped around me and a flashlight in my hand. I was the Statue of Liberty, and all the family danced around me. It was a great celebration. We were so happy because all the news had been dark up until then.

As the war continued all of us kids acquired cast-off military uniforms from friends and relatives, and we'd wear them with the patches and the braids and the medals. I remember one time walking downtown and receiving a salute from a soldier walking past who probably thought I was a lieutenant. I guess we all identified with our older brothers and our fathers, so khaki became the normal garb for young kids my age. On weekends we would play war games out in the pasture with cast-off helmets, and nobody wanted to be the Axis.

Saturdays and after school were always taken up with activities for the war effort—like scrap drives and collecting tin and tinfoil, even string, and taking grease down to the butcher shop. The whole idea of saving and rationing was drilled into us, that our doing with-

out was saving lives overseas. It was the notion that we were all bound together to save and conserve in order to help our fighting men.

There was a shared sense of commonality during the war, that we all had the same goal. If you weren't in this group you were really on the outside. I remember even getting in fights because my mother, who was from Kansas—a traditionally Republican state—would sometimes question whether to vote for Roosevelt. I would say something like that at school and get into all kinds of scuffles, because if

you weren't for Roosevelt during the war you were not patriotic. He was the man who was going to take us through the war, and anybody who seemed to be against him was sort of un-American.

There were other tensions at that time, between servicemen and civilians. My brother came home one night while on leave, and there was a big party at our house where we all sat around the piano and sang patriotic and popular songs. Around two in the morning my brother took the girl he was with home. On the way back he stopped some shipyard workers and asked for a light—the shipyard workers would get off at all hours, day and night. Anyway, when my brother stopped them, one of the workers hit him over the head with a flashlight. Now, that's the story I got. All I remember is opening the door for my brother and seeing him all bloody. And he kept saying, "These goddamn civilians, they're making all the money and we're over there fighting." So that tension was very much there. The people who were not in the armed services were looked at as people who were getting wealthy from the war. Yet when you talked in terms of the Allies versus the Axis Powers, that conflict was submerged. It was there on a sort of neighborhood level, but not on a national one. On a larger level there was a solidarity, a unity, in the United States, a feeling that we're all in this together, and, by God, through our technological know-how and our determination and our downright good Americanism, we were going to win.

ESTHER BURGARD

It was very easy to get people to volunteer to help toward the war effort, because that was the main effort in all our lives, to end the war before it reached our shores. I was also very concerned about my three sons, and all the other sons who were available to be drafted into the war. My oldest son, John, was not drafted, but he volunteered right away for the air force. As a matter of fact, he hadn't finished high school when he volunteered.

Anything I could do for the war effort I wanted to do. The Red Cross was doing a tremendous job. Everyone had to do their share and I wanted to do mine. They asked me to go door-to-door in the neighborhood and solicit funds, so I said I'd try. I took my youngest son with me, he was just a little boy, and we went from house to house. We had very few people who would not donate. Even when a woman's husband had donated someplace else, usually she would want to donate, too. Everyone gave according to their means. The area the Red Cross asked me to cover was quite a large district in North Long Beach, but I was able to get some of my church ladies to help me and we were very successful.

I also sold war bonds during the war. I belonged to a Catholic organization called the Young Ladies Institute, and one of their projects was to sell war bonds. We set up a table on the corner of Broadway and Locust in Long Beach, and we had bunting on it and plenty of literature, and there were three to four of us there all the time. We really did sell war bonds, one right after the other, almost like selling apples.

Another thing I spent a lot of time doing was standing in line. So many things were rationed, coffee and sugar and flour, that any time you would see a line you would automatically get in it. My little boy would ask, "Mother, what are we standing in line for now?" and I'd say, "I don't know, but we'll soon find out."

VERNON SIETMANN

There was a great shortage of supplies during the war where I lived in Marshall County, Iowa. Automobile and truck tires, farm equipment and many more items were under federal regulation. You even had to register the serial numbers of your auto tires with the county board.

Tires were rationed and very hard to get. You could get what we called reclaimed tires that were reprocessed rubber. The quality was very poor, and sometimes they didn't run over a hundred miles. Anyone who had any

Library of Congress

extra old tires was required to turn them in. In some cases people went out to a ditch where the old tires had been thrown and discarded. They dug them out and sent them in, so you can see why they didn't last very long. In those days tires on the combines and wagons were the same size as tires on cars, so in the off season farmers would often remove these tires illegally and put them on their cars so they would have a way to get to town. They had to.

Because of the shortages everyone was called upon to turn in all the extra iron he had that wasn't vital or useful. There were scrap drives organized in the county, and on a certain day people would get together and make an effort to bring in all the surplus they could find. In our courthouse square in Marshalltown we had four or five old Civil War cannons, and even they were sent in and melted down for the war effort. That was quite a sacrifice, but that was how strong the feeling of cooperation was for the war effort.

FRANCES VEEDER

I grew up in an upper-middle-class family, lived in New York City, Beverly Hills and Europe. I'd been raised to feel that I was acceptable everyplace. During the war I followed my husband, who was in the service. In one small town where he was stationed, my mother had a friend. And my mother said, "Oh, you must go to see her; she'll help you get some lodging." We were staying in a terrible hotel there and lucky to have that.

I went and I knocked on the woman's door. She opened it and I started to introduce myself: "I've just arrived in town." She looked me over and she said, "We don't rent to army wives." And she slammed the door in my face.

When my sister and I lived together before I was married, my fiancé and my sister's boyfriend, who was a captain at Fort Lewis, came for dinner in uniform. The next day our landlady gave us notice, said she would not rent to anyone who "entertained soldiers."

So, on one hand you had all this patriotism, we're going to beat the Japs and the Germans, and on the other, as a practical thing, a lot of people looked upon the GI's as dirt.

Another contradiction was when we went home on leave to my in-laws in Beverly Hills. There was a war out there, but it wasn't beating on the doors and walls of Beverly Hills. When we came home they would try and celebrate for us by getting a lot of black-market food. It used to upset me and I'd get very angry inside. I had been raised conservatively and not to be rebellious, but that really made me sore as hell, because they would laugh and giggle about how "the butcher had to pinch my bottom, that's what this lamb cost." Some of my husband's family bragged that they could get "all the butter and tires we want." And they and their friends never seemed to have any difficulty traveling. They always could get a compartment on the train. These were the things that made you chew your nails.

SHIRLEY HACKETT

Before the war we were blasé. The whole country was having a good time. We were not prepared for war. Yet when Pearl Harbor was attacked you saw this country do something that was almost unbelievable. In less than a year I watched the United States transformed from a peaceful country to an

America Calling: Take Your Place in Civil Defense • 79

enormous manufacturing nation, from having Sunday picnics together to buckling down seven days a week to build what was needed for the war. You don't know what this country can do when people are pulling together, breaking their necks to do what they can.

There was a great coming together of people, working as a team, being proud of what you were doing because you knew it was contributing something to the war effort. Everybody did their share, from the oldest gentleman on the street who was working as an air raid warden and watching over us during blackouts to little children who saved things that were crucial at that time—paper, tin cans, scrap, anything that could be reused for the war. Buying war bonds was almost like breathing. I don't recall many people who didn't have them.

We all pulled together in a way that I have never seen happen any other time in this country. It wasn't something you could put your finger on, but it was a feeling that definitely was there, and everybody was connected with it.

·5·

WHY WE FIGHT

We are fighting to cleanse the world of ancient evils, ancient
ills. That is the conflict that day and night pervades our lives.
No compromise can end that conflict. There has never been—
there never can be—a successful compromise between good
and evil. Only total victory can reward the champions of
tolerance and decency and freedom and faith.

—Franklin D. Roosevelt

They were bad, we were good, and God was on our side.

—James Covert

World War II was the last of the good wars, the only one in this
century to be overwhelmingly supported by the American
people. Several factors account for the fervor with which Americans
rallied behind the war. First, the Japanese attack on Pearl Harbor
grossly violated the American sense of fair play. Not only had Japan
attacked without warning, but her envoys in Washington were kept
uninformed of their government's true intentions, thus undermining
any meaningful peace negotiations with the United States. Moreover,
Americans held the Japanese and their government in low esteem.
Japan's militaristic quest for empire was an affront to American
principles of anti-imperialism and self-determination. If Japan

succeeded in winning control over an East Asian empire, it would effectively nullify the long-standing American policy of an "Open Door" for American commercial and investment opportunities in China. Finally, many white Americans accepted the racist theory of a menacing "Yellow Peril." The initial successes of Japan during the first six months of the war reinforced all of these factors and practically assured that persons of Japanese ancestry living on the West Coast would be forceably moved to interior "relocation camps."

The American animus against Hitler and Nazi Germany and Mussolini's Fascist regime in Italy focused upon both dictators and their totalitarian regimes rather than on the German and Italian people. Hitler's theory of a master race and his systematic destruction of European Jews during the war bore out the contention of the Nazi dictator's earliest critics that he was the personification of evil. Mussolini was regarded as a comic buffoon, as well as the lackey of Hitler.

American military and civilian leaders weighed all of these popular feelings, but their strategy for winning the war was predicated on a "Europe First" policy. The war-making potential of Nazi Germany and its submarine warfare in the Atlantic was correctly deemed to be more dangerous to the U.S. than Japan's advances in the Far East. Indeed, the prospect of Nazi Germany dominating Continental Europe threatened America's major economic interest there. The Nazi industrial prowess and the possibility that Germany might be able to harness its science and technology for the "winning weapon"—an atomic bomb, for example—intensified U.S. fears of a Nazi conquest. These realistic considerations of American policymakers were shared by many citizens.

The war was presented as a conflict of philosophies: America's democratic principles versus the totalitarian principles of the Axis. President Franklin D. Roosevelt eloquently articulated the ideas for which we fought, which he expressed as the Four Freedoms: freedom of speech and expression; freedom of religion; freedom from want; and freedom from fear. The ordinary citizen reduced these four principles to one maxim: God is on our side.

OURS...to fight for

FREEDOM FROM WANT

National Archives

SAVE FREEDOM OF WORSHIP

EACH ACCORDING TO THE DICTATES OF HIS OWN CONSCIENCE

NORMAN ROCKWELL

BUY WAR BONDS

National Archives

SAVE FREEDOM OF SPEECH

BUY WAR BONDS

National Archives

OURS...to fight for

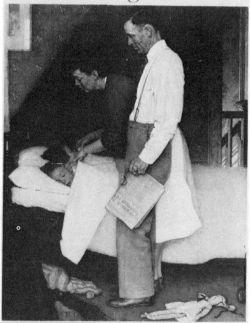

FREEDOM FROM FEAR

National Archives

ELLIOT JOHNSON

We were fighting to save the free world and keep it free. France was certainly gone, next would be England, then they would certainly come over to our shores. I didn't live in California, but I know the people in California were sure they were going to be invaded. Before we went overseas we learned they had picked up traces of a submarine off the coast of California. So to some extent America was threatened physically in our minds.

We were fighting for the U.S., France, England, the other free nations. And we had the help of a very wonderful friend—that was Russia, who, at the time, we thought was a very strong ally.

WILLIAM PEFLEY

I remember one man who had been recruited to the Portsmouth Navy Yard—he was in his seventies. I talked to him one day and said, "You've already had a hard life. You've been through it all. Why come here?"

He said to me, "Listen, Pefley, I got a son over there. I got a daughter at home and a wife. This country is going to get it sooner or later. I felt I had to put in some kind of effort. I wasn't doing anything back on the farm. I'm not as fast as you younger men, but I can get something done."

So they gave him a job handing out tools. We had many people like that, older men who came out of retirement to help the war effort. I even had a retired banker working under me. It amazed me to meet this man, who had

a job with a coat and tie before, working on my crew in overalls.

But we felt our country was threatened. We knew that there were German submarines off our coast. You could stand on the shore on Virginia Beach and see them. They caught one in a submarine net right near the naval base. Let me tell you, that's getting close. In the five-mile area between Portsmouth and Chesapeake, Virginia, they had an ammunition depot, the world's largest supply center, the naval base and the navy yard. If they could bomb two or three of those they'd completely put us out of business. So we felt we had to do something to protect our coast. I think everybody had this feeling. Many a time we worked nights in a blackout where we almost had to feel

THIS IS THE ENEMY

H. MELZIAN DREW JAP ATROCITY AS GRIM WARNING

our way to what we were doing. But we felt we had to do what we could. Otherwise we were going to be next.

JAMES COVERT

Growing up, my experience of World War II was the good guys versus the bad guys. It was very clear in everybody's mind who was right and who was wrong. Eisenhower referred to it as a "crusade," and in a sense it was. It produced a kind of moral outrage. To me it was like a medieval morality play. They were bad, we were good, and God was on our side.

Looking back on it now, I have to separate my own personal experience from fact. Hitler didn't cause World War II; it was a complex set of circumstances. The policies in Europe were very complex; it wasn't the good guys and the bad guys. There was plenty of goodness and badness to spread around.

But internally, it's almost a different feeling.

Pearl Harbor really brought an intense hatred of the Japanese in our family, because on December 7 a boy that we had grown up with, who lived across the street, was killed on the U.S.S. *Arizona*. He was in the boiler room when the bomb hit the ship. From the moment we found out, suddenly the Japanese were the enemy to us personally. It wasn't just a group of people out there, but they had really affected our lives in a very dramatic way.

The war against the Japanese became kind of a racist fight, whites against the yellow race, and the yellow races were inferior. In Europe it was a little different. You felt that Europeans were good people. They just followed the wrong leaders.

FRANKIE COOPER

I think the reason that the American people were ready to accept any of the propaganda they read in the papers was two words: sneak attack. Pearl Harbor. We couldn't take this. We couldn't bear the thought that those "evil little Japanese" had attacked a powerful nation. We couldn't take it. That was the basis of all our hatred.

WILLIAM MULCAHY

During the war I was as gung-ho and as patriotic as everybody else. I felt that we had been invaded, that we were in danger, that enemies were interfering with and endangering our way of life. Our men were being sent overseas, many of them to be killed, and it was vital that we not only defeat our enemies but assist our allies in their fight.

I'm a shade more cynical today about the reasons for our entrance into the war. We are all aware that some of the factors of war are financial. There's no question about it. Even though millions of men may die, many millions of dollars are also made during war. I still believe World War II was worth fighting, but I cannot accept the fact that we should let this kind of thing happen again.

DELLIE HAHNE

To this day I have a terrible ambivalence about the war. I don't know whether we should have fought it or not. On the one hand Hitler had to be stopped. He represented everything that was evil—death, destruction, lack of freedom. He was against everything we stood for, everything that made a good life. And I know this man would not have been stopped unless the United States had fought in the war.

On the other hand, I'd say, isn't there any other way to resolve our differences? Isn't there any way to stop a madman other than with death, with killing? I wish I knew . . . I wish I had the answers.

During the war the propaganda was all black and white; there was no gray. I remember an article in the *Reader's Digest* at that time entitled "One Small Unwilling Captain." It was a letter from a Japanese to his American friend in which he described himself in these terms. He said, "I am a small man. I am an unwilling man. I am a captain in the Japanese Imperial Army and I do not want to do this." This was the first time I had seen any gray, and it made me think: Is it possible that they're not all the bastards they're depicted? It was quite a jolt to see that article in, of all places, the *Reader's Digest*, because ninety-nine percent of what was thrown at us was propaganda of the most blatant kind where our enemies were pictured as senseless, heartless, cruel. It was the equivalent of the Americans being told by the government that the Germans had chopped off the hands of the Belgian children in World War I propaganda, which I had laughed at when I was in high school. And I thought, is it possible that the government is doing the same thing to us and now it's my turn to swallow this stuff? It gave me a lot to think about.

JOHN ABBOTT

I felt the whole country was going crazy. The whole attitude seemed to be that war was glorious. The sickness of war brought people together. Everybody seemed to be crazily enamored with it. Songs were written, dances created. War was so popularized that everybody was doing it. Not to do it, not to join in that laughter—you just stood out, something seemed to be wrong with you.

When I was at CO camp in New

THIS IS THE ENEMY

Hampshire, we'd go into the closest town to shop and get a haircut. The second time we went to the barber, there was a sign in his window that said, "No yellow bellies, conscientious objectors or skunks allowed in here." That really made you feel like shit. I mean, you'd see these things in movies, in old Westerns, but here it was happening to you. I really felt ostracized.

I couldn't understand how people, individually or in groups, didn't resist more, or consider other methods than using guns. Guns don't settle anything. I've always felt wars never settle anything. Wars just beget wars.

As far as Hitler was concerned, I'm one person, I'm not the savior of the world. I can only do for myself. I can only do what I think is right, and that's all anybody else can do. I felt I had to do my very best to hold on to myself and the few things I knew were real.

As alone as I had felt many times in my life, when the United States got into the war, and all the drums started

"THIS WORLD CANNOT EXIST HALF SLAVE AND HALF FREE"

FIGHT FOR FREEDOM!

National Archives

beating, I felt even more separated from other people. But somehow or another, I thought, for once maybe they were the ones who were going crazy and I wasn't.

SYBIL LEWIS

I married during the war years after leaving Sapulpa and coming to California, and shortly afterwards the fellow I married was drafted. When I found out my husband had to go to war I had very mixed feelings. Fighting for what? I thought. You read all about patriotism, and being a good American, and keeping up the homefront. Let's preserve democracy, and let's fight for freedom. But you must remember that I had never really experienced any equality in Oklahoma. I didn't have this feeling about democracy and patriotism. Yet that was what it was all about in terms of my husband going to war.

They had bombed Pearl Harbor, and now he had to go and fight for his country.

I could understand that intellectually but emotionally I had a lot of anxieties about what was going to happen to him, and what it was doing to our lives, and whether he was coming back in one piece, or whether he was coming back in bits and pieces. I went along with it—I had to go along—but deep down in my heart I didn't have this loyalty to my country, this patriotism, because, let's face it, I had never really experienced some of the things in life that maybe were worth fighting for. Whenever I heard people talk about preserving democracy, I could not help but think about Sapulpa, Oklahoma, and what my childhood had been like.

·6·

DEMOCRACY AND HYPOCRISY

I'm for catching every Japanese in America, Alaska, and
Hawaii now and putting them in concentration
camps. . . . Damn them! Let's get rid of them now.

—CONGRESSMAN JOHN RANKIN
Congressional Record, December 15, 1941

Hitler jammed our white people into their logically untenable
position. Forced to oppose him for the sake of the life of the
nation, they were jockeyed into declaiming against his
racial theories, publicly.

—ROY WILKINS, Executive Secretary,
National Association for the
Advancement of Colored People

World War II severely tested America's commitment to its
democratic ideals, especially in its treatment of blacks, persons
of Japanese ancestry on the West Coast, and conscientious objectors.
Each group felt the sting of official and unofficial discrimination, and
each sought in its own way, and with varying degrees of success, to
make democratic beliefs conform closer to reality.

Blacks were struck with the nation's hypocrisy in waging a war
against fascism and racism abroad while practicing racial

Democracy and Hypocrisy • 93

discrimination at home. At the outbreak of the war American Negroes were, for the most part, desperately poor and hardly any closer to equality than they were before World War I. In May 1941, A. Philip Randolph, president of the Brotherhood of Sleeping Car Porters, and other black leaders called for "a thundering march" on Washington to "shake up white America" and protest the lack of job opportunities for blacks in defense industries. The march was canceled five days ahead of time, only after President Franklin D. Roosevelt issued an executive order banning discrimination in defense industries and government based on "race, creed, color, or national origin." Roosevelt's executive order, the first presidential intercession on behalf of equal rights for blacks since Lincoln's Emancipation Proclamation, also created a Fair Employment Practices Committee to enforce the ban. Although the FEPC had the authority to investigate complaints, it had little power to compel compliance. Still, noted black historian John Hope Franklin has concluded that "its existence had a salutary effect on the employment status of Negroes."

The FEPC scored a major triumph in 1944 in Philadelphia, the country's second-largest war production center. When the local transit company hired eight black trolley-car drivers, a wildcat strike by protesting white drivers shut down the city's entire public-transportation system. Roosevelt responded by calling in eight thousand soldiers to break the strike and keep the buses and trolleys running. The strike was broken, and the black drivers retained their jobs.

Blacks found the military services no more willing to promote equality of opportunity than society at large. President Roosevelt condoned the segregation of white and black soldiers and allowed the Navy, the Marines and the Coast Guard to limit the number of blacks admitted to these services. Black sailors, marines and coast guardsmen were generally excluded from the officer ranks and assigned to menial duties. Nevertheless, many blacks were exposed to positive aspects of American society during their tour of duty and returned to civilian life with new—if not always attainable—expectations.

The most serious breach of civil liberties during wartime involved the relocation and internment of more than 110,000 persons of Japanese ancestry living on the West Coast. President Roosevelt ordered the forcible evacuation in February 1942 of anyone who had at least one Japanese great-grandparent. The internees, two thirds of them American citizens, were then imprisoned in ten relocation camps in remote and desolate parts of the country. The government justified its action on grounds of national security and public safety. In fact not a single case of sabotage by Japanese in the United States had occurred. In the court of public opinion, however, where racial antagonism against the Japanese ran high, the West Coast Japanese were convicted of real or potential disloyalty. When the evacuation order finally came under review by the United States Supreme Court in December 1944, the High Court upheld the validity of exclusion, but in another related case the justices held that while the government could temporarily detain a citizen, it lost that right after a citizen's loyalty was proven.

The conscientious objectors of World War II provided another challenge to American democracy by testing society's tolerance of the individual's right to resist war. The federal government offered the draft-eligible CO a choice of service in the military as a noncombatant or confinement in one of the civilian public-service camps established by the historic peace churches. The alternative to these choices was a court-ordered prison sentence. More than 5,500 men went to jail for terms that ranged from a few months to several years. Many of them chose prison rather than the camps because they did not want to comply in any way with the Selective Service System.

ALEXANDER J. ALLEN

When the war began, there were a number of blacks who were not enthusiastic about fighting it. They were sensitive to the inconsistency of a country that professed to be fighting for democracy and yet was not practicing it at home. But I felt then, and still feel, that the future of American blacks is in this country, and that our destiny is bound up with the destiny of the rest of the U.S.

Joe Louis, I think, spoke for most blacks and for most Americans when he said, "We'll win because we're on God's side." There were those who noted that he did not say, "God is on our side." That's an interesting distinction, and he made a point of it.

Certainly the blacks, as well as anybody else, and perhaps better than most, understood the negative side of fascism and racism. I was in Cleveland in school with Jesse Owens, and I remember when Hitler left the stadium at the 1936 Olympics because Jesse had defeated the best that Aryan society had been able to produce. So blacks were aware of what was wrong with Hitler and what was wrong with Mussolini and understood the reason for opposing the Nazi war machine as it began to take one country after another in Europe. But at the same time, blacks were extremely concerned over the fact that racism and bigotry and discrimination were a continuing practice in this country. Fascism was not a monopoly of Hitler, or of Mussolini, or the Japanese. It was something that we saw every day on the streets of Baltimore and in other places. We did not see much sense in the war unless it was tied to a commitment for change on the domestic scene. It made a mockery of wartime goals to fight overseas against fascism only to come back to the same kind of discrimination and racism here in this country.

So black leaders decided to fight a two-front war—one against the Axis and the other against bigotry at home. Both of them had to be defeated if this country was to live out its ideals. That was the philosophy of the Double V Campaign, which stood for victory at home and victory abroad. We felt it was an absolute necessity to take advantage of every opportunity to achieve change during this period of ferment, when people were perhaps more sensitive than they might otherwise be to the way the United States was viewed by its allies and by other people in the world.

In January of 1942 I went to work in Baltimore as the industrial-relations director of the Baltimore Urban League. It was an impressive title for a one-man operation. There was no department except myself and the secretary. But we worked trying to open up jobs for blacks in the building trades and the defense industries. In the beginning it was slow going. All the problems of racism and racial discrimination that were part of peacetime carried over to the war industries.

The Maryland State Employment Service, which became a branch of the U.S. Employment Service during the war, was part of the problem rather than a part of the solution. Even though President Roosevelt had signed an executive order that said all defense workers should be given equal consideration for job vacancies, that was just so much verbiage. Actual practice in Baltimore was that black workers were denied entrance to 39 Hopkins Place, where the best jobs were. Blacks were sent around the corner to the annex on Lombard Street, where they handled common labor and unskilled work. Even if you had a graduate degree in electronics, you would still be sent to the black entrance. And there were police to enforce it. If you resisted you might very well be arrested, as a number of people were. So many of the blacks would come to the Urban League offices to look for jobs, because they knew we were trying to place people in war industries. We'd go to work at the Urban League in the morning and the lines of people waiting to be interviewed would be two or three blocks long.

Trying to persuade the employers to hire black workers, you met with a lot of ignorance, and a lot of resistance. Many employers didn't have the courage to step out in a way that could conceivably subject them to criticism or abuse from their colleagues. To some degree there was a feeling that "I can't afford to be the first one. If somebody else would do it first, then I'll go along."

The sign reads:

IF NEGRO MEN
CAN CARRY GUNS FOR
UNCLE SAM
SURELY
THEY CAN DRIVE MILK
WAGONS FOR
BOWMAN DAIRY

Negro Labor Relation League

That's not the kind of thing anybody likes to say about himself, though, so instead you'd get "Well, the time isn't right," or "Black workers don't perform," or "We're afraid that our white workers will walk out." Under Baltimore city law at that time, you not only had to have separate toilet facilities on the basis of sex, but you had to have separate toilet facilities on the basis of race. So they'd say, "Well, we'd like to do it, but we can't afford to set up a whole new set of toilet facilities." So one of the campaigns that the Baltimore Urban League undertook was to change the municipal ordinance. Eventually, we succeeded in doing that.

For me the war period was a very compelling, very exhilarating era. There was a feeling that you had hold of something that was big and urgent and was not going to be here forever. There were opportunities for change which would not exist after the war was over.

And we did begin to see changes. In some places employers got a little religion. They began to realize the inconsistency and inequity of discrimination. Sometimes it was pressure from the government. A lot of times it was pressure from local citizens, black and white, who felt a commitment, sometimes through the Urban League, sometimes through other organizations. But mainly what

contributed to the change was the economics of the situation. Some companies just ran out of white workers to hire.

The pressures of labor-market shortages simply forced many employers to change their attitudes toward what they might call marginal workers—blacks, other minorities, women—in nontraditional capacities. The denial of opportunity to people who were competent and desirous of work just didn't make sense economically. War orders were pressing, they had jobs that needed to be done, so employers began to tap this long-neglected part of the labor market.

In 1942 the number of blacks in manufacturing industry in Baltimore was nine thousand. By 1944 they had increased to thirty-six thousand, which was a jump not only numerically but also percentagewise, from six percent of the work force to fifteen percent. After VJ Day the number dropped back to twenty thousand blacks, but they were twelve and a half percent of the work force. So the retention rate was far beyond the original expectation. Even though the peak had been passed, the employment picture for blacks was far better at the end of the war than it had been at the beginning of the war.

HENRY FIERING

As the Depression receded, you had a large influx of blacks into industry, although they were mainly relegated to menial jobs. My union, the United Electrical Workers, and a few others made it a policy to place special emphasis on the advancement of blacks on the basis of equality of opportunity, but the weight of the mores of the times militated against it.

You have to realize that the people who came into these industries came off the farms; they came out of the hills of Kentucky and Tennessee, and out of the South. Just because they came to work in the cities didn't mean they had changed their social beliefs. They had the same biases and prejudices that

they always had. They had to be educated.

There was a union I organized during the war at the Hoover Vacuum Cleaner plant in North Canton, Ohio. I succeeded in negotiating their contract for them and it was a very good contract, so I came out of it in good shape in terms of my relationship with the workers. One day I got a call from their leadership that the plant was shutting down because the company had hired some black women and there was a violent reaction by the white workers, both male and female, in the plant.

This was a lily-white community; they wouldn't even permit a black into town. But with the need for labor and the

issuance by Roosevelt of his Fair Employment Practices order, the company had hired a few black employees. But as soon as a black worker entered the shop, the three thousand other white employees shut down the plant.

When I got the call that there was trouble, I went down and walked into a storm. There wasn't much problem with the management. They were following the governmental directive, which was why they had hired the blacks in the first place, but they were frightened. Of course, my committee was frightened, too. I hate to say it, but it was so. I convinced them as to what

was right, but I couldn't get them to go out and confront their members, and they were leaders of the workers.

There was a mass meeting during working hours, and I took them on. I remember to this day a screaming, hysterical audience of three thousand people calling me everything under the sun and threatening me, but I knew I had the kind of standing that would make them stop there. They would not attack. It took a couple of hours, and although I did not convince the workers that it was right, I did persuade them to go back to work, that there was no alternative. When I look back at the hysteria that took place, I'm amazed that they accepted it, but they did. And it wasn't long after that there were more black women hired into that plant. Blacks and whites worked together, and there was never any other major problem. The people learned to work together very quickly.

You had that same kind of experience in lesser form in many other plants. During the war you began to see a bold change in the relationship between blacks and whites inside the shop. Compared to what it is today, you might say it really wasn't that significant; but for the time it was.

WILLIAM BARBER

I was born in Columbia, South Carolina. There wasn't much work in Columbia, so when I was nineteen I decided to try my luck someplace else. I had a couple of aunts and uncles in Philadelphia, so in '37 I went there.

My first job was as a butler in Chestnut Hill. My second job was as a short-order cook and a bartender at St. Anthony's Club on Twenty-second and Chestnut. I stayed there until June of '41. St. Anthony's Club was a fraternity house and so many of their members were drafted into the service that they had to let someone go, and since I was last hired I was the one to go. But the steward of the club got me a job with the Philadelphia Rapid Transit Company (PRT).

When I first went with PRT, I was a laborer. I worked on the tracks with a pick and shovel and a jackhammer. I was one of the smallest guys on the job, and my foreman made a water boy out of me; plus, I had to put coal oil in the lamps and set the lamps out for night work. I worked there for about a year, but I felt I could do better. At

that time you could go to Second and Wyoming after work and take up welding and grinding, which I did, so I worked my way up to welder and grinder.

Of the jobs that were actually available for blacks, that was about the best you could do. At the time, I was not able to become a bus driver, a trolley operator, a supervisor, a dispatcher, a clerk or a receiver or anything in other departments. But during the war things began to change.

There were a couple of write-ups in the paper about different places that didn't have any blacks, such as the cab and transit companies. They also had announcements in the paper of different meetings of civil-rights groups. I attended a couple of the meetings and they persuaded us to put in applications for trolley drivers. The biggest reason the company claimed there wasn't any black trolley operators is that it never had any blacks actually file an application. So forty or fifty of us went up there one morning and filed applications. We all went through an ex-

The first black transit car drivers in Philadelphia. William Barber is fifth from the left. *Courtesy of William Barber*

amination, and out of that number only eight of us passed.

About two weeks later we were notified to come to different locations throughout the city. The night before my first day it was announced over the news that they had accepted eight blacks to be trolley operators, and it was in all the newspapers. The following morning I got up to catch a trolley car to report to my location. There were ten or twelve people on the corner, and there wasn't any vehicle running in the city. I went back home, turned on the radio and I heard that all the trolley operators and the bus drivers had gone on strike on account of eight black drivers. So I walked down to the depot.

Once I arrived the whole area was blocked off by whites. Myself and two more gentlemen who were appointed to that location made an attempt to go into the building. At first we thought there was going to be some violence, but the guys moved aside. We three knocked on the door—it was actually locked—and the superintendent unlocked it and let us in. He explained the situation and said, "We want you all to sign this paper and you'll get paid for eight hours' work." So we did and every morning of the strike we had to go in to sign this particular paper in order to get paid.

The strike was not sanctioned by the union heads. The union tried to get members to accept us, but they were against the union and had a wildcat strike. The white drivers said they definitely did not want blacks on the trolley cars or buses because they were inferior, they smelled, they carried a certain amount of disease, and just about anything they could possibly say about a black. As far as they were concerned, it was perfectly all right for blacks to clean the toilets, but they did not want us operating the buses or the trolleys.

So there it was until Roosevelt sent the troops in. They tacked signs up on the bus doors: "AS OF NOW, THIS IS GOVERNMENT PROPERTY." They gave the drivers twenty-four hours' notice, "Either you go back to work or you go to war." So naturally, they decided to go back to work. For the next seven or eight days, every trolley car and every bus that left the depot or garage had two soldiers on it. One in the front, one in the back, with fully loaded carbine rifles with clips on the belt. And they were on those trolley cars twenty-four hours a day. The biggest reason they had those troops on there was that those white fellows were afraid that the black people were going to jump them. A lot of those routes went through black neighborhoods, and the white drivers refused to take a trolley car unless they had protection. They figured once they got out there they would be bodily

harmed unless they had soldiers to protect them. I feel that was a big reason for the troops. It wasn't for our protection. It was for the white trolley operators. The troops stayed on for about a week, until things cooled down.

At first, I must admit, I had a pretty rough time of it. On a lot of those routes the people were very nice, but on some routes it was like you went into a different country. I had people get on and attempt to pay their fare and see that I was a black man, then they'd step back and say, "I don't ride with no niggers," just like that. Then they'd step back off the trolley car and wait on the next one. I'd have others get on and pay the fare and throw it right on the floor. I even had people spit on me. I'd pull up to a corner and open the doors and they'd spit inside and say, "Go on down the street, nigger." I'd just close my door and go on down the street. I thought, "Well, I'll just take that as long as they don't hit me."

Once, though, I got very angry. This woman said she wanted to get off at Broad Street. I was a conductor, and I rang the bell at Broad Street. We let out about four or five people, but she was sitting in the back and didn't get up. By the time we pulled up to the next stop she was up, and she said, "Didn't I tell you I wanted to get off at Broad Street?"

I said, "Well, miss, I called Broad Street. I let off about four or five people."

And she said, "You know what, you black so and so, I'll spit in your face."

So I stood up out of the booth and I said, "Miss, I'll tell you what, and I want all these people on the car to hear this. Now, if you spit in my face this morning, the way I feel, one of us is going to heaven or to hell." So I opened the door and she got off and everybody said, "You told her right."

After a while, though, people got used to having a black driver and they just took it as it went. I stayed on the job almost forty years, so the way I look at it, anytime a man is on a job that long, he must have been doing something right. As it went along I think I had more white friends than I did blacks.

At one time after I had passed the examination for trolley driver, I almost decided not to go through with it. To be truthful, I was losing money accepting the job. As a welder and grinder I was making ninety-two cents an hour, and at that time they were only paying sixty-four cents an hour on trolleys. So I was actually taking almost a thirty-cents-an-hour cut. The biggest reason I continued was the principle of it. I figured that by doing that I would become somewhat like a pioneer and would prove to people that I actually could do the job. And by breaking the ice it would make a better opportunity for the blacks to continue to be hired. At the time they hired the first eight, they refused to accept another black application for the job for at least six months, because they wanted to see just how we would make out. But we made out all right.

I give a lot of the credit to Roosevelt. If it wasn't for him sending the troops in, ordering those men to go back to work, I figure nine times out of ten, I would never have become a driver. The strike would have continued and they probably would have said, "Well, the whites don't want you. You just got to go back to your old job."

Roosevelt was tops. And Mrs. Roosevelt. I was crazy about her. When both of them passed away, I shed tears, especially when he did. I was operating a trolley car when I heard that he passed away. And I teared. I wasn't the only one. We'd pull up to the corner and people would get on the trolley with tears in their eyes and they knew I had heard the news because I had a handkerchief to my face. I figured he was one of the greatest presidents we ever had.

MARGARET TAKAHASHI

When the war started I was married and had two children and was expecting a third. My husband, Jimmy, was gardening and going to school studying landscape architecture, and we had started a nursery in Los Angeles. We had been working on it day and night for about a year, and we were just starting to sell. Then everything went up in the air.

I was born in Japan. My mother was from Ireland and my father was from

INSTRUCTIONS
TO ALL PERSONS OF
JAPANESE
ANCESTRY
Living in the Following Area:

All of that portion of the City of Los Angeles, State of California, within that boundary beginning at the point at which North Figueroa Street meets a line following the middle of the Los Angeles River; thence southerly and following the said line to East First Street; thence westerly on East First Street to Alameda Street; thence southerly on Alameda Street to East Third Street; thence northwesterly on East Third Street to Main Street; thence northerly on Main Street to First Street; thence northwesterly on First Street to Figueroa Street; thence northeasterly on Figueroa Street to the point of beginning.

Pursuant to the provisions of Civilian Exclusion Order No. 33, this Headquarters, dated May 3, 1942, all persons of Japanese ancestry, both alien and non-alien, will be evacuated from the above area by 12 o'clock noon, P. W. T., Saturday, May 9, 1942.

No Japanese person living in the above area will be permitted to change residence after 12 o'clock noon, P. W. T., Sunday, May 3, 1942, without obtaining special permission from the representative of the Commanding General, Southern California Sector, at the Civil Control Station located at:

Japanese Union Church,
120 North San Pedro Street,
Los Angeles, California.

Such permits will only be granted for the purpose of uniting members of a family, or in cases of grave emergency.

The Civil Control Station is equipped to assist the Japanese population affected by this evacuation in the following ways:

1. Give advice and instructions on the evacuation.
2. Provide services with respect to the management, leasing, sale, storage or other disposition of most kinds of property, such as real estate, business and professional equipment, household goods, boats, automobiles and livestock.
3. Provide temporary residence elsewhere for all Japanese in family groups.
4. Transport persons and a limited amount of clothing and equipment to their new residence.

The Following Instructions Must Be Observed:

1. A responsible member of each family, preferably the head of the family, or the person in whose name most of the property is held, and each individual living alone, will report to the Civil Control Station to receive further instructions. This must be done between 8:00 A. M. and 5:00 P. M. on Monday, May 4, 1942, or between 8:00 A. M. and 5:00 P. M. on Tuesday, May 5, 1942.
2. Evacuees must carry with them on departure for the Assembly Center, the following property:
    (a) Bedding and linens (no mattress) for each member of the family;
    (b) Toilet articles for each member of the family;
    (c) Extra clothing for each member of the family;
    (d) Sufficient knives, forks, spoons, plates, bowls and cups for each member of the family;
    (e) Essential personal effects for each member of the family.

All items carried will be securely packaged, tied and plainly marked with the name of the owner and numbered in accordance with instructions obtained at the Civil Control Station. The size and number of packages is limited to that which can be carried by the individual or family group.

3. No pets of any kind will be permitted.
4. No personal items and no household goods will be shipped to the Assembly Center.
5. The United States Government through its agencies will provide for the storage, at the sole risk of the owner, of the more substantial household items, such as iceboxes, washing machines, pianos and other heavy furniture. Cooking utensils and other small items will be accepted for storage if crated, packed and plainly marked with the name and address of the owner. Only one name and address will be used by a given family.
6. Each family, and individual living alone, will be furnished transportation to the Assembly Center or will be authorized to travel by private automobile in a supervised group. All instructions pertaining to the movement will be obtained at the Civil Control Station.

Go to the Civil Control Station between the hours of 8:00 A.M. and 500 P.M., Monday, May 4, 1942, or between the hours of 8:00 A.M. and 5:00 P.M., Tuesday, May 5, 1942, to receive further instructions.

Japan. They met when my father came to the United States to go to college and my mother came from Ireland to work. They met on a train, fell in love and got married. They had three children; then they went on a visit to Japan and had me. They thought if they stayed and I was a boy I'd inherit, but since I was a girl, forget it. Plus we were mixed, and they don't like mixed people in Japan. So they came back to the United States.

Jimmy's parents were both Japanese, but he was an American citizen, for he was born in Covina, California. Anyone born here was a citizen. Since I was born in Japan, I wasn't, and Japanese were not allowed to become naturalized at that time. But we didn't feel Japanese. We felt American. That was the way we were raised.

After Pearl Harbor we started to get worried because the newspapers were agitating and printing all those stories all the time. And people were getting angrier. You kept hearing awful rumors. You heard that people were getting their houses burned down and we were afraid that those things might happen to us. My husband worried because he didn't know if people would kick him out of his jobs. You didn't

know when the blow was going to fall, or what was going to happen. You didn't quite feel that you could settle down to anything. Your whole future seemed in question. The longer the war dragged on, the worse the feeling got.

When the evacuation order finally came I was relieved. Lots of people were relieved, because you were taken care of. You wouldn't have all this worry.

People would come to the door and ask if the house was for rent. I got so mad once I hollered at them and the lady said to me, "No wonder they're kicking you out."

We had the baby on Easter Sunday, and it was a boy, and I was really happy about having a son. I had two daughters first, and I had always wanted a boy. Then three weeks later we were evacuated.

You could only take one suitcase apiece, but people who had gone to camp before us were able to tell us what to bring, so we were a little better off than others. My husband bought foot lockers, so our luggage was pretty big and we took sheets and things that the other people hadn't taken.

We sold our nursery stock to a different nursery, and all the lath houses we'd built, but we didn't get much for them. The rest of the stuff we stored with a friend who was reliable. A lot of people I knew gave things to friends to keep and they never saw the friends again, but ours was a good one.

Library of Congress

The day we were taken to camp we had to go to a special designated place to get the bus. This friend of ours took me and the baby so that we wouldn't have to walk. Most people just walked. We got on the bus and everybody was sitting there, and I was thinking, Gee, everybody's so brave, nobody's crying, and I wasn't going to cry either, because Japanese frown on weakness, so I wouldn't look at anybody. And then this colored lady came up and looked in the bus window and she said, "Oh, look at the poor thing, she has a tiny baby." And then I started to bawl, and I bawled the whole way to camp. I felt like a fool, because nobody else cried. They didn't even cry when I cried. They just sat zombielike. They could hold it in that much.

We were taken to Santa Anita Racetrack, and they had built barracks for us. The first people who were taken to Santa Anita had to live in the stables. They had it bad, because the stables had a lot of fleas, and they smelled. But they had showers. We had to walk there to take showers and wash at first, and it was almost a mile from our barracks.

When we first arrived, we were examined by doctors, and they made you open your mouth and I didn't want to open my mouth, so this doctor pulled it open, and I kicked him in the leg. I felt good about that.

The first meal was spaghetti without meat, and yams. Plain boiled yams. I'll always remember that. Nothing tasted good. The whole time we were in camp, nothing tasted good.

We were in Santa Anita a few months, and my five-year-old, Winkie, my old-

est daughter, came up to me one day and said, "Momma, I don't like this neighborhood. Can't we move?" And I just felt we had to get out of there. We had heard a rumor that Father Flanagan of Boys Town was hiring people. So, being a Catholic, I felt familiar with him and I thought he would help us. I couldn't stay in camp any longer. I just couldn't. So my husband wrote him a letter, and he wrote back right away and told us to come. That was Father Flanagan's mission in life—to take the rejected or unwanted. He had a home for homeless boys near Omaha and he needed workers, for all of his workers were being called up to the Army.

We wrote back and forth for several months, and nothing happened. We just couldn't get permission to leave. We'd go up to the office and say, "When are we going to get to leave?" and they'd say, "No orders have come out." So finally we telegraphed to the head of the camp. They were going to move the whole camp out in a few days. Our group was to go to Amache, Colorado, and we said, "Oh, God, we aren't going to get to go to Boys Town." It was very tense. I thought they wouldn't let us go. But finally they sent a telegram and we got permission. The telegram was signed by Herman P. Goebel, Jr., I'll never forget that name.

So we went into town and got the train tickets. And my husband was given permission to go back to Los Angeles and get his truck, and he picked up a lot of our belongings and drove to Nebraska himself. We took the train. He thought it was safer. Everybody was warning, "Oh, they're going to massacre you." There was a lot of fear, but I didn't have any. And everybody on the train was very nice. I don't think anybody even paid any attention.

My husband went by way of Arizona, and he stopped at a motel and people started to gather around and talk and look at him, and he got worried. So he asked where he could get something to eat, and instead he just took off and drove straight through to Nebraska. He said he stopped once and slept by the side of the road, but he was worried because we had heard that in Arizona several people had had their cars burned.

We arrived in Boys Town at night, and Father Flanagan met us at the train. I expected him to look like Spencer Tracy, but he looked like Eddie Rickenbacker. He was a very tall, gentle, warm man. When you first met him, you could feel this warmth. I've never felt that from another human being. He was so full of love that it radiated out of him. It was startling.

Then my husband came three days later, and we settled in this farmhouse on Boys Town property and started right in to work. We lived on a real farm with a pump and cistern, and there was a place you could plant your garden. We had a victory garden with the Bishop of Omaha. We raised the vegetables and gave them to him. We learned to can, and to cook on a cook stove, and what a real winter was. I just loved it there. I didn't want to come back, but my husband wanted to be his own boss, so after the war, in 1947, we moved back to Los Angeles.

When I think back to the internment, I want to call it a concentration camp, but it wasn't. We have a neighbor who escaped from Auschwitz during the war, and there's no comparison. In our life it was only four months, and that's not long.

But the evacuation did change our philosophy. It made you feel that you knew what it was to die, to go somewhere you couldn't take anything but what you had inside you. And so it strengthened you. I think from then on we were very strong. I don't think anything could get us down now.

HENRY MURAKAMI

After Pearl Harbor we were ordered not to go out fishing. We put away all the nets, tied the boats, and all you had to do was stay home and watch what was going on. It was worse than terrible. You could do nothing. Day after day you just had to stay around the house, and that's all.

On February 11, I was outside the house, holding my year-and-a-half daughter in my arms. And a big flock of tall American men came around. One

of them had a piece of paper in his hand, and he started asking me who lives where, where is this man, and so on. So I said, "What is this?" and he said, "We're just asking a few questions." I asked, "Is my name on the list?" And he asked, "What's your name?" So I told him. He was checking the names, and he found it. So right there he said, "You come with us for just a little while and you'll come right back." I called my wife and she came on the porch and I asked the FBI man if I could go in and put my shoes on. I had no socks, just Japanese slippers. And the FBI man said, "No, you don't need to change. You'll come right back." I believed what they said. I couldn't

argue. So I handed the baby to my wife and I went with them.

They took us to the immigration office in San Pedro. We were there two days and two nights, then they put us all in old trains. Two days and two nights more we traveled. No windows, all closed; you couldn't look outside. And suddenly the trains stopped and the guards said, "Get out." We came out, and all you could see was white, nothing but white. You couldn't even see houses or buildings. Just snow. They said eight feet high. And we found out it was Bismarck, North Dakota, and it was twenty-nine degrees below zero, and I was walking on the snow in my bare feet and slippers.

They took us to Fort Lincoln, and we had to go to the mess hall where hundreds of people were standing in line. You know how hard it is to stand only fifteen or twenty minutes in cold like that? Within a week I had frostbite. I couldn't walk anymore.

Why? We hadn't done anything wrong. We obeyed the laws. None of us were spies. We didn't know anything about those things. But we were all arrested because we carried fishermen's licenses.

After I was at Fort Lincoln a few weeks I received a letter from my wife that she had had forty-eight hours' no-

tice to evacuate from the island. She was eight months pregnant and there was nothing she could do. So she abandoned everything. Pregnant and with four children, how much could she carry? So she took the children and one suitcase and they all went to the camp the government had built at the Santa Anita Racetrack.

They were there about sixty days, then they were sent to Manzanar. In July I was sent to Manzanar and joined my family, and my new son who was born in May. And we were really joyous.

Manzanar was easier than Fort Lin-

coln. You didn't feel so much like you were in a concentration camp, but when I came there in July it was hot and windy. You can't imagine how windy it was. It would blow the heck out of you.

The camp was divided into thirty-six blocks, all separated, and each block chose their own manager. Right away I was appointed manager of Block 9, where all the fishermen lived. This was about the roughest block. They had a fight almost every day. I stayed at Manzanar for a year, but I just couldn't take it anymore.

I heard the United States was calling for help for work in Chicago. The government paid the bus fare to Chicago, and I decided to go.

The people at the camp called me all kinds of names because I volunteered for the United States government. They called me a dog, a crook, everything. When I left Manzanar, many of them didn't even say goodbye. But I took it because I had to think of the future too. What about after the war? I wasn't a citizen yet, but I had to think of my children. They were all future American citizens. So I thought I should do the best I could. That's why I worked for the government during the war.

I went to Chicago and started work at the Fort Bushnell Lumber Company on Summit Road. They were doing one hundred percent manufacturing for the government, building shipping crates for the B-29 engines and ammunition crates.

There is one incident I remember. The general manager wanted me to take the job of foreman of one of the departments. The trouble was, a lot of the Polish workers refused to work under me because I was an enemy alien. So the general manager said, "Okay, whoever can take Henry's job, come on out." But no one came out. So the general manager said, "Well, then I have to let Henry keep the job, because he knows how to do it." So we kept working that way until the war was over. One six-month period I worked almost twenty hours a day. The Army gave me an appreciation certificate for doing a good job. So you can imagine how hard I worked.

After the war I came back to California, but I couldn't fish anymore. I had no gear to start with. I had no money. How could I go back to fishing?

None of the old Japanese fishermen ever went back.

My own loss I can say, was $55,000 or more. Minimum. In 1940 I bought three new sets of nets. One was for tuna, one for mackerel, and one for sardines. The mackerel and sardine nets each cost $15,000; the tuna net cost about $25,000, because it had all heavyweight webbings. I worked so hard to pay for them. I bought everything by cash. I didn't like that credit business.

Each of the nets we kept in a big flatbed truck on the street where we lived. The day I was arrested I saw with my own eyes my three sets of nets sitting on the flatbeds. I saw them. When we were sent to Fort Lincoln I asked the FBI men about my nets. They said, "Don't worry. Everything is going to be taken care of." But I never saw the nets again, nor my brand-new 1941 Plymouth, nor our furniture. It all just disappeared. I lost everything. But I don't blame anyone. It was a war. We had nothing to do with the war, but we were its victims.

JOHN ABBOTT

Once you were declared a CO, you could either join the Army as a noncombatant, go to camp or go to prison. I didn't want to have anything to do with the military, but I was too chicken to go to jail, so I decided to try the camps.

The draft board sent me a railroad ticket, and I took the train to West Hampton, New Hampshire. The camp was way out in the woods, thirty or forty miles from any town. It was a Quaker camp, and there were maybe two or three hundred men there, living in old Civilian Conservation Corps bunkhouses. We were supposed to be doing "work of national importance," but we used to call it "national impotence." We'd go out and clean up campgrounds, empty the privies, make trails or sweep pinecones or dirt off the roads. Or they'd take us out and tell us to dig for some pipe they said they needed to find. We would spend most of the day out there in the field digging for the buried pipe. At the end of the day they would come back and say, "Well, I guess you didn't find it there. Fill the ditch back up."

I was not very happy at the camp. The camp system was just to keep CO's out of the way of the general public. We were not objecting to war there. There was nothing for us to do there except be slaves, as we worked without pay. I felt we should be doing something for peace, to show our antiwar position, not hiding away in a camp forty miles from the nearest town.

The camp was not right for me, and I said so, in camp meetings and to other people. I was argumentative, telling everybody that we were in the wrong place, so they sent me to another camp,

Courtesy of John Abbott

take the consequences, whatever they were. Staying in camp any longer was to comply with Selective Service, and compliance with Selective Service was participating in the war effort. So I walked out of camp one day and went down to Pasadena and got a job working at the Huntington Memorial Hospital doing gardening and laundry work.

I worked at the hospital for three or four months before the FBI finally came and got me. They put me in the Los Angeles County Jail, and I had a hearing and a trial before a judge. The judge pleaded with me to go back to camp, but I told him I couldn't return because the principle involved was compliance with Selective Service. The judge sentenced me to two years in federal prison.

It's ironic that later on, while I was sitting in a prison cell in the federal penitentiary in El Reno, Oklahoma, serving time because I refused to kill people, my older brother wrote me that he was working in Los Alamos, New Mexico, on a secret device that he could not name, that was going to shorten the war and save lives. That was, of course, the atomic bomb they dropped on Hiroshima.

in California in the Angeles National Forest. From the time I got there I purposely worked at trying to disrupt the camp, trying to show the men that we ought to be someplace else, that we weren't doing anything to fight the war.

I finally recognized that although I couldn't go to prison when I was first sent to camp, I had to leave now and

·7·

ROSIE THE RIVETER

I went to work in the riveting group . . . I remember my
brother, who was in the air force at the time, and his friends
laughed at me one day, thinking I couldn't learn this
mechanical stuff. I can still see them, but it only made me
more determined. I think it probably hurt their pride a little
bit that I was capable of doing this.

—RACHEL WRAY

On the eve of World War II women comprised twenty-five percent
of the American labor force. By 1944, the peak year of female
wartime employment, they constituted thirty-six percent of the work
force. In those three years five million women joined the fourteen
million others who had already found work outside the home. The
new recruits to the labor force included women who left their jobs as
maids and cooks for employment in defense plants, housewives who
had never worked for a wage, and young women entering the work
force for the first time. The new workers were white, black, Hispanic,
single, married, college-educated and school dropouts. As the
country's largest labor reserve, women were actively recruited by both
government and industry.

By far the best-known female occupation in the defense industries
were the riveters who assembled the thousands of airplanes produced
during the war. Riveters usually worked in pairs: one woman shot

116 • **THE HOMEFRONT**

the rivet into the metal plates with a gun, and another "bucked," or flattened, it on the opposite side. "Riveting and bucking" teamed thousands of women together at Lockheed, Boeing, Convair, North American Aviation and other airplane factories around the country. In Los Angeles, the major aircraft manufacturing center of the nation, one out of ten women in the city worked in an aviation plant at the height of the war. "Rosie the Riveter," the mythical heroine of the war, whose muscles bulged almost as much as her coveralls, was celebrated in song, films, posters and magazine covers and became the stereotype of the female defense worker of World War II.

In fact the labor shortages that resulted from the military's demand for manpower opened up thousands of jobs for women in many industries that had formerly been the exclusive domain of males. Women became welders, mechanics and crane operators. They assembled ammunition, bombsights and jeeps. They drove trucks, locomotives, buses and tractors; they pumped gas at filling stations, operated drill presses and stamping machines. Cowboy became cowgirl, and lumberjack lumberjill. Professional positions too opened up for women during the war. Newspapers, radio stations, symphony orchestras, even the male bastion of the stock exchange, began to employ females.

At the same time, working women continued to perform "women's work": cooking, cleaning, sewing, shopping and all the other chores involved in running a household. If they had young children, they retained the responsibility of caring for them during their "off-duty" hours.

However successful women were in the performance of their tasks at work and at home, they frequently encountered sexism on and off the job. Many men feared that working would masculinize women. Columnist Max Lerner publicly worried that the war was creating a "new Amazon," who would "outdrink, outswear, and outswagger the men." Hostility toward women was common at the plants. Often they were intimidated, harassed and insulted, and they were generally paid less than men for the same work. Women who remained at home criticized them for wearing slacks, for "neglecting" their children and for working alongside, and therefore presumably tempting, married men. Black women suffered the added burden of racism from both men and women.

Still, most women persevered, and many thrived. They enjoyed spending and saving the money they had earned and the sense of economic independence that came from receiving a decent wage. They gained self-confidence from the new skills they acquired and satisfaction from the work accomplished. At the end of the war many surrendered their jobs with great reluctance. A 1944 Labor Department study reported that eighty percent of the women interviewed desired to continue working and in the same kind of job after the war. Whether or not women willingly returned to their domestic roles after the war, the experience they had gained in the defense plants altered the way they viewed themselves and their future.

SYBIL LEWIS

When I first arrived in Los Angeles, I began to look for a job. I decided I didn't want to do maid work anymore, so I got a job as a waitress in a small

black restaurant. I was making pretty good money, more than I had in Sapulpa, but I didn't like the job that much; I didn't have the knack for getting good tips. Then I saw an ad in the newspaper offering to train women for defense work. I went to Lockheed Aircraft and applied. They said they'd call me, but I never got a response, so I went back and applied again. You had to be pretty persistent. Finally they accepted me. They gave me a short training program and taught me how to rivet. Then they put me to work in the plant riveting small airplane parts, mainly gasoline tanks.

The women worked in pairs. I was the riveter, and this big strong white girl from a cotton farm in Arkansas worked as the bucker. The riveter used a gun to shoot rivets through the metal and fasten it together. The bucker used a bucking bar on the other side of the metal to smooth out the rivets. Bucking was harder than shooting rivets; it required more muscle. Riveting required more skill.

I worked for a while as a riveter with this white girl, when the boss came around one day and said, "We've decided to make some changes." At this point he assigned her to do the riveting and me to do the bucking. I wanted to know why. He said, "Well, we just interchange once in a while." But I was never given the riveting job back. That was the first encounter I had with segregation in California, and it didn't sit too well with me. It brought back some of my experiences in Sapulpa—you're a Negro, so you do the hard work. I wasn't failing as a riveter—in fact, the other girl learned to rivet from me—but I felt they gave me the job of bucker because I was black.

So I applied to Douglas Aircraft in Santa Monica and was hired as a riveter there. On that job I did not encounter the same prejudice. As a matter of fact, the foreman was more congenial. But Maywood, where Lockheed was located, was a very segregated city. Going into that city, you were really going into forbidden territory. Santa Monica was not as segregated a community.

I worked in aircraft for a few years, then in '43 I saw an ad in the paper for women trainees to learn arc welding. The salary sounded good, from a dollar to a dollar-twenty-five an hour. I wanted to learn that skill and I wanted to make more money, so I answered the ad and they sent me to a short course at welding school. After I passed the trainee course, they employed me at the shipyards. That was a little different than working in aircraft, because in the shipyard you found mostly men. There I ran into another kind of discrimination: because I was a woman I was paid less than a man for doing the same job.

I was an arc welder, I'd passed both the army and navy tests, and I knew I could do the job, but I found from talking with some of the men that they made more money. You'd ask about this, but they'd say, "Well, you don't have the experience," or "The men have to lift some heavy pieces of steel and you don't have to," but I knew that I had to help lift steel, too.

They started everyone off at a dollar-twenty an hour. There were higher-paying jobs, though, like chippers and

crane operators, that were for men only. Once, the foreman told me I had to go on the skids—the long docks alongside the hull. I said, "That sounds pretty dangerous. Will I make more than one-twenty an hour?" And he said, "No, one-twenty is the top pay you'll get." But the men got more.

It was interesting that although they didn't pay women as much as men, the men treated you differently if you wore slacks. I noticed, for example, that when you'd get on the bus or the streetcar, you stood all the way, more than the lady who would get on with a dress. I never could understand why men wouldn't give women in slacks a seat. And at the shipyards the language wasn't

the best. Nobody respected you enough to clean up the way they spoke. It didn't seem to bother the men that you were a woman. During the war years men began to say, "You have a man's job and you're getting paid almost the same, so we don't have to give you a seat anymore, or show the common courtesies that men show women." All those little niceties were lost.

I enjoyed working at the shipyard; it was a unique job for a woman, and I liked the challenge. But it was a dangerous job. The safety measures were very poor. Many people were injured by falling steel. Finally I was assigned to a very hazardous area and I asked to be transferred into a safer area. I was not granted that. They said, "You have to work where they assign you at all times." I thought it was getting too dangerous, so I quit.

The war years had a tremendous impact on women. I know for myself it was the first time I had a chance to get out of the kitchen and work in industry and make a few bucks. This was something I had never dreamed would happen. In Sapulpa all that women had to look forward to was keeping house and raising families. The war years offered new possibilities. You came out to California, put on your pants and took your lunch pail to a man's job. In Oklahoma a woman's place was in the home, and man went to work and provided. This was the beginning of women's feeling that they could do something more. We were trained to do this kind of work because of the war, but there was no question that this was just an interim period. We were all told that when the war was over we would not be needed anymore.

WINONA ESPINOSA

In July 1942 I left Grand Junction, Colorado, where I grew up, and came to San Diego with my brother-in-law and my sister. I was nineteen, and my boyfriend had joined the Army and was in Washington State. In my mind San Diego sounded closer to Washington than Colorado, and I thought that would make it easier for us to see each other. I also wanted to do something to help the country get the war over with, and I knew there were a lot of defense jobs in San Diego.

I applied for a job at Rohr Aircraft, and they sent me to a six-week training school. You learned how to use an electric drill, how to do precision drilling, how to rivet. I hadn't seen anything like a rivet gun or an electric-drill motor before except in Buck Rogers funny books. That's the way they looked to me. But I was an eager learner, and I soon became an outstanding riveter.

At Rohr I worked riveting the boom doors on P-38s. They were big long doors that had three or four thicknesses of skins, and you had to rivet those skins together. Everything had to be precise. It all had to pass inspection. Each rivet had to be countersunk by hand, so you had to be very good.

I found the work very challenging, but I hated the dress. We had to wear ugly-looking hairnets that made the girls look awful. The female guards were very strict about them, too. Maybe you'd try to leave your bangs sticking out, but they'd come and make you stick them back in. You looked just like a skin head, very unfeminine. Then you had to wear pants—we called them slacks in those days—and you never wore them prior to the war. Finally, all the women had to wear those ugly scarves. They issued them, so they were all the same. You couldn't wear a colorful scarf or bandana.

I worked at Rohr for almost a year, then when I got married and pregnant I went back to Grand Junction for a while.

When I came back I went to work for the San Diego Transit driving buses and streetcars. I just saw a sign on a bus downtown one day that said, "I need you," and I went and applied. I hadn't even been driving very long. I only learned to drive a car after I got to San Diego, and I didn't know anything about driving a big vehicle like that. But the war really created opportunities for women. It was the first time we got a chance to show that we could do a lot of things that only men had done before.

The transit company had a three-month school. They had classroom lessons and training in the field. You had to learn the automotive aspects of the bus so that if it broke down you could call in to tell the mechanic what was wrong so he could come and fix it. You also had to learn all the bus routes and all the streets where the buses stopped.

For the training classes they took us out to what is now Spring Valley. There was nothing out there but sagebrush and an old dirt road, and we would practice stopping the bus and opening the door to let people on and off. One of us would be the driver and the others would pretend to be passengers so we could practice giving change and transfers.

In Grand Junction there were no blacks at all, so I had my first contact with them in San Diego. I remember in transit school they taught us that in a lot of states the colored people had to ride in the back of the bus and that in California they could ride wherever they wanted to. I had a lot of colored people get on and ask me if they had to sit in the back of the bus. I guess they came from the South and weren't sure what the rules were.

I drove buses and streetcars for about two and a half years. In fact, I was driving a bus the day the war ended. I let everybody ride my bus free that day.

RACHEL WRAY

I grew up on a farm in northeastern Oklahoma, knowing nothing but the Depression. My father lost the farm and we moved to town just when I was starting junior high school. I lived there until the eleventh grade, when I was forced to quit school to go to work.

When I was nineteen I fell in love with a boy from Oklahoma. George was also from a depressed area and joined the Navy to get ahead. He was stationed in California, and I decided to come and join him. I felt there would be more opportunity in California, and I was determined that I was going to have a different life.

I had twenty-five dollars when I left Oklahoma. I answered an ad in the paper looking for riders to California and paid twelve dollars for the trip. I arrived here with twelve dollars to my name and lived with friends until I could get work.

I got a job as a pastry cook at a restaurant in Whittier, a very exclusive place. I was making fifteen dollars and board a week and was very proud of myself. George and I were planning to marry. Then Pearl Harbor was attacked, and his ship was immediately sent out to fight in the Pacific.

After he left I knew I had to make it on my own. I saw an ad in the paper announcing the opening of a school for vocational training in aircraft. I was looking for the opportunity to learn something else, and I wanted to earn more money. I worked during the day cooking and went to school at night studying bench mechanics and riveting, how to read blueprints and use different aircraft tools.

After about three months the instructor said, "There's no use in you spending any more time here. You can go out and get a job." He gave me my graduation slip, and I went down to San Diego to look around because George's mother lived there. I went to Convair, which was Consolidated Aircraft then, and they hired me.

I was one of the first women hired at Convair, and I was determined that I wasn't going to lose the job and be sent back to working as a pastry cook. Convair had a motto on their plant which said that anything short of right is wrong, and that stuck with me. I went to work in the riveting group in metal bench assembly. The mechanics would bring us the job they had put together, and we would take the blueprints and rivet what they brought us.

They would always put the new people with another person, a "lead man." The man I went to work for was really great. He saw my determination, and he would give me hard jobs to do. The other girls would say, "Joplin, don't give her that, I'll do it." But he would say, "I'm going to break her in right, I'm going to do it the hard way." He told me later that he had made a mistake and been too easy with the other girls.

I tackled everything. I had a daring mother who was afraid of nothing, horses, farm implements, anything, so maybe I inherited a little bit of that from her. I remember my brother, who was in the air force at the time, and his friends laughed at me one day, thinking I couldn't learn this mechanical stuff. I can still see them, but it only made me more determined. I think it probably hurt their pride a little bit that I was capable of doing this.

Pretty soon I was promoted to bench mechanic work, which was detailed hand riveting. Then I was given a bench with nothing to do but repair what other people had ruined. I visited a man recently who's seventy-four years old, and he said to my daughter, "All we had to do was foul up a job and take it to her and she'd fix it."

I loved working at Convair. I loved the challenge of getting dirty and getting into the work. I did one special riveting job, hand riveting that could not be done by machine. I worked on that job for three months, ten hours a day, six days a week, and slapped three-eighths- or three-quarter-inch rivets by hand that no one else would do. I didn't have that kind of confidence as a kid growing up, because I didn't have that opportunity. Convair was the first time in my life that I had the chance to prove that I could do something, and I did. They finally made me a group leader to help break the new women in.

Our department was a majority of women. Many of them had no training at all, particularly the older women. We had women in our department who were ex-schoolteachers, artists, housewives, so when we could give them a job from the production line the job would have to be set up for them. I'd sit them down and show them how to use the drill press, the size drill to use, the size of screws, the kind of rivets, whether it was an army rivet or a navy rivet—a navy rivet was an icebox rivet, the army rivet was not—and so on. Then I would go back and check to see if the riveting was okay, and if there were any bad rivets they had to take them out. Most of the time I had to take them out myself. As a group leader that's what I did, and I did it at the same time I was doing my job as a bench mechanic. There were four male group leaders and myself. Theoretically we should have been classified as group leaders and paid for that type of work, but we were not. I felt that was discrimination and we were being used by the company and fought against it.

Shortly after I went to work at Convair I was chosen by the people in our work group to sit on the wage review board. The company had automatic wage reviews, and when I first started those were the only raises that we received. The women were lucky, though, if we got a five-cent-an-hour increase on a review. Some of the women got three cents, some of the women even got two cents, and some of the women were passed over. To us it seemed that the men's pay automatically went up and ours didn't. I was fortunate enough to get raises, even a ten-cent raise, and I actually had an assistant foreman come up to me and say, "Don't say anything to the other girls about getting a raise." I told him, "I don't discuss my personal wages, but how about the other women who are deserving, too?" So on the wage board I fought for the other women as much as I fought for myself.

Some of the things we did change. For example, they were forced to classify you because of your work. And somewhere in the back of their minds they had the idea that they were not going to make a woman anything but a B mechanic. As a B mechanic you could only go to a dollar an hour, and they were determined that no woman would ever become an A mechanic or an A riveter. But we really fought that, and we proved to them by bringing them on the job that we were doing A mechanic work and producing more than the men. So I got my A mechanic classification and a raise to a dollar-fifteen an hour.

Another thing we fought for was the two-hour break. For the first two years we were timed when we went to the rest rooms. You had to ask permission every time you went, and you had matrons checking to make sure you didn't loiter or overuse your time. Finally they instituted a ten-minute break every two hours.

I also sat on the safety board the whole time I was at Convair, for the safety requirements they demanded of women were more unreasonable than what they demanded of men. In the beginning we had caps and uniforms we were supposed to wear, but the women rebelled at that. We felt we could be safe and wear the clothes we wanted. Eventually the company did become a little more relaxed about dress, so we won some victories there too.

HENRY FIERING

During the war you saw millions of women coming into industry for the first time, but the mores of that era maintained that women were not as valuable as men. So the general wage levels of women were lower than those of men. Before the war there was no awareness of the issue. I'm thinking even in terms of myself, and I think I'm socially aware. Before the war my main concern was the general work conditions and the positions of the men. We had a plant which employed women too, but it wasn't until more and more women entered the work force during the war that they began to make some noises about the issue.

My union was one of the unions that made equal work for equal pay one of the big planks of its programs. As far as the men were concerned, there was a selfish motive involved, too, for unless women were paid the same rate of pay they would be used to undercut wages of the men. We didn't have a great need to convince the men this was so. Our union, and a number of others, adopted the policy that women be paid the same rate as men for doing the same work.

The pressure from the unions persuaded the War Labor Board to establish the principle of "equal pay for equal work." Interestingly, however, the employers resisted the order. When we sat down to bargain with them, they would ask, "Can a woman lift as heavy a box as a man?" And so they would whittle away at the principle. To get a settlement we had to make some concessions, work out compromises. It wasn't quite a hundred percent equal pay at the time, but it was about ninety, ninety-five percent equal pay. And we lived with that all throughout the war.

ADELE ERENBERG

When the war started I was twenty-six, unmarried, and working as a cosmetics clerk in a drugstore in Los Angeles. I was running the whole department, handling the inventory and all that. It seemed asinine, though, to be selling lipstick when the country was at war. I felt that I was capable of doing something more than that toward the war effort.

There was also a big difference between my salary and those in defense work. I was making something like twenty-two, twenty-four dollars a week in the drugstore. You could earn a much greater amount of money for your labor in defense plants. Also it interested me. There was a certain curiosity about meeting that kind of challenge, and here was an opportunity to do that, for there were more and more openings for women.

So I went to two or three plants and took their test. And they all told me I had absolutely no mechanical ability. I said, "I don't believe that." So I went to another plant, A.D.E.L. I was interviewed and got the job. This particular plant made the hydraulic-valve system for the B-17. And where did they put women? In the burr room. You sat at a workbench, which was essentially like a picnic table, with a bunch of other women, and you worked grinding and sanding machine parts to make them smooth. That's what you did all day long. It was very mechanical and it was very boring. There were about thirty women in the burr room, and it was like being in a beauty shop every day. I couldn't stand the inane talk. So when they asked me if I would like to work someplace else in the shop, I said I very much would.

They started training me. I went to a blueprint class and learned how to use a micrometer and how to draw tools out of the tool crib and everything else. Then one day they said, "Okay, how would you like to go into the machine shop?"

I said, "Terrific."

And they said, "Now, Adele, it's going to be a real challenge, because you'll be the only woman in the machine shop." I thought to myself, Well, that's going to be fun, all those guys and Adele in the machine shop. So the foreman took me over there. It was a big room, with a high ceiling and fluorescent lights, and it was very noisy. I walked in there, in my overalls, and suddenly all the machines stopped and every guy in the shop just turned around and looked at me. It took, I think, two weeks before anyone even talked to me. The discrimination was indescribable. They wanted to kill me.

My attitude was, "Okay, you bastards, I'm going to prove to you I can do anything you can do, and maybe better than some of you." And that's

Rosie the Riveter • 127

exactly the way it turned out. I used to do the rework on the pieces that the guy on the shift before me had screwed up. I finally got assigned to nothing but rework.

Later they taught me to run an automatic screwing machine. It's a big mother, and it took a lot of strength just to throw that thing into gear. They probably thought I wasn't going to be able to do it. But I was determined to succeed. As a matter of fact, I developed the most fantastic biceps from throwing that machine into gear. Even today I still have a little of that muscle left.

Anyway, eventually some of the men became very friendly, particularly the older ones, the ones in their late forties or fifties. They were journeymen tool and die makers and were so skilled that they could work anywhere at very high salaries. They were sort of fatherly, protective. They weren't threatened by me. The younger men, I think, were.

Our plant was an open shop, and the International Association of Machinists was trying to unionize the workers. I joined them and worked to try to get the union in the plant. I proselytized for the union during lunch hour, and I had a big altercation with the management over that. The employers and my lead man and foreman called me into the office and said, "We have a right to fire you."

I said, "On what basis? I work as well or better than anybody else in the shop except the journeymen."

They said, "No, not because of that. Because you're talking for the union on company property. You're not allowed to do that."

I said, "Well, that's just too bad, because I can't get off the grounds here. You won't allow us to leave the grounds during lunch hour. And you don't pay me for my lunch hour, so that time doesn't belong to you, so you can't tell me what to do." And they backed down.

I had one experience at the plant that really made me work for the union. One day while I was burring I had an accident and ripped some cartilage out of my hand. It wasn't serious, but it looked kind of messy. They had to take me over to the industrial hospital to get my hand sutured. I came back and couldn't work for a day or two because my hand was all bandaged. It wasn't serious, but it was awkward. When I got my paycheck, I saw that they had docked me for time that I was in the industrial hospital. When I saw that I was really mad.

It's ironic that when the union finally got into the plant, they had me transferred out. They were anxious to get rid of me because after we got them in I went to a few meetings and complained about it being a Jim Crow union. So they arranged for me to have a higher rating instead of a worker's rating. This allowed me to make twenty-five cents an hour more, and I got transferred to another plant. By this time I was married. When I became pregnant I worked for about three months more, then I quit.

For me defense work was the beginning of my emancipation as a woman. For the first time in my life I found out that I could do something with my hands besides bake a pie. I found out that I had manual dexterity and the mentality to read blueprints and gauges, and to be inquisitive enough about things to develop skills other than the conventional roles that women had at that time. I had the consciousness-raising experience of being the only woman in this machine shop and having the mantle of challenge laid down by the men, which stimulated my competitiveness and forced me to prove myself. This, plus working in the union, gave me a lot of self-confidence.

SHIRLEY HACKETT

I had a job with the telephone company and I was making thirteen dollars a week, but I immediately realized that I could not continue to support myself on that salary. I had to make more money because I was on my own, had to pay rent and everything else, so I applied for a job at a war plant.

I knew nothing about what it was like to work in a factory. I remember the first day I walked in there. It was a real shock to my system. The factory made ball bearings and it was extremely dirty. There was oil on the floor, and the area where we worked was very crowded; every inch of the plant was covered with machinery for vital work. The noise was so bad that you could not hear each other without yelling. I thought, I'll never get used to this.

The job I had was previously a man's job, very tough and very dirty. I worked inspecting ball bearings. Some were small and some of them were so big you could barely handle them. We had to put them on a gauge to see if they met the specifications they were supposed to. The ball bearings were made out of steel, and we wore heavy gloves, but it didn't make any difference. The ball bearings weren't the finished product, they were rough steel and ripped the gloves. You had to work very fast—this was piecework—and within three hours these thick gloves would be in shreds. By the time your foreman would bring over new gloves your hands would be bleeding all over the place. That was one thing you had to watch constantly—that you didn't cut your hands so badly you couldn't work.

The trays of ball bearings weighed a lot, and the women were not allowed to lift them. So the men had to bring your work to you, but they didn't like us in there taking their jobs. They didn't like that at all and let us know about it. In order to make life miserable for us and get us to quit, they would do everything they could to delay bringing the ball bearings to you. And we were doing piecework where speed was essential. Another thing the men tried to do was take advantage of you sexually. As they reached over to give you a tray of ball bearings, they'd rub against you in any way they could, try to feel

SECRETARIES OF WAR

or touch you. If you didn't let them get smart with you, they'd let you sit there waiting for that tray. It was really a bad situation, so consequently I began to lift my own trays, until one day I got smart. Some of the women who were there before me knew the ropes, and one of them said to me, "If you're going to be crazy and pick up your own tray, just lift it and drop it. Do it two or three times and spill ball bearings all over the floor. Then the big man will come down, and you know who's going to get it."

So I learned from the women who had been there longer how to get around these things. I was determined I was going to make it in that factory, because I was doing something useful and I could make better money than I ever had before. We received very good salaries. You could work as many hours as you wanted. Every state had laws about how many hours women could work, but during the war the government looked the other way and we were allowed to work as many hours as we could stand up without falling down. I can recall working as much as sixty, seventy hours a week. I got paid time and a half overtime and double time sometimes. There was always more work to do than they had people to do it. I was willing to work that hard because it was an opportunity to make money and save it, and we never knew if after the war we'd get the chance to make this kind of money anymore.

FRANKIE COOPER

The first job I had lasted only a month. The foreman was sort of a frantic-type person and wanted me to start my machine at ten minutes to seven, and I refused. I told him, "I've only been here a month and I'm already making my quota and I have no intention of starting my machine early." He said, "You know I can fire you," and I said, "You know I don't care." So he fired me.

Then I heard of an opening at American Steel for a crane operator, on a small ten-ton crane. I applied for it and got it. Then I had to learn it. The men said, "You won't learn it. Women can't do that job." But they were wrong. I think I was the fourth woman hired in the mill.

It wasn't an important or dangerous job, just moving gun mounts and gun barrels around and cleaning up the floor in what they called the Navy Building. The important work was inside the foundry where they poured the steel. It was all men in the foundry. You had to have seniority to run one of those fifty-ton cranes, because there was so much responsibility involved.

One day there was a terrible accident at the plant. One of the crane operators lost a load of steel, poured it all over. It just streamed everywhere, put a lot of lives in danger. After the accident they took him to the doctor and he was examined carefully. They found that he was losing his eyesight, that he couldn't see that far away in the brightness to pour the steel. They had to take him off the crane and needed an immediate replacement. They looked around and there wasn't anyone but women. The men they still had were on jobs where they couldn't be replaced.

By this time I had moved up to operating a fifty-ton crane, and I had learned the language of the foundry, the sign language with which you communicate to your rigger or chainman. So they offered the job to me, and I took it. Pouring steel was the hardest job in the mill, and the men said, "It's too big a responsibility for a woman. She'll never last." But I did.

The hardest part for me was sanding the rails. The rails are what the wheels of the crane run on. They're way up in the air over the concrete floor, and they have to be sanded every eight-hour shift because if your rails get too slick your hook will slide. That was the first time I had a crane with railings, and when I found out that the operators had to sand them I was almost scared to death. I thought, I can't do that. I can't look down at that concrete and put this little bucket of sand up and down. I just can't do it. And one of the men said, "Well, that'll get her. She'll never sand them tracks." That's what made me sand them. After that I had to. I had to show them I could do it.

It took a while to be accepted. We had a big coke stove, and we'd gather around it to get warm. On occasion,

when I had time to come down and take my breaks, the men would stand so close together around the stove that there wasn't room for me. So I just leaned up against the wall. The wall was warmer than where they were standing, anyway, because it had absorbed the heat from all the hours the fire had been going. So I would lean up against the wall and laugh at their jokes. And I would offer them a doughnut if I had one, and so forth. So, actually, I made the overtures. And after a while they began to accept me.

There was only one man who never liked me so well. But he was an older man, and to be young to some people is an embarrassment. To be young and a woman he couldn't tolerate. But I just sort of minded my own business. And I learned to be a good craneman. To gain their respect you had to be as good or a little better than they were on the job.

I was never absent, and I wasn't unique in that. There was very little absenteeism where I worked. If I woke up in the morning and I didn't feel too good, and I really didn't want to work, I could make myself go by thinking, What about those boys who are getting up at five o'clock, maybe haven't even been to bed? Maybe they're leaning their chin on a bayonet just to stay awake on watch. I don't even know their names. They don't even have faces to me, but they're out there somewhere overseas. And I'm saying that I don't feel like going to work today because I've got a headache? That would get me out of bed and into work. And by the time I'd stayed there a couple of hours, it was okay. I was going to make it that day. So I never stayed home.

There was only one really difficult problem with working. That was leaving my two-and-a-half-year-old daughter. When a mother goes away from home and starts to work for her first time, there is always a feeling of guilt. Any mother that has ever done this has had this feeling. I couldn't cope with it at first. I was so particular about who was going to take care of my little girl. At that point in the war, there weren't a whole lot of day-care centers. Mostly you had to find a neighbor who would take care of your child. But in a strange city, I just couldn't see taking my little girl to a strange person. So I was continually hunting somebody to take care of her. I finally found a good day-care center. But in the meantime, once or twice, I even brought her home to my mother in Kentucky. So I was separated from her for two or three months at a time. And then I would find maybe a good day-care center, or somebody that I trusted; I'd get acquainted with them, and then I'd bring her back. But women from the beginning of time who've worked have had to leave their children, and they're still doing the same thing, and they still have this great guilt complex. My personal feeling is that sometimes it's good for the child. It teaches children to rely on themselves, to learn to do a little more for themselves. And my child was a little on the spoiled side anyway. She needed to be with other children and other grownups, away from me. So when I look back on it now, I think that it was a plus for me, to have her learn about different people and be with them, because she was an only child.

That's the reason I relate so much with women who are trying to get into nontraditional jobs today, because during the war we had those jobs out of necessity, and then after the war they were no longer there.

Women have actually had nontraditional jobs since the first wagon train went across the country. When they arrived at the place where they wanted to settle, they helped cut the logs, they helped put them together, they helped put the mud between the logs of the cabins and they made a home and had their babies inside. And every time a war comes along women take up nontraditional work again. During the Civil War they worked in factories, they helped make musket balls, they made clothing for the troops, and they kept the home fires burning the way they always have. World War I came along and they did the same thing. After the war was over, they went back home. World War II it was exactly the same thing, but the women were different in World War II: they didn't want to go back home and many of them didn't. And if they did go back home, they never forgot, and they told their daughters, "You don't have to be just a homemaker. You can be anything you want to be." And so we've got this new generation of women.

INEZ SAUER

I was thirty-one when the war started, and I had never worked in my life before. I had a six-year-old daughter and two boys, twelve and thirteen. We were living in Norwalk, Ohio, in a huge home in which we could fit about two hundred people playing bridge, and once in a while we filled it.

I remember my first husband saying to me, "You've lived through a depression and you weren't even aware that it was here." It was true. I knew that people were without work and that lots of people were having a hard time, but it never seemed to affect us or our friends. They were all the same ilk— all college people and all golfing and bridge-playing companions. I suppose you'd call it a life of ease. We always kept a live-in maid, and we never had to go without anything.

Before the war my life was bridge and golf and clubs and children. One group I belonged to was a children's-improvement group. I sat one night at the meeting and looked around at the group of women—there must have been thirty of us sitting there—and each one of us had maids, and our children were all at home with the maids. We were sitting there discussing how to improve our children, and they would have been far better off if we'd been home taking care of them.

When the war broke out my husband's rubber-matting business in Ohio

had to close due to the war restrictions on rubber. We also lost our live-in maid, and I could see there was no way I could possibly live the way I was accustomed to doing. So I took my children home to my parents in Seattle.

The Seattle papers were full of ads for women workers needed to help the war effort. "Do your part, free a man for service." Being a DAR, I really wanted to help the war effort. I could have worked for the Red Cross and rolled bandages, but I wanted to do something that I thought was really vital. Building bombers was, so I answered an ad for Boeing.

My mother was horrified. She said no one in our family had ever worked in a factory. "You don't know what kind of people you're going to be associated with." My father was horrified, too, no matter how I tried to impress on him that this was a war effort on my part. He said, "You'll never get along with the people you'll meet there." My husband thought it was utterly ridiculous. I had never worked. I didn't know how to handle money, as he put it. I was nineteen when I was married. My husband was ten years older and he always made me feel like a child, so he didn't think I would last very long at the job, but he was wrong.

They started me as a clerk in this huge toolroom. I had never handled a tool in my life outside of a hammer.

Some man came in and asked for a bastard file. I said to him, "If you don't control your language, you won't get any service here." I went to my supervisor and said, "You'll have to correct this man. I won't tolerate that kind of language." He laughed and laughed and said, "Don't you know what a bastard file is? It's the name of a very coarse file." He went over and took one out and showed me.

So I said to him, "If I'm going to be part of this organization, I must have some books, something that shows me how I can learn to do what I'm supposed to do." This was an unheard-of request. It went through channels, and they finally brought me some large classified material that showed all the tools and machinery needed to build the B-17s. So gradually I educated myself about the various tools and their uses, and I was allowed to go out and roam around the machine area and become acquainted with what they were doing. The results showed on my paycheck.

I started at Boeing at forty-six and a half cents an hour. That was remarkable, women working and earning that sort of pay. After I had worked there a few months, Boeing themselves upped my salary to sixty-two and a half cents an hour, which was really thrilling. No one would believe it, myself least of all. From then on I had steady increases. Eventually I became chief clerk of the toolroom. I think I was the first woman chief clerk they had.

The first year I worked seven days a week. We didn't have any time off. They did allow us Christmas off, but

Thanksgiving we had to work. That was a hard thing to do. The children didn't understand. My mother and father didn't understand, but I worked. I think that put a little iron in my spine, too. I did something that was against my grain, but I did it, and I'm glad.

Since I was the chief clerk, they gave me the privilege of coming to work a half-hour early in the morning and staying over thirty to forty minutes at night. Because I was working late one night I had a chance to see President Roosevelt. They said he was coming in on the swing shift, after four o'clock, so I waited to see him. They cleared out all the aisles of the main plant, and he went through in a big open-air limousine. He smiled and he had his long cigarette holder, and he was very, very pleasant. "Hello there, how are you? Keep up the war effort. Oh, you women are doing a wonderful job." We were all thrilled to think the President could take time out of the war effort to visit us factory workers. But it gave us a lift, and I think probably we worked harder.

Boeing was a real education for me. It taught me a different way of life. I had never been around uneducated people before, people that worked with their hands. I was prudish and had never been with people that used coarse language. Since I hadn't worked before, I didn't know there was such a thing as the typical male ego. My contact with my first supervisor was one of animosity, in which he stated, "The happiest day of my life will be when I say goodbye to each one of you women as I usher you out the front door." I didn't understand that kind of resentment, but it was prevalent throughout the plant. Many of the men felt that no woman could come in and run a lathe, but they did. I learned that just because you're a woman and have never worked is no reason you can't learn. The job really broadened me. I had led a very sheltered life. I had had no contact with Negroes except as maids or gardeners. My mother was a Virginian, and we were brought up to think that colored people were not on the same economic or social level. I learned differently at Boeing. I learned that because a girl is a Negro she's not necessarily a maid, and because a man is a Negro doesn't mean that all he can do is dig. In fact, I found that some of the black people I got to know there were very superior, and certainly equal to me—equal to anyone I ever knew. I learned that color has nothing at all to do with ability.

Before I worked at Boeing, I also had had no exposure to unions. After I was there a while I joined the machinists' union. We had a contract dispute and we had a one-day walkout to show Boeing our strength. We went on this march through the financial district in downtown Seattle.

My mother happened to be down there seeing the president of the Seattle First National Bank at the time. Seeing this long stream of Boeing peo-ple he interrupted her and said, "Mrs. Ely, they seem to be having a labor walkout. Let's go out and see what's going on." So my mother and a number of the people from the bank walked outside to see what was happening. And we came down the middle of the street—I think there were probably five thousand of us. I saw my mother. I could recognize her—she was tall and stately—and I waved and said, "Hello, Mother." That night when I got home I thought she was never going to honor my name again. She said, "To think my daughter was marching in that labor demonstration. How could you do that to the family?" But I could see that it was a new, new world.

My mother warned me when I took the job that I would never be the same. She said, "You will never want to go back to being a housewife." At that time I didn't think it would change a thing, but she was right, it definitely did.

I had always been in a shell; I'd always been protected. But at Boeing I found a freedom and an independence I had never known. After the war I could never go back to playing bridge again, being a club woman and listening to a lot on inanities when I knew there were things you could use your mind for. The war changed my life completely. I guess you could say, at thirty-one I finally grew up.

BARBARA DE NIKE

My sister and I were living together in Fayetteville, New York, while our husbands were in the service, and we had three babies with us. Stuck in a house with three kids under the age of three, we got quite stir crazy. There was a factory in Fayetteville, Precision Die Casting Corporation, that was making munitions and asking for people to come to work. So we got the idea of sharing a job between us so that one of us could get out while the other stayed home with the kids. We decided to try it.

We listed the skills that we both had. We could both type, answer the phones, do filing, things like that. We made our little list, and my sister went over and talked to the personnel lady to see if it would be possible for us to share a job. She said it would be, but the only thing they had open right then was filing. My sister said, "Fine, we would be glad to try that." So we took the job.

It turned out that to them filing meant putting on heavy gloves and knocking a burr off an aluminum casting with a long metal file. Well, that was a surprise to us. It was a very tiring physical job. You came home just totally exhausted, with your shoulders aching and your hands covered with blisters.

We stuck at it for about three months, until finally an efficiency expert came in one day and timed a job my sister was working on. She was taking an aluminum casting, drawing it across a piece of sandpaper and dropping it into a drawer. You had to do it with two hands, and you did it over and over again until your arms were ready to fall off. The efficiency expert timed her for a few minutes, multiplied that to the hour, and set that as the hourly rate for this job. It was ridiculous and unfair, a completely impossible rate to maintain, so my sister came home that night and said, "I have quit our job. You can go back if you want to, but I can't stand it." And that was the end of our little defense work.

DELLIE HAHNE

I had about two dozen jobs during World War II. I wanted to do things that were fun and jobs that I knew I'd never get a crack at unless there was a war on. I did everything but work in factories, because I knew I could not stand eight hours a day adjusting bolts. I drove a taxi, worked on a newspaper, as a waitress, and in a dry-cleaning shop.

I even pumped gas for a time. Standard Oil put us through a training course. I learned how to lube cars. I was so green I thought the dipstick for checking the oil was kept in the station. The first time I had to measure oil I was looking all over for it, and I found out it was right there in the car. That came as a surprise. But the hardest time I had was with the women. Many did not like to see liberated women. They'd drive in and say, "Well, isn't Joe here?" And I'd say, "Am I not as good as Joe?" And the answer was "No, you're not." And Joe told me he could go out and take a monkey wrench and drop it right on the hood of the woman's car and she would smile sweetly. So he said, "Don't let it bother you, it's going to take a while."

Archives of Labor and Urban Affairs, Wayne State University

WILLIAM MULCAHY

During the war I worked for RCA in Camden, New Jersey, and supervised the manufacture of the nose-cone portion of the proximity fuse. It was a very specialized electronic assembly operation and required a great deal of dexterity and a very delicate touch. For that reason it was almost entirely a female operation. At RCA we had never put together such a work force in such a short time. We were hiring at the rate of twenty-five to thirty a day and wound up with about eight thousand women and some fifteen men. The fifteen men included stock clerks, foremen, assistant foremen, inspectors and so on.

I had women working in the plant from the Philadelphia Main Line who had never done anything but go to Bryn Mawr, but who rightly felt that working in a war plant was the appropriate thing to do. We had several women like that from the Main Line who were driven to work by chauffeurs. One in particular remains in my mind, a very lovely young woman who wore her fur coat to the plant in the winter. She always dressed magnificently, but, by God, she sat on the end of that line and she worked away with that soldering iron and those pliers, just the same as the black girl down the line who came from the center of Camden.

I gained a real respect for women's capabilities during the war. Their suggestions of how to better do their jobs surprised so many of the oldsters who felt that women just did what they were told to do. Their respect for the intellectual and physical capabilities of women was definitely heightened.

Prior to the war the idea of a woman supervisor, God forbid, was horrible. But during the war we made many women group leaders and salaried supervisors because, by that time, we had learned that women could do things that we had never dreamed they could do: supervise, manage, chew somebody out, not go into hysterics if things went wrong. Since then I think it has become relatively common in industry for women to supervise large groups of other women.

Unfortunately, when the war ended, despite the skill and patriotism the women had displayed, we were forced to lay them off. I will never forget the day after the war ended. We met the girls at the door, and they were lined up all the way down Market Street to the old movie theater about eight blocks away, and we handed them a slip to go over to personnel and get their severance pay. We didn't even allow them in the building, all these women with whom I had become so close, who had worked seven days a week for years and had been commended so many times by the Navy for the work they were doing. It seemed to all of us who were not dyed-in-the-wool, hard-bitten factory men that this was a pretty cavalier way of doing it, but there was nothing we could do. There was no further work. All our contracts were canceled.

MEN OF DEFENSE

We were in a survival mode. People knew that, and they worked together to get the job done. We had a common purpose. We worked as a team. We had the skills. We had the machinery. We had the materials. We had the know-how. We achieved.

—DON JOHNSON

During World War II America outproduced the rest of the world, Allied and Axis powers combined. By 1944, the Willow Run aircraft factory near Detroit, the largest in the world, was turning out a B-24 bomber every sixty-three minutes. In the shipyards of the West Coast ten-thousand-ton Liberty ships were being launched at the rate of two per day. Before the war had ended American factories had turned out some 300,000 airplanes, 87,000 warships, 102,000 tanks and self-propelled guns, nearly 400,000 artillery pieces, and 47 million tons of artillery ammunition. At the same time American farmers produced enough to feed not only the U.S. military and civilian populations but also millions of our allies overseas. This miracle of production, achieved by the "men of defense" and their feminine counterparts in the factories and on the farms, was no less important to America's victory than the valor of its men in uniform.

During the war the work force increased sharply, climbing from 46.5 million in 1940 to over 53 million in 1945. People from all

Culver Pictures, Inc.

National Archives

Educational Audio Visual, Inc.

professions were drawn into the war effort—white-collar workers, scientists, lawyers, teachers. Unemployment virtually disappeared. There were jobs for even the marginal workers—teenagers, the aged, the handicapped, convicts. With job security insured by the labor shortages and the insatiable demands of the military for war materials, union organizers increased the membership of unions from 9.5 million to 15 million during the war. Union leaders provided government and management with a no-strike pledge in 1941 as evidence of organized labor's good citizenship. With the notable exception of John L. Lewis' United Mine Workers strike of the coal industry in 1943, the unions generally honored the no-strike pledge for the duration of the war.

Business, particularly the biggest corporations that were most capable of fulfilling large defense contracts on schedule, grew even larger during the war. Moreover, the managerial skills and organizing talents that served large corporations so well in producing war goods would enable these firms to retain their lead and dominate the market after the war.

Farmers were proud of the government's wartime slogan "Food will win the war and write the peace." Agriculture had fared badly during the 1930s due to both the depressed economy and severe climatic conditions. The Depression left many farmers dispirited and doubtful about their future. But the good weather of the 1940s and the wartime demand for food and fiber gave farmers a new lease on life. Farm production increased by fifty percent over the previous high production period of World War I, and farm income rose dramatically, too, until the government imposed ceiling prices on agricultural products. By the end of the war many farmers had retired the mortgage on their farms, and they entered the postwar period with renewed confidence and efficiency.

The production effort was not without its human cost. Inexperienced workers operating dangerous machinery and the paramount importance of speed resulted in a high rate of industrial accidents. In January 1944, the federal government announced that the toll of personal injuries in the factories exceeded those of the battlefield.

However dangerous or important their tasks, the men of defense who served their country on the homefront could never quite shake the doubts they had about their exemption from military service. Those who were able-bodied and were exempt because the knowledge or skills they possessed were deemed vital for the war effort also lived with the uncertainty that their exemption could end overnight. Men who were classified 4-F, or disqualified for military service because of a physical or mental impairment, shared the same doubts about their contribution to the war effort as the able-bodied who served their country in a civilian capacity.

JOHN GROVE

I had received a parental-support draft deferment in 1940. On December 8, 1941, that was terminated, and as a research scientist I was "frozen" into my job at the Shell Chemical Company fertilizer-munitions factory, where we were manufacturing ammonia from natural gas and air. By 1943 my three younger brothers were in the air force, and although I was getting deferments I didn't feel that I was doing that much for the war effort. I was beginning to realize, too, that I had considerable technical ability, which I had never recognized before, and I felt that I was wasting it where I was.

By sheer coincidence a man who had been a superior of mine at the company, but who had somehow disappeared, came in one day wearing a badge: UCRL. I saw the badge and realized immediately what it stood for— it had to be University of California Radiation Lab. Another friend of mine, a very able man, saw the badge and immediately went and got a job at the University of California. About two weeks after he got the job, I asked him what he was doing. He said he couldn't tell me, but that it was very important,

and he urged me to apply; so I did. I was interviewed by the man who later became my boss. He said, "I can't tell you what you'll be doing. All I can tell you is that there is nothing more important in the United States than this project. If we fail, Germany will probably win the war."

I knew that if I went to work at UCRL I might be throwing my career away at Shell and that when the war was over I probably wouldn't have a job. My salary was frozen, and I would have to work a minimum of fifty-four hours a week, and frequently overtime with no extra pay, but I eagerly accepted the job. I felt that as a scientist I could do more than fire a rifle, and here was an even greater opportunity than I had hoped for to make a contribution.

It took me about two weeks to realize what I was working on. I was given a mysterious product to purify, and as I went through this chemistry of purification I naturally wondered what it was. My boss said, "Well, you're purifying T." And I said, "Well, that's a joke." He said, "T stands for Tube Alloy. It's the Tube Alloy Project* and T is what you're purifying." Well, as I went

---

*Tube Alloy was the code name for an Anglo-American body set up to handle all aspects of nuclear energy.

through the chemistry and began to study the method of purification, I began to realize more and more that the only thing T could be was uranium.

The payoff came when I had been there a couple of weeks and my boss brought in this huge steel container, or target, he called it. It weighed maybe twenty pounds, and I could see that it had gone through tremendous temperature. He said, "This is from the new 184-inch cyclotron. The power just came on today. You're going to have to clean that off with concentrated nitric acid. Don't spill anything." As I was working on it, trying to clean it off, I became aware that my boss was standing right over my shoulder, drinking a Coke. I thought to myself, This is strange. Then all of a sudden his hands started shaking and he said, "Don't spill anything. It's worth three million dollars." I gulped, "Three million dollars?" So I had something else to think about.

That night I went home and put it all together. Obviously it's uranium they're sending through that cyclotron, I thought, and they're separating out the two isotopes. The one I'm working with is uranium 235, and the reason it's worth three million dollars is that it cost an awful lot of money to set up that 184-inch cyclotron. Even an experiment like they've just run must have taken a tremendous number of man-hours, and they can't afford to have some fool like myself drop it and spill it. Then I asked myself, Well, why are they separating uranium? There was only one answer. They were

trying to build an atom or uranium bomb.

Even though I realized the nature of the project, I didn't talk to my superior or anyone about it. I just did my job. But now that I began to understand the chemistry, well, I was able to greatly improve our methods. Eventually, my boss and the other assistant and I began to speak guardedly about the project among ourselves. I don't think we ever used the term "bomb" or "A-bomb" or anything like that. We three were very careful because we didn't want the people under us to know any more than they had to, because we were well aware that the future of our country could be jeopardized by overheard secrets. We knew that the less said about it, the better. And, of course, we never talked to anyone outside the work place. It was understood very clearly when I went to work at UCRL that we would not talk to even our wives or husbands about the job.

It was during one of these guarded discussions at the laboratory that my boss told me that the Germans had a four-year head start on us on the bomb. We knew that we could not let them develop an atomic bomb first, because it was very clear to us that, if we did, that would end the war. Or perhaps, even worse, they might drop it on us. Our main goal was to try to beat the Germans to it. I saw the bomb as a defensive weapon. If we got it before the Germans, or if we developed something superior to what they might come up with, then they would have to surrender; but if they got it and we didn't, we would certainly lose the war.*

My initial job at the laboratory expanded rapidly. By March 1944 we had designed and occupied a building in the Berkeley Hills, nearly a thousand feet higher than the UC campus. We were operating twenty-four hours a day, 364 days a year. I was averaging fourteen hours a day, or one hundred hours a week, of course at no extra pay. I was now assistant director, also researcher, glassblower, inventor and general flunkey, with three shift supervisors working under my direction. The work was demanding, dangerous and delicate.

The working with uranium really wasn't that dangerous, as long as we didn't get too much uranium 235 around, but there was a sister department, the so-called "Physics" group, which would take purified uranium from us and run alpha counts. From their counts they could tell what percentage of uranium 235 was in the material we handed to them. They used radium to do this and had one quarter of the world's known supply down in their department.

One day a colleague who was running this group came to me and said, "I need a volunteer. All of us are shot." I said, "Shot?" He said, "Yes, we've all been irradiated to the point where we can't take any more radiation. Oak Ridge† wants this radium. They want it now. And what Oak Ridge wants, they get. Will you volunteer?" I said, "Sure. I've nothing to lose."

So he led me down to this room. There were seven big lead boxes in it, each one weighing seven tons. Each one had a glass vial, or capsule, of radium in it, up on a ledge, in working position, protected by a lead shield. My job was to walk around those lead shields, hook each vial with a six-foot-long rod, move it down into a lead box, and then cap it with a lead shield, to be transported to Oak Ridge.

He said, "The radiation will be coming out like a pencil. You'll get it mostly through your eyes. It's deadly, so rehearse it. And for God's sake, don't drop one of these glass capsules."

I said, "I won't."

There was a nylon loop on each capsule, and you had to catch it with the hooked end of the long rod. I rehearsed the procedure, and then I went in and, one by one, looped all seven vials. When I got down, he said, "Well, you averaged a little over a minute for each chore. You've got seven or eight minutes of gamma radiation through your face."

A couple of days later he came around and said, "Well, John, you don't have

---

*In late 1938 scientists at the Kaiser Wilhelm Institut in Berlin demonstrated that slow neutron bombardment of uranium split the uranium atom. Scientists of several nations were quick to see the military implications of this development and lost little time in sharing their concern with military and political leaders. The United States, however, did not initiate the supersecret $2 billion Manhattan District—the code name for the building of atomic bombs—until June 1942. Adolf Hitler, confident in the blitzkrieg tactics of Nazi Germany, withheld funds from German scientists who otherwise might have beaten the U.S. in the race for the development of an atomic weapon. The war in Europe ended more than two months before the U.S. tested the world's first atomic bomb at Alamogordo, New Mexico, on July 16, 1945.

†Oak Ridge National Laboratory, Oak Ridge, Tennessee, where scientists separated the rare uranium isotope needed for the world's first nuclear weapons.

to worry about having any more children, because you aren't going to have any for at least ten years." I said, "You're joking?" He said, "No, you got a ten year's dose. We had a film badge on you, and that's what you got."

The next year I was very sick four times, but I don't know to this day whether it was due to the radiation or not, because they never gave me blood tests and no records were kept. In my mind, though, I was doing no more than my brother who was in the South Pacific or my brother who was fighting in Europe. It was wartime and the job had to be done.

As the war progressed, we knew we were getting closer and closer to succeeding with the bomb, but we had one big scare when the Germans launched the Battle of the Bulge in December 1944. During the German siege of Bastogne I was stunned to open my copy of the *San Francisco Chronicle* and read on the front page that the German High Command announced that they had dropped a "Uranium Bomb" on American forces in Belgium, totally destroying them, and calling on the American armies to surrender. Apparently *Time* magazine also carried the story, but, of course, U.S. censors seized all available copies of both publications.*

On the ride up the hill to the radiation lab in a little UCRL bus we all talked it over. We agreed that it was a phony story, a propaganda ploy, one of Herr Goebbels' paper bombs, not a real one. If the Germans really had the bomb, they would have dropped it on Allied headquarters in London, or on the Russian army standing on the east shore of the Elbe River, poised to strike at Berlin. We discussed it on the bus and laughed it off. "Boy, if they have to use propaganda, then they must be far from achieving that bomb."

But my own boss cracked up when he read the story. He was so serious about this project that when he heard this it was too much for him. He went on a monumental drunken spree. For three weeks I had to run the laboratory while he was recovering from "the German flu" and shield my absent superior from the Big One (Dr. Ernest O. Lawrence, UCRL director).

A few months later, in March 1945, a coded message told me that our project was successful, our first A-bomb was being assembled and would fire. My only thought was, Thank God, it looks like we're going to beat the Germans to it.

---

*The story, of course, was false.

EDWARD OSBERG

My draft board called me in December 1940 and gave me a month to get my affairs in order, so I gave up my chiropodist practice in Chicago and prepared to enter the Army. I appeared before the draft board again in January of 1941, but they said volunteers had already filled that month's quota, so come back in February "ready and able to serve your country." I returned in February, but by then my wife and I were expecting our first child. That changed everything. I was reclassified 3-A, for we were not in the war yet, and at that time they were not taking men with children. When we entered the war, I knew my 3-A classification was subject to change at a moment's notice, but after the birth of our child I wasn't as eager to enter the Army. We all had the same patriotic feeling, though. We didn't want to be out of it. You didn't want to walk down the street and have people think, Here's a slacker. Unless you were in the service or doing a very important defense job, you felt a little bit ashamed to tell people what you were doing.

So in the fall of 1942 I enrolled in the industrial-safety-engineering course at the Illinois Institute of Technology sponsored by the Engineering, Science, and Management War Training Department of the United States. I don't know why I selected safety

engineering; it was something that was in the back of my mind, and I thought that if I ever got into industry, safety engineering and accident prevention would be something that I would like more than operating a drill press.

I took the course at night, Tuesday and Friday evenings, from seven to ten. I made the acquaintance of a young man in my class who was an electrical-shop foreman with wide mechanical experience and knowledge. He tutored me privately in the terminology and practical workings of machine shops, forges, foundries and general assembly-line work. I studied hard and asked a lot of questions, and pretty soon I began to see some shape and form in all this chaos.

In the meantime, since I had given up my office in anticipation of going into the service, I had taken another job as club chiropodist at the Chicago Athletic Association. I was anxious to do something more important, though, than cutting the toenails of millionaires. I had heard about the Dodge Chicago plant of Chrysler Corporation being constructed on a square mile of farmland on the Southwest Side, and I went out there and applied for a job as a safety inspector.

The boss of that department, Mr. Oscar Bristol from Detroit, told me frankly that my chances were very slim.

He said he had already hired five of the ten safety inspectors he would need and that there were hundreds of applicants for the remaining jobs and, of all of them, I had the least mechanical qualifications. Noting my look of disappointment, he asked if I had any experience in selling shoes. I said I had some, and he said perhaps he might be able to use me in the safety-shoe department. So I left with a little hope.

Three months later he called me in again and said, "I'm putting you on in safety inspection in the Foundry and Forge Division." I almost dropped through the floor. He said, "It's going to be a tough assignment, but you write well, you talk well, and I think you can manage this job." Then he treated me to lunch in one of the many lunchrooms.

I really was not prepared for what I was getting into. I came on the job the first day with my safety glasses and safety shoes and I saw things I had never dreamed were in this world. Here were 155,000-pound hammers that would take a solid cubic yard of red-hot molten steel and, in twenty-two blows, would mold an aircraft housing out of it. They shook the ground, and they shook the building. There I stood, scared to death, and I was to be the man to protect all these fellows from harm and injury. I wished I were back in my chiropody office.

But I learned quickly, as everybody did during the war. One day there was a terrific accident. One of the portions of these huge hammers broke, on the twenty-first or twenty-second blow, and punctured the operator's midriff and

his spleen. I had to write up the accident report, and I hadn't the slightest idea how to start it. I went to the general foreman and I told him, "A few weeks ago I was a foot doctor at the Chicago Athletic Association. Now I'm standing here with this white star. I'm supposed to be the safety inspector for this forge plant and I haven't any idea of how to write this up."

He said, "All right, son, come into the office and I'll draw a picture for you. This thing's called a shim." He spelled it for me. "It broke off at this point here. As it broke off it sheared, so it became just a bayonet going through him."

I wrote down all the things as he explained them. He said, "The rest you can tell yourself, because you know more about the body than I do." I went back to my office and wrote up the report, and my boss was quite pleased with it because it was complete. He called me in and asked me how I'd written the report. I told him what I'd done, and he said, "That's always the way to do it." So instinctively I had done the right thing. From then on, whenever I made out accident reports or recommended safety procedures, I always asked the foreman or the general foreman for advice, for nomenclature and other information. My reports ended up on Mr. Bristol's desk, clearly written as though I knew what I was talking about—and it was still all Greek to me.

In a plant of over thirty thousand people, where you're turning out huge seventeen-cylinder Wright Cyclone engines for B-29 bombers, naturally you're going to have a lot of accidents. I saw some very, very bad ones. I remember one very lovely red-haired girl, a drill press operator. Everybody liked her, but she was vain. There was a safety law that women had to tie their hair up and wear a tight bandana. One day she ignored it. She wanted everybody to see her beautiful hair, no doubt, but it became hopelessly intertwined in the bit shaft and the grease and oil, and she lost all that gorgeous red hair plus a big part of her scalp. There was no one there to turn off the machine and she couldn't reach the control button herself. If she is living today, she is wearing a steel plate in her head and a toupee.

I saw many accidents in Foundry and Forge, of course. There were magnesium burns, aluminum burns. There were injuries from material falling off ladders. There were accidents involving the sniffing of fumes. One of the worst accidents I remember involved one of our maintenance men. He was oiling the gears of the hundred-ton sand mixer in the aluminum foundry, and he got his fingers in too far. Little by little the machine pulled in his fingers and hand until finally his arm was jerked off at the shoulder girdle. It was a ghastly thing. When he was brought into the first-aid station, the nurse just about fainted.

The arm was in the barrel, being chewed up more, so all work was stopped on the floor, and because I was the safety man I had to climb into this gigantic metal sand barrel—it was about twelve feet in diameter and thirty feet long—and get the arm. I picked up the mutilated, bloody, sand-flecked arm, put it in a sack and carried it to the first-aid station.

The safety inspectors worked nine hours a day, six days a week, every single day of the war, and nine hours a day wasn't enough to do all the things on our agenda. Besides writing accident reports, we made recommendations for safeguards and safe procedures, covered all the first-aid stations, checked out safety equipment, tested gas masks and chlorine installations, tested furnaces and heat-treat apparatus. We authorized the wearing of safety glasses, shoes, leather aprons, gloves and other safety equipment. We checked and tested all chains, ropes, cables, hoists, et cetera. We also worked with the industrial hygienists in locating dangers or toxicities in all vapors, dusts, smokes, fogs, sprays and dipping tanks. And we reported all skin and general body outbreaks and allergies.

Probably the most dangerous thing I had to do personally was, once a month, go up on the roof of both the magnesium foundry and the aluminum foundry and turn off all the gas-fired furnaces. There were certain steps I had to take, and I had a piece of paper with me to make sure that I observed each one. My boss told me, and it scared the life out of me, that if I missed one of these steps I would be blown to kingdom come.

I remember two or three times when I came to the last step, when I fired the furnace with a match, I would close my eyes and pray. Nothing ever happened. I'm still here. But I was really plenty scared, and I thought, Boy, I'd rather be with MacArthur in the Pacific right now. I'd be safer.

There were other times when I had to go into the chlorine room to inspect for leaks. I would wear an airline respirator with air from outside. To this day, when my wife uses Clorox in the kitchen, I get that sickish feeling in my stomach from forty years ago. It brings it back so forcefully that I'm almost nauseated for a couple of hours.

Chrysler Corporation is well known for its safety procedures, and they employed all those procedures at the Dodge plant. But we were making airplane engines, and that was a little different than cars and trucks. This wasn't a question of something being on the drawing board for three or four years. They had to go, go, go. Whenever engineers and general superintendents devised a new process to make something faster or better, they went ahead and did it. They didn't care if it killed someone or if the fumes and dust were dangerous. That was our job, to protect them. Yet, even under these wartime pressures, I don't recall anyone dying in the plant during the war.

Working as a safety inspector was a tremendous experience for me, a tremendous learning experience. I enjoyed my work and I felt that it was a necessary job. I was rather proud that I could do this in place of not being in the service.

I was also pleased about my hours. I only had to work fifty-four hours a week. I had Sunday off, and I wasn't very far from the plant. My income went up from a hundred eighty a month to three hundred fifty a month, which was absolutely fantastic. Everything was coming up roses for me. In fact, I felt a little bit guilty at times, when I read the papers and saw what was happening to our servicemen overseas, and here I had it just great.

HENRY FIERING

I became involved in the labor movement during the Depression. Being unemployed sharpens your thinking. I was a young guy with a lot of energy and I was receptive to all kinds of ideas. Living at that time in New York, which was a hotbed of radical thought, I became associated with people whose political thinking was to the left, and I drifted in that direction. In 1933 Congress passed the National Industrial Recovery Act. Section Seven of the NIRA gave people the right to organize, and I figured that was a good way for me to go. So I became a voluntary organizer for the Textile Workers Union.

I was infused with the idea of social change, and like many other people I saw the labor movement as a means to that end. So I threw myself into it. Even though I worked during the day to make a living, I still devoted most of my time to labor organizing. By the time the war started I was a full-time organizer for the United Electrical Workers.

Roosevelt understood that to wage the war effectively he would need to work out with the unions a means to continue war production with a minimum of interruption. So he went to the unions and asked for a no-strike agreement. When the three top leaders of the CIO met with the President to work out a deal about the no-strike clause, they wanted to be sure that the unions were protected. They wanted their key people to be exempt from the draft as a guarantee of continued growth of the union. One of that committee of three was the leader of my union. I was called to New York and told that they had agreed to exempt me from the draft. Nobody had consulted me about it, but I didn't argue with it. I acceded to the conditions that were made for me. Still one is bound to have ambivalent feelings about going into the Army, and I had conflicts about what I could best do, where I could make the best contribution.

The impact of that exemption was that I worked like hell during the war period. You wanted to make your work meaningful. You wanted to feel you were making a contribution to the war effort, to the country, to the working people. So you worked seven days a week, twenty-four hours a day sometimes. You did what you were told, went where they sent you, oftentimes at the expense of your family, but you did it because you felt you had to do your part.

As the war geared up, the unions, of course, threw their full support to it, but they didn't do it at the expense of their own interests. They had to consider that they were here today, they wanted to be here tomorrow, and they wanted to utilize the advantage that the war situation created to guarantee that they would strengthen their position in the country.

The policies of the War Labor Board encouraged organization, but the War Labor Board did not do the organizing for us. You've got to understand what the mood of the people was, coming out of the Depression, to understand why the work force that came into the war production plants was so eager to organize. The essential thing that people learned out of the Depression was that rugged individualism was a hoax. They knew because they were one-on-one during the Depression and they starved for it. The biggest lesson they learned out of the Depression was that if they were going to survive they had to pool their strength. It was the only way to compete with their employers. Now they were determined they were going to protect themselves, so organizing during the war was relatively easy.

The workers began to feel more and more secure. There was no shortage of jobs, and the important thing was to get people to fill them. It put us in a good bargaining position. The workers were no longer afraid of their employers, and they would challenge them out in the open. We'd circulate membership cards in front of the management and dare the management to do something about it. Sometimes they did, so you had a tussle, but that was rare.

When the country started to go on a war footing, management resistance eased up, too. Employers were no longer afraid that the unions were going to cut deeply into their profits, because government guaranteed profits. I don't mean to say they opened their arms to unions, but their resistance lessened.

I remember a two-year period, 1942–43, where we went through some sixty-six or sixty-eight plants, organized them and held elections. We lost one! One. Now, this represented tens of thousands of people. As a matter of fact, during that four-year period we orga-

nized 75,000 people, and that's just a small group of organizers. That was large plants, small plants, national companies like Westinghouse and General Electric as well as independent ones. Just multiply that by forty-eight states and as many unions to see what was going on in the United States.

Of course, the upshot of it was that by '45 we'd organized somewhere around five million more people than we had in 1941. It was just a huge mass movement into the unions: auto, steel, electrical, rubber, meat packing, utilities, everything that is important in our country.

You began to see people who were

nothing during the Depression, who were starving, begging, groveling in the dirt, and by the end of the war they were standing on their own two feet. It was just a marvelous thing. Everybody was better off.

Another thing that happened during those years—and it began during the latter years of the Depression—was that working people of the country really participated in the political process. They were the hub of the coalition that Roosevelt organized, and they became the mass base of the Democratic Party.

Before that, to engage in political activity that was contrary to the thinking of the employers might jeopardize workers' jobs as much as if they were organizers of the shop. Now you had political independence, and people used it. You had a mass participation of people in the political process. I haven't seen citizen participation of people in the political process to the degree I saw it in those years. The war effort heightened people's political interest and sharpened their desire to participate.

ROGER MONTGOMERY

I got out of high school at the age of seventeen and tried to enlist in the Marine Corps, but I didn't make it through the physical. When I turned eighteen I was examined again, and again I was turned down. I'd had a history of ear trouble as a kid, and my eardrum had a tiny hole in it. For some reason a punctured eardrum was an automatic exemption. They didn't look any further.

As a teenager in those days, to be a man you had to be in the service, and it was very much a blow to my ego not to be taken. I felt very definitely inferior, uncomfortable, as though I were not fully a young male. Most of my good friends in high school were joining up right and left or being drafted, and I felt very bad about not being among them.

I was very much concerned with political events, though, and aware that there was work to do elsewhere, so I became involved in the homefront activity. After I was rejected for the Marine Corps in January of 1943 I immediately started at Oberlin College. They were admitting new students every semester and took me right away. Practically from the day I arrived at Oberlin, I got involved with the left group on campus.

A Communist-led steelworkers' union in a nearby city had intentionally made contacts with left progressive students on the campus, and I volunteered to do some work for their union. I wrote articles for their weekly paper, stuff like that, but I wanted to do more. In the fall of 1943 I went to the leadership of the union and told them I wanted to work in a defense plant. They said to me, "What we want you to do is to go to work in this next town in a plant that isn't unionized and to work for us as an inside-the-plant organizer." I thought this was a perfect job for two reasons. I was producing for the war effort, and at the same time I was able to do something that was in tune with my political ideas.

The plant was a very large machine-tool-products company in Elyria, Ohio. I worked primarily in the grinding-machine department, where we did very high-precision grinding of machine tools. As a labor organizer my job was to talk union in the shop and to try to identify potential members. Then I would give their names to the union organizing people, who would contact them on the outside.

One of the things I had to do before I could be an effective organizer was to perform my job well enough so that I could get done all the production I was supposed to do to reach my quota and still have time left over to wander around and talk to other people in the plant. It took a couple of months until I felt confident that I could do my job.

Around this time the man in the personnel office who hired me noted that I had a college background and was not the usual working stiff. So the management called me in and told me the plant was having union organizing problems and they wanted me to identify who was involved with the effort. They said I'd get some bonus if I'd keep tabs on what was going on and if I observed any union organizing activity during working hours. I don't remember how I dissembled, whether I told outright lies or not, but I didn't expose

myself. Before it went very far, I suspect other people in the plant realized that I was possibly on the other side, and they dropped the matter.

I don't think I frightened management very much, though, because I certainly wasn't hassled in any way. In those days everything was cost-plus, and there was not the kind of really violent antiunion feeling that was characteristic of the thirties. All things being equal, management would just as soon not see the plant organized, but I doubt that they saw the union as a big threat.

The whole climate was such that, overall, the labor movement was a positive thing. Most unions abided by the no-strike pledge; they helped in the production effort. Unions represented the symbolic voice and body of the people that were producing the arms and ammunition. In that sense they were viewed in a positive light.

People felt good about themselves and what they were doing because everybody was manifestly doing something that supported the war effort. We walked in the door, and there were banners telling us how many of this and that we had shipped to kill the Nazis or shoot up the Japs. We all had the feeling that every time we shipped something off there was another nail in Hitler's coffin.

Not everyone was happy, of course. In those days the color line was very strong, and all the blacks in this plant were sweepers or had other menial jobs. The only college graduate I knew among the hourly-rate wage force was a black guy who cleaned up the men's toilet. I didn't know him well, but I certainly

The war will be won with weapons built this year ..... DONALD NELSON

EVERY DAY!
EVERY HOUR!
EVERY MINUTE COUNTS!

Only 278 Days
REMAIN IN THIS YEAR
TO DO THE JOB!

KEEP 'EM FIRING!

detected a good deal of alienation in him. For him it was a good job, but he was so much better educated than anybody else there that it was very obvious that it was not the way he thought he ought to be living.

But for most people the combination of good pay and good spirit made life very positive. Personally I had a feeling of pride in what I was doing and confidence that, however small, it counted. You were doing something that was contributing to the larger good. This gave you a sense of community, of common purpose. You could sit down with somebody and start off with a feeling that you were part of something important, something larger than yourself.

ELLIOT JOHNSON

There were some fellows for whom I wrote and read all their letters for nearly four years. One of these men was the son of a miner, and it was through him that I had my first experience with unions. The man's father wrote to him while we were overseas and said the miners were going to go on strike for more money. And the son had me write back and say, "That will hurt us badly because we need those materials. If you do go on strike, I'll never speak to you again." The mother wrote back and said the father went on strike, so from then on we would write to his mother, and when he would get letters from his father he would tear them up. He maintained that feeling throughout the war. The last time I saw him was when we were separated from the service, and he still would have nothing to do with his father.

DON JOHNSON

Besides the severity of the work load, there was an additional strain during the war—the uncertainty of your military status. You had no control over your military status. You were exempted by a review board, and that review kept on being repeated and repeated. So in addition to the extended hours that you worked, you had to live with the uncertainty that suddenly the military might call and your life would be changed completely.

Frequently when the news would come in from overseas, especially when you would hear of associates who went off and were injured or killed, one would question whether this was something that you should be doing or should have done. It still remained that one didn't make that decision, someone made it for you. Short of defying the system and enlisting, that was something you did not control.

It was a time of your life when you saw there really wasn't any way that you could do anything else but hang on to the goal that you had a part to play, and you would persevere and do that part. It was a period when American industry had the greatest increase in productivity of all time. I believe, in large measure, it was because we as a nation were threatened. We were in a survival mode. People knew that, and they worked together to get the job done. We had a common purpose. We worked as a team. We had the skills. We had the machinery. We had the materials. We had the know-how. We achieved. And I believe given a similar set of circumstances, we could do it again.

The war years left a lasting mark in that there was a sense of urgency developed, a commitment to accomplish something. A rule was established that said, "You can do it if you put forth the effort." I learned that rule during the war and it never left me. When faced with taking on additional responsibilities, I learned to be able to achieve. In the situation we were in, with limited number of personnel, people had to be given more responsibility, more tasks, more challenges. Expectations of their performance were raised, and people responded. Many of those peo-

ple still carry those skills, those drives, with them. They are high achievers because of it.

In my own case, the opportunity to learn skills that I might never have learned otherwise had a substantial impact on my career. I came out of the war as a section supervisor in manufacturing-engineering activity. After the war I was promoted to the manufacturing-development staff at the GM technical center and eventually ended up at the Buick Motor Division as a general superintendent of final car assembly and pressed metal, one of the top fifty executives in that division of the company, and all this without having a formal engineering degree to begin with.

The skills and experiences gained by managers like myself during the war carried over into the postwar period and had a real part in the expansion of the economy that occurred. Despite the tremendous disruption the war caused, GM came out of it strengthened. Their work force was more skilled, and they were strengthened by the technological advantages of lighter metals, plastics, and by new plants and equipment that had been acquired through expansion made during the war. And the strengths that GM gained during the war years were repeated by American industry in general.

GEORGE PEABODY

I went to work at Lockheed in '38. At that time you had to have two years of

college to get almost any kind of job there, even to sweep floors. I had two years of college and was hired as a junior learner, taking any job to get in. Soon they discovered that I had capabilities in excess of what I was hired to do. Almost immediately I was considered for advancement.

By '39 I was a die maker, then a pattern maker. In '40 I was a tool planner learner, in '41 a tool planner junior, in '42 a tool planner sheet metal B, and in '43 a tool planner sheet metal A. I thought I was going places, and I was. I was enjoying a feeling of self-esteem because I was showing that I was capable of doing something, I was being productive and useful, and I was being well paid for it. I was coming out of a depression into a state of prosperity, and pretty happy about that.

My income increased very rapidly because of the number of hours I worked. When I first went to Lockheed it seems to me my wages were something like forty-two cents an hour, and I would work eight hours a day. By 1944, as I remember, it was eight hours a day on Saturdays and Sundays and ten to twelve hours a day all during the week. We didn't have a day off. Even though the wages per hour didn't increase a great deal, the take-home pay was tremendous by comparison.

Rain or shine, it didn't make any difference, there was a fellow who would come by our house to pick me up in his car. He'd have two guys in the front seat with him already and one man in the rumble seat in the back. I was the second person to sit in the rumble seat. We'd cover ourselves over with waterproof sheets to keep dry during the rain. That's the way we went to work early in the morning hours and the way we came home late at night.

There was no resentment of the long hours, because we were paid well for them. Morale at that point of the game wasn't even a word in our vocabulary. I was earning good money, and my wife felt that I was involved with something that was improving our situation. We had just had a baby. What more can a guy ask for? A nice wife, nice baby, good opportunities, which were reflected in my advancement at Lockheed, good pay, and maybe contributing something to the war effort besides. I didn't really need to have anyone talk to me about morale. I was morale itself.

I worked at Lockheed for five years. Since I had a wife, a child and a defense job, my military classification was 3-A. Then there was a law passed that required everyone, regardless of defense-related jobs, marital status or number of children, to serve in the armed forces if they hadn't reached a certain age by a certain date. I fell into that category by four months. So suddenly I became 1-A. As soon as I was reclassified, Lockheed said to me, "We have negotiated, we've cajoled, we've done everything we can to keep you here, because we can't afford to lose you, but we haven't been able to change your classification, so we thought you ought to know that you're going to be drafted."

Here I was, skilled, capable, knowledgeable. I had proven my worth for five years in the defense-industry position I held. I had a pregnant wife and a growing son to whom I owed responsibility, my mother was a member of my draft board, and I thought my being drafted would be the most stupid thing I'd ever heard of, but since it had to be, it had to be. I didn't want to be drafted, though, and put into just any branch of the armed forces. I wanted to go where I wanted to go. So, voluntarily, I terminated from Lockheed and joined the U.S. Marine Corps Reserve, hoping to find my dad, then a prisoner of the Japanese in the Philippine Islands. A year later I was wounded on a combat patrol on Iwo Jima, shot in the right leg between the hip and the knee.

Schomburg Center for Research in Black Culture, New York Public Library.

WILLIAM PEFLEY

I started at the navy yard as a third-class machinist and worked my way into what is known as a progressman. My job was to see that every overhaul of a ship would be done on time. During the height of the war it was very important that we got every single ship that came in there out quickly so they'd be fighting again. A lot of times we'd have a Dutch ship, or one of our destroyers, slip in after dusk, and we'd have to completely pull the shaft, put a new propeller on it, do a little engine work and get it back out before daybreak, so the Germans, who were patrolling off the coast, didn't know that it had been there. This was very secret, and we put all the men we possibly could work to work on it.

Many a time the men would work eight hours and you needed some of them, the experienced ones, to get the ship out in time. So we'd ask who would care to work straight on through. And just about everybody there would volunteer and work until they could almost go to sleep on the job. Many times I had to work sixteen hours without stopping, down in a cold drydock, to make sure everything got done. When your eight-hour shift was up, you just didn't stop if you knew that ship had to catch a convoy.

We not only worked twelve, sixteen hours a day, but lots of weeks and months we wouldn't even have a day off. We never minded working seven days or what our hours were, for while we were working in the yard the people aboard the ships were out there actually fighting. It made us feel like we were only sacrificing a little bit. Your best friend might be out there on one of those ships, maybe getting bombed. You felt like you had to help him while he was out there helping you.

A friend of mine, who was in the naval reserves, was called back in as a commander during the war, and he told me that he could get me a lieutenant's rank if I came in, because he knew my experience. I went to the commander of the navy yard and I said I wanted to join the service. He said, "No, we will not release you. You're just as important in here as you are out there aboard a ship, because somebody must do this job." So I stayed at the navy yard throughout the war.

When the war was over I received a certificate from the United States Navy in recognition of my "service to the Navy and to the country." When I received the certificate I felt that other people appreciated that even if I didn't go to war I was doing my part on the homefront and that my efforts were of great value to this country. It made me very proud to receive that certificate.

During the Depression I was really feeling bad about this country. People

I talked to who lived through the same hardships were very bitter. They felt that the President, the leaders of the country, had let them down, that something should have been done to keep this from happening. But when the war broke out, and I saw what people could do when they all pulled together, and the sacrifices they were willing to make, it made me really love this country again. It made you think you were living in a great country. It made you proud to be an American.

I remember I was working down in the engine room once when they brought in this big, strapping red-headed fellow. He had strange sunken eyes and a frightful look. I asked him what his problem was. He told me that he had had such a terrible time during the Depression that to make a nickel or dime he had developed the muscles of his stomach so that you could break a rock on it with a sledgehammer. And he had gone around the country doing that in order to survive. Now, he said, he felt like he was at the end of the line.

After he worked there for six or eight months, I saw him again and he had completely changed. His face was full, he looked happy, and he told me, "I feel like now I do have a country, and I'm working hard as I can to save it."

WILLIAM MULCAHY

I spent the war at RCA supervising the Madame X, or proximity fuse project. It has been said by those in the military that if it were not for the atom bomb, the proximity or VT fuse would have been credited as the weapon that won the war. The fuse sent out a constant signal which bounced off an object, in this case an airplane, and when the plane came close enough the fuse would set off the bomb. Its advantage as an antiaircraft weapon was that it did not require extraordinary gunnery excellence or training. Because the radar set off the exploding mechanism, all the gunner needed to do was get a few rounds near the plane and the bombs would go off.

Later in the war—and this is not a chapter that is too pleasant to talk about—they began to use the device as an antipersonnel weapon. My first inkling of this was a glaring headline in one of the Philadelphia papers: "NEW ALLIED WEAPON LITTERS THE FIELD WITH GERMAN DEAD." The proximity fuse was a supersecret navy project, and there weren't many of us who knew what this particular device was and how it operated. It shook the hell out of us to be honest. As an antiaircraft weapon, it seemed somewhat impersonal, but filled with shrapnel rather than gunpowder and reset as an antipersonnel weapon, it was much more disturbing. It was our first realization that this was killing people, literally cutting them in half—it was a devastating weapon—

and it really did bother us. It didn't change my attitude toward the job, because I still felt it necessary to win the war—we were losing thousands of young men too—but I must admit that it did shake my equilibrium badly and made sleep a little more difficult. In fact, I had a lot of trouble sleeping for a while.

LAURA BRIGGS

When we moved back to the farm from California, it soon became apparent that the status of the farmer had changed. Where before we had been looked down upon, now we were important and looked up to because we were a crucial industry. We had to feed our country. Before, the farmer was struggling along, barely surviving, but now, because of the great demand for farm products, the farmer could at last make a living. Suddenly he became, on the homefront, number one right alongside the businessman.

My father never went back to the horse operation. He immediately started hustling around to dealers and putting his name on lists for machinery. Machinery was frozen—it was hard to get—but because farming became such an essential industry they did release some equipment to men like my father who they knew would use it.

They had just started coming out with self-propelled combines which threshed grain much more efficiently than the old machines. Dad had his name on priority, and so did a cousin of ours, but Dad was considered a little more reliable, and a better farmer, and

he got the combine. So in addition to his farm work he went around threshing to help get the farmers' grain out. At the same time he was going out, buying more land and putting in more crops—and always juggling to get enough labor to get it all done.

Manpower became crucial. Anybody who could carry a hoe or drive a team or a tractor helped out. They let schools out in the fall to help with the harvest and other times when necessary, and the teachers helped, too. Families helped each other. I worked all the time other than going to school. I pitched hay, hauled beans, picked spuds. When I was fifteen years old I picked four hundred half-sacks of spuds a day. And I mean that is a man's work, but you had the incentive to do it. It was patriotic and you got well paid besides. At six cents a half-sack of spuds, I made big money. One summer I earned three hundred dollars to buy myself school things for the next year. The first time I was able to do man's work in the fields and get a lot of money, I thought that was just great—better than drying dishes and bringing in the kindling.

I remember in '44 we had no way to get the hay in, and my father was really desperate. Dad had a big family, twelve brothers and sisters, and they all came over to help. My aunt was about sixteen, and she joined in and pitched hay all day long just like a man. I couldn't have done it myself, but she did it. My dad had tears in his eyes to think his sister had to work like that, and he paid her twenty-five dollars that day. "I wish I could pay you more," he said. "You're priceless to me today. I hated to see you do it." She just looked at that check and couldn't believe it. That was a fortune. Ten to twelve dollars a day was top hay hand's wages at that time.

As farm prices got better and better, the farmers suddenly became the wealth of the community. When we started getting into the area of six dollars for a sack of potatoes, that was really phenomenal. Farm times became good times. Dad started having his land improved, and of course we improved our home and the outbuildings. We and most other farmers went from a tar-paper shack to a new frame house with indoor plumbing. Now we had an electric stove instead of a woodburning one, and running water at the sink where we could do the dishes; and a hot water heater; and nice linoleum, not that cheap stuff that cracked after a few weeks. We bought a vacuum cleaner too. The guy who sold us this Electrolux came out one Saturday afternoon when Mom was in town buying groceries, and he cleaned the whole house. That was his thanks for her buying and paying cash for this vacuum cleaner.

He even had a little gadget with a jar on it that sprayed floor wax, and, oh, God, that was really wonderful. It was just so modern we couldn't stand it.

We also started buying more things from the store. Before, a farmer's wife was considered lazy if she bought bread in a store instead of baking her own. But women started doing that and not thinking too much about it. They also bought a few fancy canned goods and ready-made clothes. Before, we got by with chickenfeed prints and flour-sack underwear. Now I even had socks to wear whenever I wanted them.

People started bathing more too, spiffing up a little. A few of the women even started going into beauty parlors and getting their hair done. And farm families began to care if their kids had a nice dress to wear to a party, just like the town kids. Now your kid had to have the best out there, too.

All of a sudden the farmer had stability. He was viewed as a professional. He was going to be paid accordingly, and he was going to be treated socially the same way too. It suddenly became kind of fashionable in town to wear jeans and denim shirts. The farmer driving in with his sweat-stained hat and with cow manure on his boots wasn't looked down on for that anymore.

Just before the war ended we even got a telephone. We were one of the last ones in the area. When you can't get together with other kids on the phone, imagine how isolated you are. I remember the first time I used the phone. I just about had a heart attack with fright. My dad always acted like it was strange. "No need to talk on them unless it's a matter of life and death anyway." I don't think he ever did call anyone in his life socially. It had to be very important business, and then you just had to say it and get off.

VERNON SIETMANN

I've lived all of my life in Marshall County, Iowa. My present farm is about three fourths of a mile from where I was born, about four or five miles from where my father was born, and about a mile from where my grandfather farmed. I started farming for myself in 1934, the worst of the Depression.

It was a very difficult time. I barely managed to survive. As we got closer to war, though, people began moving from the farm to defense factories in the towns. Money became more plentiful and farm prices began to increase. Then the war began and there were new adversities.

My classification in the military was 3-A, which was a common classification for people involved in agriculture and necessary work on the homefront. Then the need for men increased, and I was reclassified 1-A. Within a thirty-day period I had passed a general military physical exam and had my induction papers to report to Fort Riley, Kansas. The day before I was supposed to get on the train for Fort Riley there was a news flash over the radio that all men over thirty-five years old need not report.

When I didn't have to report to the service I was elated. I did not frown on going into the military if it were necessary, but I didn't have my crops planted and I had not made provision for anyone else to do it, so being drafted would have meant a complete abandonment of my farm program, which was quite a price to pay.

There were times afterwards when I would toss it around in my own mind wondering whether I should be overseas or not, but then when night came and I saw what I'd accomplished that otherwise would not have been done—and which needed doing in order for the full-out war effort to be successful—I never really felt that I hadn't done my part.

The war increased the demand for food products, and the government made an all-out effort to keep the farmer in full production. Rationing of fuel was relaxed for farmers and, as much as possible, restrictions on farm equipment.

To raise production on my own farm, I bought a new tractor which helped me do a better job. I increased the size of my equipment and I decided to raise more hogs. I went from around a hundred hogs a year up to five or six hundred, which was quite a few for that time.

At the same time I put in a lot of extra effort in helping repair farm

National Archives

equipment and keeping other neighbor farmers in the field. During the war the local blacksmith who repaired most of the farm machinery went to the Coast to work in a defense plant. I had a shop in town, which I still have, for my own use, but when the blacksmith left I sort of stepped in and became general fixer in the community. People would bring their equipment into the shop to repair, but a lot of times the equipment couldn't be moved to town, so I had to go into the country and fix the piece where it had broken down.

The automobile was not an agricultural machine, but people had to have it to get back and forth to town, so I even undertook to fix a Chrysler fluid drive, which was a forbidden thing according to the factory. We would take the drum apart, though, put in new seals, put it back together again and get the farmer going down the road in his old car just as though it were a new one. The shortages and adversities of the time brought out ingenuity that would never have surfaced otherwise.

They made an innovator of you. During the war I learned a lot about how to make things work better, and as a result I have about fifteen U.S. patents at the present time. If I hadn't gone through that experience of the war, I doubt if I would have had the know-how or ingenuity to continue to do this.

We worked long hours during the war—I wouldn't say all night, but well into the morning hours when the rush was on. In doing repair work you would break the Sabbath quite often and also work into the night so that when daylight came a particular person could have his equipment fixed and be able to do his work as he had before. We worked harder, but I think we also became better farmers during the war. We became more efficient, we increased our acreages, and had better crop varieties. Of course, our income also increased. It was the best I had experienced during my life up to that time. I think that, if I remember correctly, I sold some corn for two dollars and sixty-one cents a bushel, and that was beyond my dreams.

· 9 ·

WARTIME ROMANCES

It was . . . a very hectic, exciting time, but there was always
an underlying sadness, a melancholy. Relationships were
extremely intense, because you didn't know
how long they would last.

—PATRICIA LIVERMORE

The romanticism of the uniform was very powerful.

—VIRGINIA RASMUSSEN

The uncertainties of life during the war intensified human
relations, especially between the young men in uniform and the
women who were the objects of their affection. For some women, the
uniform seemed to make every boy a man, every man a hero. Small
wonder that the male civilians turned envious of men in uniform, and
why men in the service could not always assess their true
relationships with women.

War generally increases the number of marriages, and the 1941
marriage rate—12.6 per 100,000 population—was the highest ever
recorded in the United States. Ten percent of those weddings took
place in December of that year. The impulsiveness of many wartime
marriages was reflected in the increased postwar divorce rate, which
surpassed the record established after World War I.

The romances of wartime were a compound of many elements: loneliness, anxiety, fantasy, sincerity, insincerity, foolishness and good sense. Some of the romances were fleeting, and others ended in marriage. Some marriages lasted and some didn't. And some blighted romances left permanent scars on the psyche of the wartime lovers.

PATRICIA LIVERMORE

I came to California from Omaha, Nebraska, in 1943 because I'd had tuberculosis. My doctor advised me to come to a milder climate, and my fiancé's ship was home-ported in San Diego. He had joined the Navy right after Pearl Harbor, and I wanted to see him before he left for overseas.

I was nineteen years old, a very innocent country girl from Nebraska. Omaha may have been a city, but it wasn't much more than a small town as far as attitudes were concerned. San Diego was something totally different. Every night—not just on weekends— if you went anywhere from Twelfth and Broadway to Sixteenth and Broadway and looked down toward the harbor, you'd view a sea of white hats. From curb to curb, you could see nothing but sailors.

When I came to San Diego, I went right to work. I saw an ad in the paper for a camera girl to take pictures in nightclubs, and I answered it. The job paid well, fifteen dollars a week salary and ten percent commission, which was fifteen cents on each picture. At that time that was very good pay, because we took so many pictures. I worked six nights a week from 6 P.M. to 2 in the morning and covered twenty-one nightclubs, and every night they were packed.

I had a journalist's camera, a Speed Graphic four by five, and it took the most beautiful pictures. I photographed servicemen and their girls in nightclubs. If they didn't have a girl with them, I'd have the waitress take a picture of me sitting with the guy. They liked that. I was very pretty then. Very pretty. A lot of guys who were alone would say, "Sure you can take my picture, if you'll be in it with me," or ". . . if you sit on my lap." I was glad to.

We had a little sales receipt where we wrote the name of the club and the customer's name and then the number of copies that they wanted made. If I was in the picture I'd talk him into buying me a copy, too; it was a dollar and a half a picture, so that made me three dollars. Often they'd hand me a five-dollar bill and tell me to keep the change. When I wrote up the slip for the number of pictures to be printed, I would circle the two, which told my boss who developed and printed the pictures that there was only one copy

Patricia Livermore, left. *Courtesy of Patricia Livermore*

to be made and I got the money for the other one. So I would actually make about three and a half dollars for myself out of that five.

It was a wonderful job and a very hectic, exciting time, but there was always an underlying sadness, a melancholy. Relationships were extremely intense, because you didn't know how long they would last. A man might go overseas and be killed, so every relationship, whether friendship or love or hatred, whatever it was, was very strong at that moment.

There were girls in San Diego marrying servicemen right and left during the war, partly because they felt sorry for them. The other reason was the serviceman's fifty dollar a month allotment—that's what the government gave the wives. A girl would marry a man. He'd go overseas and make out the allotment to her before he went. While he was gone, she'd go down to Tijuana, Mexico, and marry another serviceman, get another allotment. Allotment Annies, we called them. Some of them married so many guys they were making as much as three or four hundred dollars a month. I knew of one girl who married six guys that way. She was very true to the first one, until she met the second, and true to the second until she met the third.

The servicemen were not really looking for sex as much as for companionship, though. Most of them were small-town boys and they were used to the girl-next-door type, and that's what they wanted—someone to talk to, someone to dance with, a companion, a friend. A lot of guys I got to know real well. As a camera girl they would talk to me where they wouldn't talk to other people.

They'd come into the club, sit down and talk a couple of minutes, or they'd say, "Hey, Pat, I know you're busy now. Could I wait till you get off and talk to you? I've got a problem." We'd go to a restaurant and have coffee or breakfast and talk. His girl had cheated on him or left him or done this or that. How was he going to handle it? Or something happened overseas. He saw his best buddy get killed. I'd try to talk to him, but sometimes they were hurt inside in such a way that it was hard for them to speak about it, and it would come out in bitterness.

They were kids, most of them, uprooted from everything they knew and loved, and sent to defend their country. Put yourself in their place. All of a sudden here you are, face to face with the enemy. You shoot and kill him, and as you look at him dying you see that he's no older than you, maybe even

younger, and he can't understand why you're killing him any more than you understand why you have to do it. Then these young men came back and their girls couldn't understand what they had been through, because the girls were too young, too, and they couldn't understand why their men had changed so. Often the men weren't able to talk about it because they were trying to protect their wives and sweethearts from what they had been through. So they had to go to a stranger and talk to them.

I think back to some of the guys that I got to know real well before they went overseas. They'd be regular customers at one of the bars, and they'd talk about their plans for after the war, they wanted to go to college, buy a little farm, or start a business. They all had dreams and hopes for the future. And then the next thing I knew, some guy would come in and tell me one of them got killed. And I'd think, Oh, God that's the guy who wanted to have his own farm when he got back. Or he wanted to go to college, or do this or that, and he's never going to. I did a lot of crying in those years, a lot of crying. I wasn't the only one.

VIRGINIA RASMUSSEN

I was a high-school junior in South Bend, Indiana, in 1941. Uniforms were everywhere. It was thrilling and glamorous, and I got caught up in all of it.

In my senior year I was dating a midshipman who was taking his training at the University of Notre Dame. When he graduated and went back to Pitts-

burgh, which was his hometown, we had one of these scenes at the airport that you always saw in the movies. He would walk a few steps and turn around and wave to me and I'd wave back. Then he'd go a few more steps and turn and wave again. It went like that until he finally entered the airplane and the door closed. That night I sat out on my back doorstep (there was a full moon, of course), and I listened to records—the ballads of the time said the things that you were feeling—and I wept all night long. It was a very dramatic experience, but it kept recurring with the various uniforms.

In 1943 I went to college at Indiana University and fell in love with another serviceman. He was in the Army Specialized Training Program, where you completed your college education and then went into officer candidate school. After OCS he was sent overseas, but before that, in early '44, we were engaged.

Then, as the time dragged on, and with all that distance between us, I began to wonder if I was really ready to be engaged. At the same time I met another serviceman in midshipman training at Notre Dame, and I fell in love again. So I became engaged to this fellow too, and I was ready to send the ring back to the first one when he arrived on the doorstep at the sorority house at college, unexpectedly. He had been wounded in France and been sent home for bone grafts. I hadn't even known that he was injured, and here he was with his arm in a cast and his ribbons, and very gaunt, and my heart went out to him. Of course I couldn't

bring myself to break the engagement then. After all, he was a wounded war hero and I felt very sorry for him. I think this was one of the feelings that most people had at that time: Here is a wounded war hero, and we must treat him with respect and care.

So we began dating, and I never did get around to giving back his ring. Instead, I sent the ring back to the midshipman, and I married the war hero.

My parents advised me to wait a little longer until I was sure, but I was determined to go ahead and get married, so I did. He was hit in September of '44 and came back in February of '45, and we were married that July. Even as I was walking down the aisle I had reservations about the marriage, but it was a large wedding, and I felt what could I do? I couldn't stop things that were in motion. It was very difficult for me to make decisions at that time.

The romanticism of the uniform was very powerful. Being an officer was very important, too. My husband went over as a second lieutenant and came back as a captain. The second fellow that I was engaged to was an ensign. They were so very handsome in their officer's uniforms. Very gallant. It was the picture that you had seen in the movies, and they played it up very big.

Many things took place then because the men were being shipped overseas. There were a lot of girls I knew in college who got caught in that—let's make his last days here happy, just in case he never comes back. I don't know how many had illegitimate children as a result of that, but I do know that there were some in my sorority who had relationships simply because they felt they owed it to this man because this might be the last he'd ever have.

You were definitely caught up in that kind of feeling. They're going over to save us, let's do our part and make them happy before they go. I think it was a very bad time for women, in particular, because they had been taught these values of "nice girls don't do that," and then they're torn because here's this man who's going to give up his life for me. And, of course, the soldiers appealed to you like that.

The result was a number of hasty marriages to servicemen during the war and a number of divorces afterwards. My husband and I were both very immature; we were both groping for someone who cared. My parents, my father in particular, were very strict disciplinarians and held me in very tight control. My husband was an only child whose mother had died when he was in high school, and he and his father were not on the best of terms. So this was an escape for both of us, a glamorous escape. In addition, there were his injuries and feeling sorry for him. It was a combination of those emotions, not really love as I would define it today, and it quickly disintegrated.

FRANCES VEEDER

I was just about seventeen when the war started, a girl, really, quite immature. I was a tremendous reader, but I had not had a great deal of life experience. I was living with an older sister in Seattle, supporting myself by working in a department store. I had had a scholarship to college, but I was restless—everyone my age was—and I dropped out. There was a feeling that you wanted to see what was going on in the world.

Then Pearl Harbor was attacked, and I think there were many, like myself, who got caught up in the war fever. It seemed that everything was intensified, more compressed—your anxieties, your loneliness, fears, passions. There was a kind of fierceness, almost

a desperation, about people meeting each other at that time. It might sound corny, but there was that attitude of "Well, I'm going to be shipping out next week, so let's stay up all night and dance."

I remember one time I was waiting for a ferryboat. I was going to see my fiancé—he was stationed way off the coast near Seattle. I had to take two ferryboats and a bus, and it took about six hours: this was real love, for he might not even get a six-hour pass. This was at the early part of the war and the news was very bad.

I was waiting there for the ferry, and there was a GI walking back and forth, cruising around the room. I guess he had a pass and he was frantic with the

idea that he wasn't going to have a girl. He had an open billfold just bulging with money and he would sort of ostentatiously come up and stand in front of a girl and reach into his pocket and take his wallet out as though he were counting his money. And, of course, the girls were usually going to see somebody already. I don't think he ever found anyone.

Another indelible scene I remember was a startling sight on a train. It was night and our train was slowly passing another. I turned and looked, and there in the dimly lit car was a GI and a woman having sex while several other GI's stood around watching or not watching. I remember some of them were looking the other way, having a drink or a cigarette. It happened so fast that I could hardly believe what I had seen. You took a breath and it was gone, yet it made a deep impression on me. You knew everybody was going to get off the train at the next stop, and that was the end of that. You were passing each other in the night.

I think the atmosphere of those times definitely affected my life. If it hadn't been for the war I don't think I would have married. I probably would have gone on to finish college and had an entirely different life.

My husband was a former school-

Library of Congress

mate at Beverly Hills High. He was homesick and isolated on one of the coastal islands near Seattle. He had been in the service for about a year and a half when we got married. While he was in the service I saw him only every three or four months. We wrote frequently and we talked on the phone only intermittently, because you couldn't get through on the lines. Every communication was so difficult. When we did meet, we didn't have time for arguments. I don't think I really knew what he was like, even though we did know each other better than a lot of people did in the military.

After we were married I followed my husband to the air force bases. It was frowned upon, but it didn't stop the wives. The Army would give you a little speech about how difficult it was; well, you knew that. The husband, of course, he was the important one and traveled on top-priority orders. So you didn't get to travel together that often, because if he had to change bases he had to be there immediately, and you had to tag along as best you could.

You really couldn't get on a plane unless it was an absolute emergency. You stood in line to get on a bus, and if the bus filled up you just waited till the next one. It got very ragged sometimes. You'd go to Union Station in Los Angeles, any train station, and there would be people who had been sleeping on the floor for two or three days, just waiting to get a train. Once in El Paso I missed three trains and had to spend the night sleeping on the marble bench in the ladies' washroom. They had a guard at the door to the ladies'

room because men would get drunk and wander in and there'd be trouble. The next morning an older man (he must have been thirty-five) took pity on me and wrapped my arm through his, announcing to the train guard that I was his wife. He was completely *nice* too, a chief petty officer on Admiral Halsey's ship, with a wife and four kids in Iowa—I saw their pictures and heard all about them for seven hours.

Traveling was difficult, but so was finding a place to stay. The towns near the bases may not have been so bad, but the lodging, the housing, was awful. There were no houses being built, and you were lucky if you got a room in someone's home, with bath and kitchen privileges, for which you paid quite a bit. The Army didn't worry about you at all.

But the thing was, you were in it *together*. That was one of the things that made it bearable, and that you were young, so you were resilient. After you had coped with so many of these situations, you felt that you could damn well cope with anything and keep your head, be innovative. It was no good sitting in a hotel and whimpering because your husband was working out at the base. He was doing his job and you had to get out and either look for a job to keep from going crazy or else you had to spend the time trying to find a better place to live.

The experience was maturing in other ways too. It opened my eyes to the problems and potential in this country, a tremendous country. When I went to Pecos in west Texas, that was my first experience with the South. To find that half the train station was for whites and half of it said "Colored." My husband had never been out of California, and he said, "Do they mean red or green?"

Yet even with the problems we had, when you traveled around you still had the feeling that it was such a great country. There was no doubt the whole thing was worth it, worth all the effort.

DELLIE HAHNE

There was this tremendous romance and glamour to the men in the service. And at the very top were the flyboys— "Off we go, into the wild blue yonder." Anybody who flew was absolute tops in the social scale, and my brother was a pilot, so it gave me a great deal of importance. I would drive out to the air base in Santa Ana to visit him on weekends. That's how I met my husband.

It was an alphabetical thing. Our family name started with an *H*, and my husband's last name started with an *H*, and all the *H*'s were put together in this particular barracks. My brother telephoned me and said that he wanted me to meet this man, so I went out to Santa Ana for the weekend and I met him. I was recuperating from a devastating romance at the time, and I was on the rebound. Six weeks later we were married. I saw him six weekends and then married him.

The social pressure for young women to marry soldiers was incredibly strong. It was in everything we did, everything we read, the songs we listened to on the radio, in movies like *The Clock*, where Judy Garland meets a soldier and, in a matter of hours, decides to marry him. The disapproval of refusing to marry a soldier is laughable now, but it existed. I felt the pressure. I told my brother after my husband proposed—this was after the fifth time I'd seen him—I said, "You know, I don't think I want to marry Glenn." And he said, "Oh, Dellie, don't say that. Not marry Glenn?" And his wife, my sister-in-law, said, "But you have to." And I didn't have the sense to fight it. Besides, I wanted to marry anyway. I had absorbed all these attitudes.

The serviceman was giving everything to his country—arms, legs, his eyesight, his blood, his life. The least you could do was give yourself to this man. And since sex outside of marriage was frowned upon, the only thing left was to marry him. It was almost your duty.

I had doubts about whether this was the man I wanted to marry, but I didn't pay attention to them. In the back of my mind I realized that we were having a marvelous time on the weekends because there was something to do every minute. But looking to the future, I wondered what I was going to do when the war was over, when the hysteria and the fervor were gone. What were we going to do every single evening? What would we talk about?

I think I had a lot of sense, but I talked myself out of it. I didn't even know what my husband did for a living. When I found out he was a carpenter, I thought, I can't marry a carpenter, so in my mind I changed it. I just adjusted reality. I turned him into a contractor; that was okay. And it never occurred to me that what I thought and what was true were so divergent. But the fervor, the patriotism, the propaganda completely blinded you, so you stopped thinking.

After I married my husband he washed out of the pilot training program, and that was a terrible shock. I think that was my first taste of reality. I didn't marry a pilot, I married a man, and this man was a sergeant in the air force, and his job was dusting off airplanes. But I followed him anyway, first to Amarillo, Texas, then to Panama City, Florida.

It was expected of you to follow your husband, even pregnant women and women with small children. That was the least you could do. You belonged to a select group—the war brides. You were giving your all to the guys who were giving their all to us.

The conditions on the railroads were horrendous. The trains were packed with women following their husbands. What broke my heart was the sight of pregnant women. They weren't women; they were girls, really, seventeen-, eighteen-, twenty-year-olds who had married soldiers and gone to say good-bye to them, or were on their way home, and they were five, six months pregnant. I would think, What in hell are they going to do? The guy is going overseas—do they go home and live with their families? How are they going to support themselves on an allotment of fifty dollars a month?

Following your husband was really very difficult. The trains were a mess. We were allowed into the dining car twice a day, morning and night. We weren't given lunch. Only the servicemen were allowed to eat lunch. In some trains we could sit in the aisles on our suitcases or in the vestibules. We never had a guarantee that we would remain on the train. There were several times when I was put off the train. I remember being put off in a place called El Reno, Oklahoma, which to me was nowhere, and I had to fend for myself. I had to find a hotel, find a way to get out the next day or whenever I could. It was a tremendous lesson in growing up.

I had led a very sheltered life. My mother was the type of woman who liked to run the show; she made all my decisions for me, and I never questioned it. The first decision I ever made on my own was on my first day in college when I had to decide whether to eat lunch at the hot-dog stand down the road or in the cafeteria. It was the first decision I'd ever had to make in my life, and I couldn't do it. I just stood in the hall, frozen.

Just shortly after that I became a war wife, knocking around the country, trying to figure out how to feed myself without ration points, coming into a strange town, finding out where to rent a room, how much to pay. I never had a checking account in my life. I opened one in my first town and didn't sign my name on the check the way I had signed it on the application card; I didn't think it meant anything. So my first check bounced. I learned very quickly how to take care of myself. I think a great number of us did, because we were forced on our own traveling from one town to another. The war produced some good things, and self-reliance was one of them for me.

INEZ SAUER

I met my second husband at Boeing during the war. He was a bombardier, a war hero coming back from the Battle of the Coral Sea to go to B-29 school. He was a front-page hero, ten years younger than I and very handsome, a second Tyrone Power, tall, black-haired and blue-eyed, and from a prominent New York family. He was Irish and had that beautiful New York accent, and he knew how to persuade a woman my age. My mother was thrilled with him. He was with the Fifth Air Force and had his uniforms specially made in Australia. They were cream-colored and, oh, they were beautiful. That was quite a romance. I was engaged to a Boeing engineer at the time, but I immediately broke it off. Two months later I married the bombardier.

Unfortunately the marriage didn't last. We had an understanding that when the war was over he was going to be a civilian. Well, he got out of the service, but he didn't stay out. He didn't like civilian life. He had entered the air force when he was nineteen and had been in it for five years, and he had difficulty readjusting to ordinary small-town life, so he reenlisted with the Strategic Air Command. I could see that with three young children my life could never follow his. I would never raise my children on Air Force bases, so I left him, and we were divorced.

BARBARA NOREK

I was twelve when the war began and my father went to work in the ship-yards in San Francisco. He worked the graveyard shift, so suddenly he wasn't around. He slept during the day and was gone all night. There was no father figure anymore after that. I remember seeing him just to say hi to.

My mother and I did not get along too well at that time, or before, and, not having my father there, it was really difficult for me. He was my stability and I missed his companionship and affection.

I rebelled against my mother's authority, and she didn't know how to handle me. She constantly threatened, "If you don't behave I'm going to tell your father." And I'd want her to tell my father, but he wasn't there; so naturally the discipline kept breaking down more and more.

When I turned fourteen, I became the best churchgoer in the neighborhood. I went Sunday morning, noon and night to church because each week a whole new crop of sailors was coming in. Every Sunday the pastor would invite young sailors in for a supper. Of course, they had to listen to the sermon afterwards, but they didn't seem to mind. Three of my girlfriends and I went to this church, and we would pick and choose who we thought were the best-looking kids of the group and invite them home with us. My mother was very good in that respect, in letting me bring the young boys home. They were kids, seventeen-, eighteen-year-olds going off to war. They thought I was sixteen. I never would tell them I was only fourteen. My mother played the piano and we sang. I got acquainted with quite a few of them that way. They'd be gone in a few weeks, and then there would be somebody else.

Barbara Norek during the war years. *Courtesy of Barbara Norek*

I wrote ten or fifteen letters a week to all these different fellows I met. It was almost a contest to see how many each of us could date. "I'm writing to ten. How many are you writing to?" In fact, sometimes I would forget which one I was writing to and not remember that I had said the same thing before, so I started keeping a file. I had an old Cardex where I had the fellow's name and his address, and then I'd write what I wrote him on each card, plus the date, and when I received a letter I posted that. Of course my school grades went down the drain because I was so busy working on the Cardex.

I started my correspondence, and as the sailors came back I would see many of them. Some of them were quite serious, thinking I was older. I had two of them come back with engagement rings. I think I was engaged to five different men within the same period of time. Then, as time went on, I'd forget. I'd lose track of who they were, and they'd come back two years later expecting me to be there waiting for them when I could not remember who they were.

I had some really bad experiences with a couple of them coming back the same day on the same ship, and coming to my home. It was almost like a situation comedy on TV, but it really did happen. One fellow came back with a big diamond engagement ring, all ready to take me off to Ohio. My mother said, "My God, she's only sixteen. You can't take her home." The sailor was very upset. "I thought she was that two years ago."

When I think back on those times, being with the sailors, it was like a drug. I was addicted to it. Having all this attention, having all these men saying that I was beautiful, that they couldn't live without me, will I wait for them? I couldn't get enough of it. I mean every day, every night, it wouldn't have been enough. At night I'd dream about sailors, and during the day, when I was supposed to be in school, I'd be daydreaming about them again. I was sailor crazy.

I had very little understanding of the war. My whole world was what sailor I was going to meet. If a big battle was going on, that meant there'd be more coming out to this port. I didn't have anyone in the family in the war, except a cousin who went later, so I was barely touched by the war except for what I was seeing.

A couple of times when I was writing to the sailors the letters would come back marked "Deceased." One even said, "Expired," and at that time I hadn't heard that word before. I recall I had to ask my mother. We looked it up in the dictionary, and it said, "deceased, dead." It was a very emotional moment, but the sad part of it was that he was one of the sailors I didn't remember, a boy I'd been writing to who, in my mind, I couldn't even picture.

I think that all during that time I was lonely, missing my father and looking for male companionship. I know I felt the loneliness of a lot of these young kids. Many of them came from the South, from very strict families. Some of them had just barely worn shoes before. I was amazed at some of the stories they told of living in the backwoods.

Some of them could barely read and write.

Spending time with them, it wasn't sex. There was a lot of necking and hugging and holding hands. Some of the boys wanted to do a little more than I did, but I didn't. Neither did my girlfriends. It was just being together at that time with these young men who were going overseas. Most of them were lonely and wanted a companion. We did a lot of roller-skating and a lot of walking. We'd go window shopping downtown and we'd go to the Golden Gate Park and walk. But mainly they wanted to talk. They'd tell you about their life, their family, and what they were going to do when they got back home. Some of them talked about fear, how they were afraid to go. A few of them actually broke down and cried. Some of them said they knew they'd never come back. Some of them didn't.

We also spent time at the naval hospital. I think going there was really the hardest experience. Some of the young men were blind or had lost arms and legs, and we'd go up there and write letters for them. I didn't do that too much, because that was too hard. I didn't want to get that emotionally involved. That was getting a little too close to the war, so I wanted to stay away from it.

And many times we would go over to Treasure Island and sit on the docks and wave at the ships as they left. I can't even describe what that feeling was. It was an excitement, yet a feeling of loneliness. Many times we would just sit there and cry, because it was very sad. Now I can understand why, but at the time I wasn't aware of what it was all about.

LAURA BRIGGS

The Mountain Home Air Base was about a hundred miles from Jerome, and it had quite an effect on the community. Soldiers would come around on leave all the time, and young girls would go to the base for dances. It troubled the community a little.

In a way it was patriotic to entertain the servicemen, but you wanted everyone else's kid to do it, not yours. The farmers and the town fathers, even the businessmen, didn't want their girls to be mixed up with strangers. They didn't feel their daughters were so-phisticated enough for that.

In Idaho you got married at seventeen or before and that was it. There were no young women over eighteen running loose, and so the flyboys got involved with the younger girls, the high-school group. There were a lot of changes in people's lives because of that—a lot of heartbreak.

If a girl got pregnant and didn't marry, then it was the end of her life. It just wasn't recognized or accepted. If farm kids romanced around, they got married and a baby was born seven months later. Well, it was premature and that was that. There were a few snickers, but they were very quiet. For a girl to be pregnant without any man around vouching for her, that was the end. She might as well jump off the cliff or Snake River Canyon, because her life was over.

I was the Elsie Dinsmore of the town, the girl in the set of books where if you kissed you were engaged. My parents kept an iron hand on me. I wasn't allowed to go anywhere. I was kind of envious really. I didn't ever get involved with the soldiers, because my parents were so strict. But not all the girls were meek and namby-pamby like me. Many of them rebelled—and they were having the time of their lives.

Rides were provided to the air base for these dances, and there was a group of girls who just took off, which was remarkable considering the trip to the base was through the desert and a hundred miles away. I would have been scared to death. I could just see my father pursuing me if I had gone. But it was a big adventure to the brave, more adventurous souls in the town.

Their daughters are probably heading the fight for the Equal Rights Amendment right now. Yet they were still young and innocent. They didn't feature themselves as getting pregnant and getting in trouble, but a lot of them did sooner or later.

I remember the biggest town scandal. One girl went right ahead and had her baby, looked the town right in the eye and carried the kid around. Every parent thought it was degrading. "How dare she not leave town?" Then there were several other girls who were suddenly paying visits to maiden aunts over in Montana. Their absence would last for a few months, and then they would come back. Or they were going to a "secretarial school." I remember laughing a few years later because I fell for all those stories, and I remember going into hysterics because someone told me my best friend had had an abortion. I couldn't believe it. To me you had to be a virgin. That's all there was to it. It was hard for me to adjust myself to the fact that anybody I would know or care about could be anything but a virgin.

ROGER MONTGOMERY

When I was working in Elyria, Ohio, I was on the night shift, which was a different world, and it was very exciting for me. I never had the opportunity before to live in a group where there were no elaborate social games. You sat down with some guy and struck up

a conversation. He asked you where you worked and he bought you a drink. Even though I was not legally old enough to drink in Ohio, I never had any problem.

The way this plant worked, everybody had a break at the same moment, so we all went over to this bar, and we'd dance, eat our meals and flirt with the opposite sex. There were people playing the jukebox and there was a lot of banter and byplay that went on. It was sort of an easy, social world. You were awake and living your life at a time of day when nothing else was going on except for a few institutions that were serving these night war workers.

Most of the women I knew were older than I by a few years, because everybody my age was in the service. The one woman who was the most intense experience of that time was a hillbilly woman who was the wife of one of the guys who worked in the steel mill. She and her husband were friends of the group in the union, and her husband was working days, and I was sleeping days, and I was sleeping in her bed some of the time.

Up until that point all the girls I ever knew were in the same social class, upper-middle-class college kids who were going to become scientists, or, at the very least, well-educated wives of scientists. What was improbable for me was the total difference of the social world at the plant. I guess I was a fairly intellectual kid, and I was used to people who read books. I had a book in my pocket in the factory. The women used to ask me what I was doing. They were very different from the young women I had known. They were interested in almost nothing except romance on several immediate levels. If you were nice, and had the right vibrations, the next thing you knew you were in bed. It was totally new to me.

I don't want to paint myself as being a great lover in this situation, because I wasn't. I was frightened to death about it a good deal of the time, but my memory of it, and my sense of the overall ambience, is that for me it was quite a liberating experience. I had never been really closely involved with people for whom personal interaction was so immediately open. You didn't have to bullshit anybody. You just had a drink with somebody and the next thing you knew, they accepted you on a level that I was totally unused to.

ELLIOT JOHNSON

One of the Southerners whom I had to read and write letters for went out to have a good time one Saturday night and he got involved with a camp follower. This corporal came in the next morning—I happened to be the duty officer—and he said, "Lieutenant, you got to help me. I did something stupid. I got drunk last night and when I woke up and looked down there was ninety-eight pounds of woman flesh beside me, and she opened her eyes and reminded me that we had gotten married. But I don't want to be married."

Well, the corporal and I went in and

tried to buy off the justice of the peace, to get him to tear up the papers and not mail them. I'd never tried to buy or bribe anyone in my life. Ten dollars more and we could have done it, but when we pooled our cash we came up ten dollars short, so the justice wouldn't undo the marriage.

We went overseas, and every week that woman wrote to the corporal. I read the letters to him. She wrote nothing but good news, happiness. Then we came home, and he was given his thirty-day leave. He went home to see his wife and she handed him this cheap little ring that he had bought when he was drunk and said, "Now let's get a divorce."

"Why did you write to me all this time?" he asked.

"It was the least I could do for you after all you were doing," she said. "But you don't want to be married to a girl like me. I'm a whore." And that terminated the marriage.

·10·

WOMEN ALONE

I lived alone for four years during the war, and they were the
most painful, lonely years I think I will ever spend.

—Marjorie Cartwright

Motherhood is a great deal like music. It's an international
language. Any mother who has lost her son or daughter
in war feels the same anguish as we did.

—Esther Burgard

Fifteen million men served in the armed forces of the United States
during World War II. The separation of the men from their
families and loved ones tested the character of all, especially the wives
and mothers of the servicemen. The long vigil of women alone was
perhaps surpassed only by the homesickness and longing for home of
the men who served overseas. Many service families tried to remain
together throughout the war as wives followed their husbands from
one post to another. But separation became inevitable when the men
were ordered to sea or to a theater of war.

The challenge of living alone was most severe for wives with young
children. Many women, pregnant when their husbands left home,
bore their children without the moral comfort and support of their
mates at their side. Countless numbers of children did not meet their

fathers until they were old enough to walk and talk. Economic
support for the serviceman's dependents who were totally dependent
upon him for support came from the federal government, which
provided a monthly allotment check calculated to meet only the basic
necessities of life. Many wives found it necessary to supplement this
income by working outside the home. Their jobs often helped to
alleviate their loneliness as well.

Letters were the universal link between women and the servicemen
away from home. In 1942 the federal government gave servicemen
free mailing privileges, but even without this aid the flow of mail
would still have reached epic proportions. Letter writing was at least
a weekly affair in most households, and some tried to write a letter or
a card every day. Letters from the servicemen helped to reassure
those at home that they were getting enough to eat, were in good
health and were out of danger, even when these conditions did not

prevail. Letters from home in turn assured the servicemen that they were missed and loved and provided news of life in their hometowns.

But bad news often accompanied the good in the exchange of letters, bringing disappointments and sorrow to the lives of many. Some women and men learned of the infidelity of their mates in a letter from the unfaithful partner or from a relative or acquaintance. And some women wrote "Dear John" letters to inform a former boyfriend that their relationship was over.

Telegrams usually brought news of a more tragic nature: a death on the homefront or the battlefield; a missing-in-action report; or news of a serious battle injury. Over 300,000 American servicemen were killed in World War II, and another 700,000 sustained injuries which left many with varying degrees of disability or impairment. No statistics, however, can measure the anguish and sorrow of families who lost a son, husband, father or brother in the war.

MARJORIE CARTWRIGHT

Three months after the war started, my boyfriend came home to West Virginia on emergency leave, we were married, and I came back to the West Coast with him. My husband was with the Seventh Fleet, on the U.S.S. *Chicago*, and their home port was San Francisco.

The men wanted their wives and families on the West Coast because they were never sure when they would come back into port and they didn't always get a long enough furlough to travel where their families were. Ship movements were secret, too, so no one knew when they would dock or when they would leave again. The men wanted to have a feeling of home when they got back. If they didn't have someone in San Francisco, then they would have to live on the ship, or on the base. And, naturally, they wanted a little loving

Marjorie Cartwright and her husband in 1946. *Courtesy of Marjorie Cartwright*

and a little caring when they came home.

I had never traveled farther than Pittsburgh before, and here I was suddenly, three thousand miles from home, in San Francisco. Almost as soon as we got there my husband shipped out and I was on my own, living in a city I didn't know and where I knew very few people. It was like being an orphan. I felt completely alone.

I got a job as a keypunch operator for Standard Oil, and I found a furnished room because it was impossible to find an apartment or housing of any kind. There was a waiting list of at least a year, and military men and families were given priority. During the day I worked at Standard Oil and at night I'd return to my room. I learned to knit at that time and spent many nights knitting socks for my husband and listening to the radio for war news. I lived alone for four years during the war, and they were the most painful, lonely years

I think I will ever spend. I look back and wonder how I ever got through those years, but when you're young you can do a lot of things that you can't do as you grow older. I spent many nights by myself in my room, crying because I was so lonely.

The occasional times my husband would come on leave, we would talk about the future. "As soon as the war is over," he would say, "I'm going to leave the Navy, and we'll go back to the East Coast, buy a home, raise a family." We had the house all built in our mind. It was a two-story brick home, with a beautiful entrance hall. There was a lovely winding stairway leading upstairs and bedrooms enough for five children. I just loved that house and carried those plans around in my mind for years and years.

BARBARA DE NIKE

My husband went into the Navy, and after he had taken his original training courses he was assigned to small-craft school in Miami Beach. Many of my friends took their kids and went home to their parents and just sat it out. But my parents had died some time before, so I really had no place to go. I lived for a while with my little boy in a housing project, Parkchester, in the Bronx. It was a decent enough place to live, but it was very hard without my husband. So finally I decided that I was going to try to go with him. We put our furniture

in storage and I went to Florida.

We were very fortunate that we were able to live in a lovely Miami Beach hotel, the Flamingo, that the Navy had taken over. I was pregnant again and that was a good time. We could go swimming in the pool and eat in the dining room. He went to school every morning and came back every evening, so I got to see a great deal of him.

We stayed there until he got orders to report to a ship that was being built in San Pedro, California. When a navy wife is living in navy housing and her husband gets orders to another station, she has twenty-four hours to leave. But I had nowhere to go, and I didn't know what to do.

I sent my sister a wire saying I was coming to California, because her husband was at Camp Roberts. I thought, Wherever she is, I can move in with her. I got a return wire in Miami saying she was on her way to the East Coast, that her husband had had orders to go to Europe. So I took my little boy, and the two of us got on the train and headed back for New York to meet my sister and her husband. In the meantime my husband was able to get in to New York. The four of us all said goodbye to each other in Grand Central Station.

I felt a great deal of resentment toward the situation my husband was in. He had orders to go to San Pedro, he had a ticket in his hand, and he went. He didn't have to take any responsibility for me or our son. He didn't have to worry about where we were or what we were doing. The military relieved all the men of the responsibilities of their families. They were told what to do and where to go; their meals were put on the table and their wash was done. But I had to leave Miami Beach in twenty-four hours and find a place to live. I resented the fact that our family had been interrupted and that our lives had been changed so drastically.

I was eight months pregnant at that point, so my little boy went to visit an aunt in Westchester County and I went and stayed with another aunt in the Bronx for about a month until my little girl was born. That was hard, because I couldn't see my little boy at all. And,

of course, my husband never saw his daughter. Finally, when my daughter was four weeks old, I moved to Syracuse, where my sister had rented an apartment. That's when our troubles really began. She had a child who was between my two in age. So it was the two of us with three little ones: a two-year-old, a ten-month-old and a four-week-old infant.

Two and a half months after we moved in, the house was sold and we got our first eviction notice. Every morning we got up, grabbed the paper and read the for-rent ads. My sister would get dressed and go out and I'd stay with the three babies. Most of the people just said no the minute they heard we had children. "Absolutely no." They just didn't rent to people with children. Finally we found a widow who had moved out of her house in Fayetteville and who let us have it very much against her own good judgment.

The widow's house had a coal furnace, and neither my sister nor I had any experience with coal furnaces. We didn't know how to stoke it to keep the fire going all night, so we used the coal very fast. The snow was very high, and there was a period of about three or four days when we couldn't get coal delivered to the house, so my sister and I went down along the tracks in the snow and picked up pieces that had fallen off from freight cars.

Three months after we moved in, the rent control office lowered the rent, so the widow said she wanted to move back. She had moved out simply to get the money, and when the money was reduced we got an eviction letter from

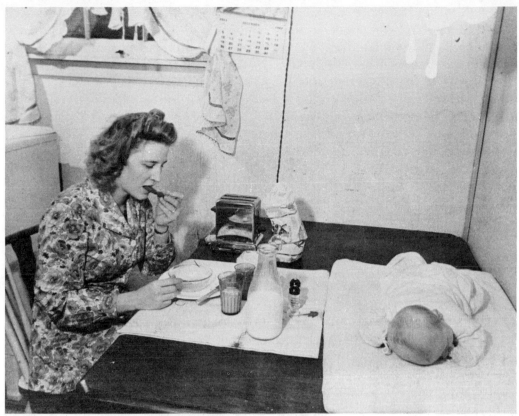

her lawyer. So there we were again. Fortunately we found another house in Fayetteville. A navy wife was leaving, and she let us move in. The new house provided the luxury of a gas furnace.

Unhappily, after four months the navy wife returned and we had to move again. My sister's father-in-law had this cottage out at a lake just south of Auburn, New York, that no one had lived in for a long time because he and his wife had been divorced. So that's where we moved in late May. The only heat was a fireplace in one of the rooms. My little girl got pneumonia and I had to

put her in the hospital. I left her in as long as I could so she'd have a warm place, but finally they just said I had to take her home.

It was a very lonely time. I felt so buffeted about. I didn't feel that I had choices. All you could do was try to cope. I think my children helped sustain me during this time. I felt if I lost my husband, I still had them. That was some support.

My husband was stationed in California when our daughter was born, and I remember as she got older the awful feeling that he didn't see the first time she walked. He didn't see her get her teeth or hear her first word. That hurt more than anything. I spent a great deal of my time writing to him, trying to make him see her and understand the things she was learning to do, learning to sit up, learning to walk, to hold a spoon—all the things that babies do. I felt that was one of the most important things I could communicate to him. But I knew that sometimes he got those letters and sometimes he didn't, and there wasn't much continuity.

In June of '45 my husband's ship was hit by a Japanese kamikaze plane in the Pacific. I received word that it was going to be brought back to Portland, Oregon, to be repaired. I wanted very much to go to Portland to be with him. We were all anticipating what was probably going to be a long war in the Pacific, and I thought this would be my only opportunity to see him.

At this point the war was over in Europe and my sister's husband had been sent home to Missouri and she had gone there to be with him. I had moved back to Syracuse and was staying with an aunt, an elderly schoolteacher, in a one-room apartment. She couldn't cope with two little kids by herself and there simply wasn't anyplace else to leave them. A friend of mine said he could arrange to have them kept in a Catholic orphanage in Syracuse. So I put them in the orphanage and took the train to Portland.

Afterwards when I returned to Syracuse, my aunt would not let me bring the children back to her one-room apartment. I didn't blame her. It was simply too much for her. So I left the children in the orphanage while I looked for a place to stay. Finally the sister at the orphanage said, "Don't come again to visit them until you can take them." It was just too confusing.

When I finally took the children out of the orphanage, it was not because I had found a place to live, but because my husband's ship was being brought around to Charleston, South Carolina. I had an old 1936 Ford Phaeton, an open car, and I piled all my things in it and I went to the orphanage and picked up the children and put them in their snowsuits, and we started off on the trip.

The first night we stayed in a hotel in Williamsport, Pennsylvania. I was trying to get their morale up and my morale up because at last we were going to be a family again. So I dressed them all up and took them down to the hotel dining room to have a nice dinner. And in the middle of dinner all of a sudden my son burst into tears.

"What's the matter?" I asked.

"I want to go home," he said, but he didn't know where he meant and I didn't know where he meant. He was just thoroughly bewildered. He had no home. He didn't know where he belonged anymore.

So we finished up our lovely dinner and we got on the road again and we went to Charleston.

SHIRLEY HACKETT

My boyfriend and I discussed getting married right after the war began, but I didn't want to and said we should wait. As time went on, though, he became more and more insistent. He didn't want to put it off any longer, especially since he was pretty sure he was going to be sent to Europe. My husband was stationed in New Orleans, came up to Connecticut for ten days for the wedding and then went right back. Then he was transferred to North Carolina, and I went to live with him there until he was shipped to Europe. It was very difficult when he went overseas.

I did everything I could to stay busy. There were always other people you could help who were really having a rough time. Being by yourself was very lonely. You couldn't plan from one day to the next, because life was very precarious. Death was always around you. It seemed to come in bunches. Sometimes, in my hometown, and this was a shocking thing, there would be as many as five or six in a day. It just didn't happen in one battle area. It could happen from one side of the world to the other, say from New Guinea to Europe. You wondered, Why did it hit like this? And why so many? Everybody dreaded a telegram. You almost hated to answer the phone at times.

You lived for the mail, yet the mail was censored, and it was not priority-shipped; it was always left for the very last thing. My husband wrote to me every day, but I sometimes didn't hear from him for three months. When the mail did come, often it was censored so much that you couldn't possibly figure out what he wanted to tell you in the letter. We knew very little about what was actually going on in the battlefield until much later. You worried because you didn't know anything. We had radio, but the war news was censored and very little was in the newspapers that told you anything.

The future became almost nonexistent. The war seemed endless. There was not just one war, but two, one on either side of you, so how do you plan? I wondered should I have gotten pregnant and at least had a child before my husband went away. You felt as if you were in some kind of trap you couldn't get out of, you were helpless to do anything about it. I couldn't plan for the future, so I did a lot of praying. That was my only consolation. I prayed to God to give me strength and hope.

You had nothing which you could hold on to and say it's going to be like that when the war ends. You knew it wasn't. All the old values and the old things that we had always been brought up to believe in, everything was changing rapidly. Women had suddenly been taken out of their protected environ-

196 •   THE HOMEFRONT

ments. All the men who had been around to protect you were suddenly gone. You had to face the world without your protector. Before if some guy made a pass at you, you told your boyfriend or your husband and he took care of it. But now there wasn't anyone around like that to lean on. So this left a lot of women feeling very insecure.

Then you had a war situation in which the women didn't know when or if the men were coming back. The men didn't know when they'd be coming home.

Inevitably you wound up with a lot of cheating on each other. But this is where the old double standard came in. The women who had cheated on their husbands while they were overseas were looked on as absolute trash and were ostracized, but if the men had cheated, and some of them made no bones about the fact that they had, you were supposed to understand. "He was in the war, so what do you expect?" My mother-in-law was a perfect example of this attitude. My husband wrote and told me that she had written to him,

Library of Congress

encouraging him to find a woman over there. She told him it wasn't healthy for him not to have sex all this time. That caused a big stink between us. She told me I didn't realize that men were just that way and she was just encouraging him to do what came naturally. Yet she had another set of standards for me. If I mentioned I was going to the movies, she would always say, "Who are you going with? What time are you going to get back?" All the time my husband was away, she watched me like a hawk.

ELLIOT JOHNSON

While we were overseas, letters from our loved ones, including our girl-friends and wives, really sustained us. The mail came in very irregular batches, though. Sometimes for several weeks we wouldn't get any letters at all, then we would get an enormous amount of mail. And sometimes the letters that had been mailed first arrived many weeks after those which had been mailed last.

But letters were a big part of our emotional stability, because they made us feel like we were still a part of the people back home, that we hadn't been forgotten. Then, from time to time, one of the fellows would get a "Dear John" letter. And that was devastating.

I remember having to read a "Dear John" letter for one of the soldiers. He was a Southerner, and his reaction was complete silence. He got up and walked away, came back and asked me to read the letter again, then folded it, put it in his pocket and walked away. I could see the lines of grief in his face, the total disbelief. And I could feel his emptiness. Then it spread to all the men throughout the company. We understood how he felt, and it made us all very insecure. Most men were insecure about how their wives would act while they were thousands of miles away.

Still, having a wife at home was very sustaining. I did a lot of dreaming about coming home to her. I wanted to buy a house and have a family, and I spent many hours thinking about exactly the kind of house I'd like to have. A very smart man I know said once that anticipation was sixty percent of life. There was this anticipation of returning to this beautiful girl. And fantasies of kids and jobs. It was absolutely sustaining.

RACHEL WRAY

I saw George in June of 1942, and then he did not come back again until June of 1944. If I got a letter a month from him, I was lucky, a censored letter in which all he could say was "I'm fine, I hope you're the same." That was the gist of the letter. So I buried myself in my work.

As much as I didn't want to admit it at the time, my work did make the time go fast. I worked swing shift, which was four-thirty in the afternoon to one in the morning, and I didn't go out.

A lot of the younger people working the swing shift would go skating, or to Tijuana, and they would ask me to go with them. "Oh, Rach, come on and go out," they'd say, but I wouldn't. They teased me and called me "Granny" and said I was being too honest, too true to George, but I never went out with other men, just the girls at work. I was living as true to George as if we were married.

I know that many women who worked alongside me couldn't hold out. They were married when their husbands left, but they didn't have whatever it takes to withstand the loneliness, so they became involved with another man. They weren't "bad girls." They were just human. Loneliness can be overpowering. But I had only one thing in my mind and that was when George was coming home.

But when he came back in '44, he was changed. The impact of the war had changed him. It's really hard to explain. He was the same person and I loved him just as much, but it was like he didn't want to get close to anyone. Maybe it was the uncertainty of war, of not knowing when the end was going to come, or the impact of losing one of his very best friends; whatever it was, he had changed. He was very quiet. He didn't talk. He had nothing to say about the war, other than maybe laugh and joke about the rations they had, one biscuit for breakfast and one biscuit for dinner, and that kind of thing. But he didn't want to be pushed at all. He didn't want anyone to throw him into a group of people. In fact, he didn't want to be around people at all. His whole personality was different.

He was home for thirty days and then he shipped out again and I didn't see him anymore until the next June, in '45. But when he left we decided that we weren't going to get married. There was no long conversation, but the decision was clear. That was a crushing blow, but I just accepted it and threw myself into my work. From then until the end of the war I didn't do anything but work.

Then, after the war was over, we were all laid off from Convair, and I said, What the heck, you can only live alone so long and pretty soon my life

Library of Congress

is going to be gone. So I met another man and we were married and had two daughters. We were married seventeen years and then we divorced, and then—this is almost an unbelievable story—George came back into the picture by sheer accident. My husband had a boat that he asked me to sell for him. The first person to answer the ad for the boat called while I was at work, and my daughter told him to come by at five.

When I came home, there was George.

We got talking and he opened up and said, "I don't know why I was such a fool," and so on, and shortly afterwards we were married. Even now my children and many people who know me say that my love for George never wavered, even when I was living with my husband. I think my husband at the time knew it, too. If it hadn't been for the war George and I would have married a long time before.

WINONA ESPINOSA

I came out to San Diego during the war to be closer to my boyfriend, who was stationed in Washington, but by the time I got here and contacted him he had been shipped overseas. He was such a long ways away, and the war felt like it was never going to end. It seemed like I was going to have to work in this factory every day and that was going to be it forever.

Meanwhile I met a nice man at Rohr. He really treated me like a brother. It was that kind of relationship. He would take me to dinner, to the beach, to meet his parents. They were wonderful. I was a very immature nineteen. I can't believe how much I didn't know. And this man was very nice to me. It made me not afraid to have a personal relationship with him.

Everybody at work would ask, "When *are* you guys going to get married?" I decided we might as well do it.

We got married, and within a year I had a baby. When I was pregnant I cried the whole time for this fellow who was overseas. I felt bad about myself that I was so "ungrownup." I needed more time under my belt before I stepped into marriage. I could handle the work at the factory, but I just couldn't handle the emotional thing between us.

As soon as I had the baby I wanted to go back home and be with my mother and dad, so I went back to Colorado.

I blame my mother to this day for my staying so long. I felt like she should have said, "Young lady, your place is in San Diego with your husband. Get back out there." But she didn't, and I loved being at home. I had this baby now and I could really love it. Finally I wrote and told my husband I guessed he needed to divorce me, because I was never coming back, and he did.

After I got married I wrote to the fellow who was overseas and told him that the war was lasting too long and that I had married someone else. Then I never got an opportunity to see him again. He was from my hometown, though, and my mother knew his mother, so I would know about him, where he was, where he went. In 1973 I was back home again and saw his mother. She told me that he was single again and gave me his address in Idaho. So I wrote to him from San Diego and told him that I was a single lady too and why didn't he come down to San Diego to visit sometime.

He called me on the phone as soon as he got my letter and he laughed, "Your voice hasn't changed at all! It's just the same. Even after thirty years." So he flew down for a weekend to see me. We laughed about how we would recognize each other, but we had no problem at all, and we just really had the best time together.

So we made arrangements to coordinate our vacation times, so that we could take a vacation together. But when the time came, he never showed up. I was worried about him and finally called his mother back in Colorado. She told me, not that day but in the course of a week, that he was so angry at me during the war for sending him that letter saying I was marrying somebody else that thirty years later he wanted to do the same thing to me. He came down and spent this weekend with me and had this happy time and had no intention at all of seeing me again. He just wanted to hurt me like I had hurt him. He had loved me so much, and I had hurt him so deeply, that he still carried it with him all those years.

DELLIE HAHNE

I was home visiting my older sister when we received a telephone call quite early in the morning asking if someone would be there to accept delivery of a telegram. My older sister was frantic immediately. She was afraid it was a death notice. I called the Red Cross and asked under what circumstances do you receive a telephone call like the one I had just gotten. They said either someone had been killed or had arrived overseas. We knew my brother was going to be shipped out momentarily, so I said, "There, that's what this telegram is. George has been sent overseas."

The doorbell rang and a very old man delivered the telegram. On the envelope were two or three stars. I saw the stars and my blood turned cold. I knew immediately that my brother had been killed. We ripped open the telegram. I can't remember the wording, but it was from the Adjutant General, somebody I'd never heard of before, who regretted to tell me that my brother had been killed. It was one of the most horrible moments in my life.

I kept saying, "I don't believe it; this did not happen," and I laughed, because it was ludicrous. Part of me knew that I was simply anesthetized, that I was numb with shock, and that when that numbness wore off I would have to face the fact that my brother was dead, that he had been killed on a training mission right here in the United States. The waste, I thought, the terrible waste.

This was a trained pilot—he knew what the hell he was doing—and they stuck him up in a C-47, a flying boxcar (so safe they could fly themselves), and they said, Fly up a thousand feet and drop these supplies. It was a night flight and one of the planes got lost and ended up directly over my brother's plane. When they got the order to drop, they dropped the supplies right through the wing of my brother's plane. At a thousand feet they couldn't recover. One man bailed out, but my brother was killed along with everybody else on the plane. He had just turned twenty-one and had never even voted.

At the funeral, the rabbi who gave the service said how wonderful it was that a Jew, in this country, could give his life helping the Jews all over the world. My sister said, "Isn't that a beautiful thought, isn't that comforting." And I said, "That's bullshit." For the first time it occurred to me: Why does a young man have to die for his country in the first place? So right there was a little crack in the patriotism, a little doubt about the righteousness of the war.

My sister-in-law was covered with guilt; she's never shaken it off. Even now when I see her, she'll say "I can't look your mother in the eye: I caused your brother's death." She feels responsible because she encouraged him to join the service even though he could have been released, and because she remembered saying that she'd rather have a dead hero than a live coward for a husband.

ESTHER BURGARD

Every Friday, after my husband had gone to work, and I had the family out to school, I'd get the typewriter out and write a long letter about what happened during the week to my son John, who was in the air force in England. I was just in the process of writing this letter one Friday when the doorbell rang. I went to the door and there was an elderly man with a telegram. He handed it to me, and I said, "Is it bad news?" He didn't answer me. He just walked away. I opened it, and when I read it, that my son had been killed, I couldn't move. I started screaming. I don't know why, but I did. I screamed and my neighbor next door heard me, and she came over. I think that only a person who has gone through this can really know the feeling that comes over you. I had prayed so hard before that he would come home, but if he didn't I prayed that I would have the courage to take it. I don't know whether I had the courage or not, but it was a terrible feeling—he was lost, he was gone.

After the war was over I joined the American Gold Star Mothers Organization. We are all very sympathetic of one another's ordeals, very compas-

Esther Burgard and her son, 1943. *Courtesy of Esther Burgard*

sionate toward other mothers, German mothers, Russian mothers, whatever nationality. Motherhood is a great deal like music. It's an international language. Any mother who has lost her son or daughter in war feels the same anguish as we did. But the organization helped fill a great void. We are dedicated to aid and comfort wounded veterans and their families, especially those who are hospitalized. In fact, "We carry the torch of freedom that our sons or daughters let fall with Death."

·11·

VICTORY: THE DAWN OF THE ATOMIC AGE

The force upon which the sun draws its power has been loosed against those who brought war to the Far East.

—President Harry S. Truman
announcing the use of the
atomic bomb at Hiroshima,
August 6, 1945

The spring and summer of 1945 witnessed cataclysmic events in world affairs. On April 12, President Franklin D. Roosevelt died suddenly of a cerebral hemorrhage and was succeeded by Vice President Harry S. Truman. On the twenty-eighth of April the German resistance in northern Italy collapsed, permitting Italian partisans to capture and kill Benito Mussolini. Two days later Adolf Hitler committed suicide as Russian forces bombarded the bunkers of his Berlin headquarters. On May 8, 1945, the Allies received the unconditional surrender of the German Forces. V-E Day—Victory in Europe—was at last a reality.

The end of the war in Europe, however, was but prelude to the next campaign: the invasion of the home islands of Japan planned for November 1945. Only President Truman and a small number of military and civilian personnel knew that the invasion of Japan might never occur, because of a powerful new weapon—the atomic bomb.

The closest Truman came to revealing the pending use of the new bomb came ten days after its first successful test in New Mexico. From Potsdam, where Truman was concluding a meeting with the Soviet Union and Great Britain, he issued with Great Britain and China an ultimatum to the government of Japan calling for the unconditional surrender of the Japanese armed forces. The alternative, the document concluded, was "prompt and utter destruction." When the Japanese government ignored the Potsdam Declaration, Truman issued his order for dropping atomic bombs on Japan.

The bombing of Hiroshima on August 6, 1945, and Nagasaki three days later numbed the American people. It was beyond the ability of most to contemplate the far-reaching consequences of a single bomb that could destroy an entire city. In the first public-opinion polls taken a few days after V-J Day, when everyone was rejoicing over the enemy's quick capitulation, eighty-five percent of the American people polled approved the use of the bombs. Only with the passage of time, and the revelation of the extent of the bomb's destruction, did many begin to question the wisdom of the government's action.

V-J Day, Victory over Japan, came on August 14, 1945, with the announcement from Washington that the Japanese government had agreed to surrender. From New York City to San Francisco, from Times Square to the Main Street of rural communities, Americans gathered to celebrate their victory. The pent-up feelings of almost four years of war poured forth in tumultuous and triumphant revelry. Amidst the merrymaking and dancing in the streets, some offered prayers of thanksgiving that the war had ended, and perhaps a few prayed that humanity might survive in the atomic age.

ELLIOT JOHNSON

When the war was over in the European theater, we were shipped back to the United States almost immediately and given thirty-day convalescent leave to be reunited with our families and loved ones. When we reported back to duty we were put aboard a train, and after we departed from the station we were informed that it was fully combat loaded. They told us, "You are going to Japan. You're going to debark from the Port of Seattle, and you are going to invade the coast of Japan."

And I knew, I *knew*, that if I went into combat in Japan I would never come back. Most of the guys, the original ones who had been in the unit from the word go, felt that we had used up our luck. We were resentful because we were being sent to Japan. What were we fighting them for? I had a deep belief, right or wrong, that I would never come home again. I felt there was one bullet over there with

my name on it. Too many of them had gone by me already.

When the train had been moving about half a day, we stopped out in the middle of the prairie. Nothing around us anywhere. We were told to debark and start playing baseball. For three days we did nothing but play baseball and practice close-order drill. At the end of the third day, we were allowed to turn on a radio. And the radio announced that the Americans had dropped this horrible new bomb on Hiroshima that had killed thousands and thousands of people. We simply couldn't comprehend it. We'd been through so much combat, and seen so much suffering, that we were sickened at the size of the target they had chosen to demonstrate the strength of this weapon.

But at the same time, we also felt enormous relief, because we knew that that effectively spelled the end of World

War II, and that we could then be free to go home to our families and resume our lives. And, in fact, they told us to board the train, that we were going back.

JOHN GROVE

A week after V-E Day all but three of us at the University of California Radiation Laboratory were dismissed. We three worked until July 1, 1945—fifteen days before the first atomic bomb was exploded at Alamagordo, New Mexico.

On July 4, 1945, I started work on the development of rockets near the Pasadena Rose Bowl. That's where I was when I learned about Hiroshima. A girl who was working under me at the rocket laboratory came in about ten minutes late and said, "Now I know what you were working on all during the war. You were working on the atomic bomb."

I said, "What?"

She said, "I heard the eight-o'clock news and they announced that they dropped an atomic bomb on Hiroshima."

My immediate reaction was, Thank God we really were successful. That proves that all the money that was spent on the project was worthwhile. That was my first thought. About two seconds later it struck home. "Oh my God, Hiroshima. They dropped the atomic bomb on a city."

I went to my superior and then I got another stunning blow. I said, "You heard the news?"

He said, "Yes."

I said, "Why a city? Why didn't they drop it on the great naval base at Truk, or some other military installation? God knows how many people they've killed. Maybe a hundred thousand, maybe five hundred thousand."

And this man, who was Jewish, said, "What the hell difference does it make? They're only Japs."

I looked at him and thought, And your people have gone through Hitler's atrocities in Europe, and you can say they're only Japs—they're not even human beings. So that was my second shock.

Of course, you can say that all of us sinned in developing and isolating uranium 235. But in wartime, unfortunately, you don't always see the forest for the trees. It never occurred to me that we would use the bomb against Japan. I didn't give too much thought to dropping it on Germany either. It was always just a defensive weapon.

A few days after the war was over, my brother came to visit me. After two years of fighting in the South Pacific, he had volunteered for the invasion of Japan and was training in Texas. He said, "Well, you probably saved my life, and also a million other Americans', because that is what we thought we would lose in the invasion of Japan."

I said, "Nevertheless it was a terrible thing. Two bombs."

He told me, "We've done worse. Our B-29's for months were flying over Tokyo and Yokohama, dropping firebombs. We were deliberately trying to burn everybody to death in those two cities. So what was worse? We could have burned maybe five to seven million people to death if we had kept on with that."

So that took a little of the sting out, but not entirely, because burning to death is bad enough, but blowing them up with atomic bombs, to me, was far worse. And it also was opening Pandora's box, if you like. I think it has to be recognized that we sinned there.

JAMES COVERT

I think it was in the evening that we received the news of the dropping of the atomic bomb. I walked out on the back porch, and my mother was sitting on the steps crying. I sat down next to her and I said, "Mother, the war is almost over. You don't have to cry anymore. My brother and Dad will be home."

But she said, "I'm crying because I think we may have done something we are going to be sorry for."

I asked her what she meant. The way she talked about it was that the bomb had changed things. A new era had been born. I remember sitting on the back steps trying to understand that. The war was going to be over, but suddenly the whole future was in question.

After the second bomb was dropped and the word came that the Japanese were going to surrender, there was a great celebration. On the radio they described what was happening downtown, the parades and the dancing in the streets. So a group of us kids went out in the neighborhood and got some bugles and washtubs and an American flag, and we held our impromptu parade. We wore our cast-off military uniforms and marched up and down the street setting off firecrackers. All the people came out on their porches to watch us. There was a feeling of great relief, of great joy.

Yet the end of the war also brought a kind of bittersweet feeling. We had won, but at the same time I sensed a kind of growing disillusionment. People began to wonder what was next. The feeling of unity that went with the war effort disappeared. The soldiers who came back, the people who worked in the shipyards began to wonder what was in store for them in the future. What could they do now? They had fought the war, now would they be able to live a different life? There was a feeling that their expectations might not be fulfilled.

MARGARET TAKAHASHI

When we were in Boys Town, the boys used to come to our house and visit. When the bomb was dropped in Hiroshima, this one boy was in our kitchen, and he said, "Ha, ha, ha, they dropped a bomb on Japan, and all the babies are dead." The way he said it really upset me. I didn't think I had that much feeling for Japan, but I broke down hearing that.

ALEXANDER J. ALLEN

I had very mixed emotions about V-J Day because of the way in which it came about. The dropping of those bombs I thought was one of the most tragic things in the history of humanity. I still can't understand why Truman and other people who made policy in those days could not have at least given a warning, saying, This is the weapon we have, let us show you what it can do; if you then refuse to surrender we will drop it on one of your cities. That seems to me entirely plausible. But to wipe out not one but two cities with no warning I think is just unforgiveable.

LAURA BRIGGS

I don't think we really wanted to think about the atom bomb very much. I think we closed it out. I know I kind of did. I couldn't sort it out in my mind. I couldn't comprehend it. And yet I knew, of course, that if anyone developed the bomb, it would be America, and if anyone would be justified in using it, it would be us. But it was very hard to think about in terms of people. Of course, the Japs were pretty rotten people, at least that's the propaganda we'd all been fed, and if anyone deserved it, they did. Sad to say, that's what we believed.

PATRICIA LIVERMORE

On V-J Day all hell broke loose. They closed the liquor stores. They closed the bars. They closed the border between here and Mexico. Any girl that was at the Horton Plaza in downtown San Diego got kissed and thrown in the Plaza fountain. I got thrown in about ten times.

Then a bunch of us got together and rented a room on the top floor of the Pickwick Hotel and went up there to celebrate. We bought a couple of bottles from the bellhop because that was the only way to get a bottle of booze. Then sombody had an idea. We went out and bought several boxes of condoms and filled them with water and dropped them out the windows on the people below. It was all we could use, because we couldn't find any balloons.

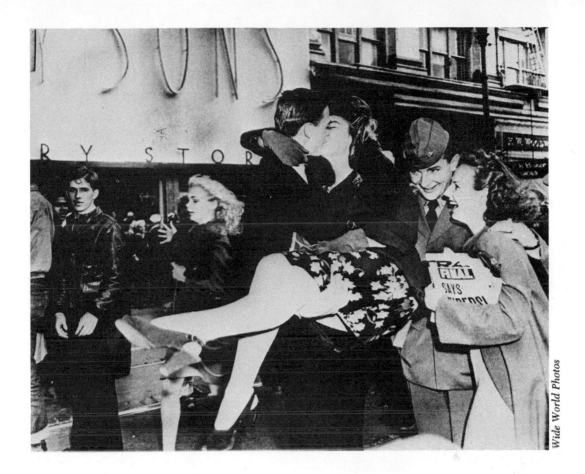

Wide World Photos

BARBARA DE NIKE

I was visiting my husband in Portland, Oregon, when we came in one evening and saw the newspaper headline with the largest letters I am sure that they could find announcing the "A bomb." That was the first time I had ever heard the word. Of course our hopes went soaring. We hoped that this would be the end of the war. We had no concept at all of the destruction. We knew it was something big, but we didn't re-alize the tremendous amount of dev-astation.

Then just a few days after that was V-J Day. The hotel where we were staying just fell apart. There was no room service, no phone operators. Ev-erybody was just running around out on the streets. It was chaos, just total chaos. A lot of people drinking, stag-gering around. To me that simply was not the response that I felt. My husband and I went to church and said a prayer of thanksgiving that the killing was over, and then we went back to the hotel and joined the party.

SYBIL LEWIS

I'll never forget V-J Day. I had followed my husband in the Army until he received his orders to the Philippine Islands, then I had returned to Los Angeles a heartbroken newlywed bride. I didn't go back to the defense plants. I had had enough of that. I saw an ad in the paper announcing openings for maids at Paramount Studio, and since I was curious about what happened in a movie studio, and the pay was good, I took the job. I was working there the day the war ended.

The word came through the movie studios like a fire. I recall very vividly following people up all these stairways not knowing where we were going. Some people had telephone directories in their hands, and other people had rolls of toilet tissue. We got to the top of the studio, and we tore pages out of the directories one at a time. This was our celebration that afternoon that the war was over. After all this excitement and fun, I recall becoming very pensive. The war was over and I knew things were going to change. I realized that the good jobs, all of the advantages that had been offered because of the war, I knew that they were over. And it was on top of that building that I said to myself, You came to California to earn enough money to go back to Oklahoma, and now you're going back and complete your education.

FRANKIE COOPER

At the end of the war I was working in the Kaiser shipyards in Oregon, as a welder. My husband and I had left Illinois because he was dissatisfied with his job and I think he also had itchy feet. I was making more money than he was and I think that had a lot to do with it. So we went west and started working seven days a week at the shipyards.

In August of 1945 we went to work one day and the foreman wanted to speak to all the women. He said, "There's a boat coming up the river and its going to be one of the first troopships coming back. When you come up on the deck, take your caps and scarves off and let your hair down and wave. This will be the first load of boys coming back from the Pacific."

We were thrilled. I think there were three thousand boys. We all waved. That was one day, and the next day I was laid off.

It was a great blow. I know the pride that I felt during the war. I just felt ten feet tall. Here I was doing an important job, and doing it well, and then all at once here comes V-J Day, the end of the war, and I'm back making homemade bread.

DELLIE HAHNE

We were in Panama City, Florida, on V-J Day. I was working on a newspaper downtown. I left the office and mingled with the crowds in the street. I wanted to see who was saying what. There was one man who was absolutely

Black Star/S. Wyman

lost. He had lived on a farm all his life and had come to Panama City to work in the shipyards. He had spent every dime he earned, because the war was going to last such a long time. He said the minute the news was released that the war was over, he was dismissed. He had a little boy, and they didn't have a dime to go home with. I think a lot of men who worked in those jobs were in the same position.

By the end of the war I had become quite disillusioned. I felt taken in by the patriotism. It was a gradual realization. I think it started with the rent gougers when I was following my husband from base to base. I thought that you paid ten dollars a week for a room, because I had never paid for a room before. Then I spoke with the townspeople and discovered they paid three or four dollars a week for a room, but army wives would pay three or four times that amount. And I thought, This is patriotism? Then I read about the tremendous profits of the munitions companies, and the people with money who could afford to buy three or four cars and store them someplace so they could get extra ration books for gasoline. Bit by bit I became disillusioned with the people who were profiteering off the blood of the soldiers and with the propaganda our government was feeding us. This came to a culmination after the war when I read that the United States was sending aid to Germany. I couldn't believe it, that we were going to rebuild and rearm Germany, our avowed enemy, and now we were on the same side. That was the last straw for me. I thought, My brother is dead, and not one damned thing has changed. The balance of power is exactly the way it always has been, except now it's the United States and Germany against Russia. My brother's death was totally useless, it didn't mean a thing.

· 12 ·

HOMECOMING

World War II was a popular war, so we all
came home heroes.

—DON CONDREN

They were the winners, the victors; they had fought the war
bravely, yet they were disillusioned.

—JAMES COVERT

The veterans of World War II returned home conquering heroes,
heralded by marching bands and ticker-tape parades throughout
the country. Yet for many readjustment to civilian life was
unexpectedly complex and painful. Anticipating some of the problems
of the returning veterans, Congress had enacted the Servicemen's
Readjustment Act of 1944. This measure—the GI Bill—provided for
the payment of tuition, books and a monthly stipend for veterans who
wanted to pursue a college education or receive vocational training.
This act also provided for low-cost thirty-year housing loans for GI's
that enabled millions to buy their own homes and also stimulated the
postwar economy. Another government benefit, for returning
veterans who could not find employment or who had difficulty
adjusting to civilian life, was a year-long unemployment-insurance
program. The "52-20 Club," the name given to it by the GI's, provided

Culver Pictures, Inc.

payments of twenty dollars per week for fifty-two weeks to unemployed veterans.

The combat veterans' adjustment to civilian life was actually much more difficult than many could have imagined. The men who returned from the war were not the same persons who had entered the service a few years before. Their wartime experiences, ranging from the trauma of battle and war wounds to the regimen of military discipline, had affected them profoundly. Their loved ones knew only that war had changed some of the men in ways difficult to understand. On the other hand, those who had stayed at home were also changed by their experiences during the war. Women who had managed their affairs without the help of their absent husbands, or who had worked beside men when jobs were plentiful and labor was scarce, were unwilling to begin or resume a career as a homemaker and a subordinate partner in a marriage. For these reasons not all homecomings were joyous occasions; instead they were the prelude to domestic strife that culminated in divorce.

Most servicemen were eventually able to overcome the shock of reentry into civilian life, but for some the continuing legacy of the war was bitterness and disillusionment.

LARRY MANTELL

Our ship was anchored in Tokyo Bay during the surrender. We were about a hundred yards off the port bow of the U.S.S. *Missouri*, where the official surrender took place. My parents had already been writing me that Congress had passed a bill establishing benefits to returning veterans. They were both very anxious to see me come back and go to school.

Before the war I had had no plans whatsoever to go to college. Financially, it was just out of the question. But the GI Bill changed everything. As a kid I had worked selling Cokes in the Coliseum and had always rooted for UCLA athletic teams, so I told my dad to find out what he could about UCLA. My high-school grades weren't good enough for me to be accepted, though, so my dad said, "Go to USC. It doesn't cost you anything." So when I returned to the States in October of 1945 I began preparing my application and establishing my transcripts for the University of Southern California.

When I left home I was a seventeen-year-old boy, and since then I had been alongside people who had had their heads blown off. The first time we got hit I was on the bridge of the ship, and a man's arm was blown off. You go

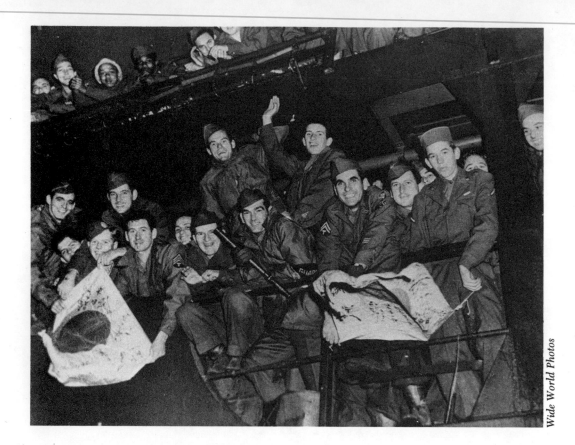

through some of those things and you wonder what are you going to be like. But when the war was over we knew that it had all been worthwhile because we had won. There was a lot of exuberance—like the excitement of marching in a Navy Day parade in New Orleans. As returning heroes, we were treated with tremendous generosity. While I stayed in New Orleans I never paid for a meal or a glass of beer or anything there.

I remember coming home and seeing a few of my friends who, for various reasons, didn't go into the service, or those who remained stateside and never had the experiences I did. I looked at them as a little less than me: You guys were fat cats staying here, making out with all the women, having all the fun, and you made money. Well, I felt I was better than they were. When the war ended and it was time to become a hero, the guys who had all the battle scars and had been through all this mess were the ones who seemed to get the most respect.

A good example of this is what happened when I went to buy a car. They didn't manufacture cars during the war years, and when the first ones came out in 1946 the lists were huge. When

I got home I really wanted a car, though, so my dad suggested we offer the dealer a little extra money. I was about thirtieth down on the list and the car dealer was really offended by Dad's offer, but he elevated me way up the list because I was a veteran and had been overseas and helped keep this country safe. Within a week, I had a 1946 two-door black Ford and it cost me nine hundred dollars. People in shops had such respect for us. Your whole self-esteem was elevated.

And as a result of the GI Bill, ten days after I got out of the service I started as a freshman at USC. Almost everything important that happened to me later came from attending college there. I met my wife, my closest friends, my accountant, my attorney, my business partners. It was the war and going into the service, a coincidence of living, that absolutely changed my life. I don't know what I would have been if it hadn't been for that.

DON CONDREN

I got out of the service in the late fall of 1945 and returned to Amarillo. After I graduated from high school I had gone to junior college for about a year and worked as a drugstore clerk until I was drafted. I had no idea what to study at junior college, though, or what to do for a living.

Being in the service had improved my expectations because all of a sudden I had the GI Bill, and I needed it. I could go to college and it would be paid for.

I read a number of articles in books and magazines that said we were becoming an increasingly technological society, that there was going to be a lot of opportunity for engineers. So I took engineering courses at the junior college in Amarillo; then I transferred to the University of Colorado, where I completed my degree. While at the University of Colorado I married, and after I graduated, my wife and I bought

our first home on a GI loan. It cost ten thousand dollars. Sometimes I tell my kids I never even had a room of my own until after I was married.

I considered the GI Bill a good piece of fortune, but I didn't consider it charity. World War II was a popular war, so we all came home heroes. The people around us looked upon us with approval. They thought we deserved the GI Bill and were happy for us to have it.

I'm not sure whether I could ever have gone to college without the GI Bill. I doubt if I would have moved away from the Texas Panhandle. The GI Bill had a major impact on the country. It set a whole new standard of improved education for a large number of people, a whole new standard of improved housing. A college graduate has higher expectations, and he finds ways to realize those expectations, or tries to. I think the GI Bill gave the whole country an upward boost economically and in every other way—at least in the late forties and early fifties.

ELLIOT JOHNSON

When the war was finally over, and we got our orders to go home, we were all very excited and eager to get out. The Army had to have one more parade, though. We all had to get into our uniforms and line up for a dismissal-and-separation-from-service parade. When it was over, we all threw our hats in the air and screamed and yelled and cheered, because we didn't want to do that *ever* again. And I recall very well one of the captains standing and looking at us without cheering. "You guys are anxious to get home and put this all behind you," he said. "But you don't understand how big a part of your life this has been. You'll put it all behind you for about ten years, and then someday you'll hear a marching band. You'll pick up the beat and it will all come back to you and you'll be right back here on the parade ground marching again." And he was right.

I have several close friends who were in the military, and all of us still feel today that we would not take any amount of money for the experience we had. But we still feel that the guys who managed to stay at home came out ahead. I felt then, and still do, a sharp resentment for those men who were physically fit and able to go but by one means or another avoided going. When I came back, after being gone for four years, they were not only married, but they had purchased their homes, very nice homes. They had made a lot of money, they had started their families, and I was just starting at the beginning and I resented that greatly. If anything, that feeling is even stronger today.

THOMAS A. SCOTT

My kid brother had joined the Army when he was sixteen. He was with the show troops down in Fort Myer, Virginia, the Sixteenth Field Artillery. When his tour of duty ran out in 1939 there was practically no work around. We hadn't gotten into the war effort yet, so I told him that if I were him I'd go see the world. The result was he went for the Philippines and was with the Fifty-eighth Bombardment Squadron at Clark Field, Manila, when the Japs hit. And, of course, he was on Bataan, and he was a prisoner of war for three and a half years. During that time all we heard from him was three little postcards saying "I am well."

One night four of us, all Port Security Force volunteers, were having dinner with our wives down at the Ben Franklin Hotel and I got a telephone call from my home. My in-laws were baby-sitting and they said, "Call Operator So-and-so in San Francisco." So I called the operator and here was Norman. He had just gotten back from Japan, from the prison camp. Christ, I was so happy I bought everybody in the Ben Franklin Hotel a drink. Then we didn't see him for another ten months after that because he weighed ninety-six pounds when he came out, so they had to rebuild him.

That was one of my prime interests in the war, why I became active in so many civilian-defense activities, to bring that kid home. I sent him over. I had to bring him back. Mission accomplished.

JAMES COVERT

When my father and brother came home from the war, they weren't as happy as I thought they should have been. There wasn't the kind of joy I expected. They were older, obviously, in years, but they were also older in the way they acted, quieter.

My father was a medical man on Guadalcanal. One of the few stories he would ever tell was an incident when they were being strafed. A GI panicked and wouldn't move, and my father went out and grabbed him, trying to save his life, and threw him in a foxhole. Just after he turned around and ran away, a bomb landed in the foxhole and killed the GI. My father felt he was responsible. A lot of people brought home experiences like that. "I shouldn't have done this; I shouldn't have done that." After the war they didn't want to talk about it, and it was hard for them to resolve that guilt.

My brother was nine years older than I, and I looked up to him. He was a soldier and I idolized him. When he came home I expected him to be joyful and happy and successful, and he was sad; he was hurt. Things had changed.

He was in the air force and was captured on Iwo Jima. The Japanese were shooting the prisoners, and he decided that as long as they were being shot he might as well be shot running away. So he ran and escaped in a miraculous fashion. He came home and never really told us this. It sort of came out in little dribbles after the war. Most of the soldiers didn't want to talk about their exploits. I was very interested in having them tell me their war stories, all the exciting action, the blood and gore. As a young boy that was the exciting thing. It was like a John Wayne movie, or seeing William Bendix in *Guadalcanal Diary*. That was the part I wanted to hear, but they didn't want to share that. They kept it all inside.

They were the winners, the victors; they had fought the war bravely, yet they were disillusioned. Those who had some kind of combat experience felt that they had been out there on the front lines, had made great sacrifices, then coming back they found there were not enough houses, and the jobs weren't as plentiful as they thought. So a period of disenchantment set in.

I remember my brother saying one time that the war wasn't over. He assumed that he would be called back in to fight the Soviet Union. He and his friends were carrying a lot of feelings that I was not able to understand as a thirteen-year-old. At that age I could not really comprehend the kind of experiences he had endured in the war.

FRANCES VEEDER

When the war was over we came back to Los Angeles and started looking for a place to live. Living with my husband's mother didn't work out too well. Our baby daughter cried all one night, and my mother-in-law found a place for us to live the next day.

Then my husband had to look for a job, and he was competing, literally, with thousands of other young veterans. I remember he tried on his civvy clothes that he had worn four and a half or five years ago, and we laughed until we cried. Nothing fit, and everything looked funny. Styles had changed, so he had no clothes and he had to buy some. We had to get a car, so we were up a creek, with very little money.

They say some of the GI's came out with a lot of money, but we didn't know many of them. My husband was a first lieutenant when he got out, and he continued in the reserve for a while, but then he dropped it; there didn't seem to be any point to it anymore.

There were so many GI's coming out to California to find a job. It was a very anxious time, after the war. At least during the war you had a real sense of purpose in what you were doing. But after the war that purpose was gone.

SYBIL LEWIS

A few months after V-J Day I received word that my husband was coming home, that he was going to be discharged in Cincinnati, Ohio. I got my bags packed as quickly as possible and I took off on the train. I was fearful

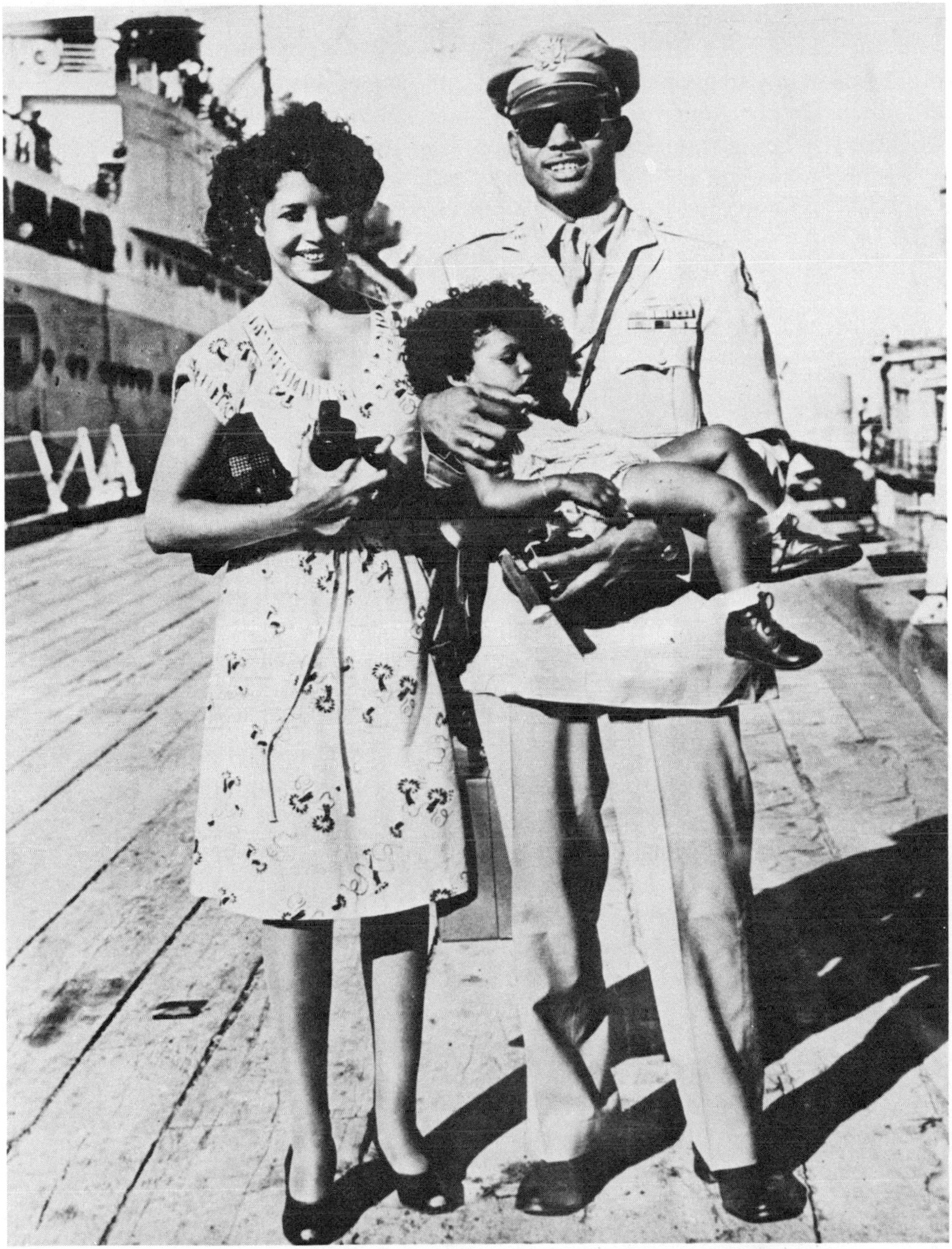

Culver Pictures, Inc.

because I had the experience of knowing and hearing that some of the fellows did not tell their wives that they had one arm missing or one leg missing. I was happy to go, and yet I wondered what it was going to be like and what he was going to look like. I had gained some weight—as a matter of fact, I was quite overweight at the time—and I was thinking about that. But what a reunion it was. My husband looked great, like he had never missed a meal, and I certainly hadn't missed too many meals. And immediately we began to make plans to return to Oklahoma to finish our education, which we did. We both enrolled in school, and it's happy times again.

MARJORIE CARTWRIGHT

When the war was over my husband was one of the first men discharged from the Navy, but all the plans we had made for the future, all of them were dashed. We didn't go back to West Virginia, we didn't build the brick house we had dreamed of, and we never had any children.

When my husband returned from the Navy, he was unable to adjust to civilian life. He couldn't cope. When he joined the service, he was like most young men, a happy-go-lucky person. He came out very disillusioned, very bitter. The doctors said he had gone through too much trauma.

The ship which he was on was involved in many of the major battles of the war. It was hit during the Battle of Guadalcanal, and he was wounded and lay helpless in the water hours before being rescued. When he came home he had terrible nightmares. It made it difficult for him to go to sleep at night. He said, "Every time I close my eyes I see my buddies being killed around me." He had one horrifying experience when one of his best friends had his head blown off right in front of him and fell into his arms.

The navy doctors tried to help him, but he started drinking heavily. He drank to forget. Looking back, I was very young and I couldn't cope, either, because I couldn't understand his problems. I've heard that from many servicemen today. When my nephew returned from Vietnam he said, "My wife doesn't understand my problems."

I think most of the men at that time were more emotionally inhibited than they are now. Men were taught to be brave and tough and not to complain or cry. Don't show emotion. Don't let your feelings out. You have to be big and strong. Men in those days could not confide how they felt, expecially after all those years of military training where they were taught to do things automatically and ignore their feelings.

My husband couldn't deal with his feelings, so he sat around and drank and brooded. The men rehashed their

Black Star/Arthur Schatz

Homecoming • 227

war experiences to each other, of course, but he felt he couldn't talk to me, that I wouldn't understand, and I don't think I could have, for I hadn't been through what he had.

The navy doctors thought that the best thing for him was to go into a military hospital for intensive treatment, probably for six months or a year, but he refused. We stayed together for seven years after the war, but things got worse and worse, so finally we divorced. I didn't know what else I could do. Staying with him wasn't helping him or changing him. I realized that I had to do something for myself, because I couldn't do anything to save my husband.

DELLIE HAHNE

When the war was over, my husband wanted to be released from the Army immediately, so he faked a psychiatric illness and got a medical discharge in two months. Then our brave new life started, which was sheer hell from the beginning.

During the war we all had a common bond. The idea was to live through the war years, get back with our husbands, have kids and raise a family. Get the war over with and get back to what we thought would be normal living.

I remember during the war reading in *Good Housekeeping*, in the makeup pages, that a woman did more than put lipstick on: she painted a brave mouth to show the world that her courage was equal to that of her man on the firing line; but after the war she was supposed to let her man assume the role of leadership which he was born to, and she went back to the house. And I swallowed it, hook, line and sinker.

My favorite daydream was that we were living in a three-bedroom house in the suburbs and I got up at seven o'clock every morning and fixed my husband's breakfast, and in my head I had a schedule of keeping the house. I'd do my ironing at eleven-thirty, and I would scrub the kitchen floor at two in the afternoon, and at the end of the day dinner would be on the table and I would be changed into a lovely cocktail dress and meet my husband at the door with martinis. I would be the hausfrau in the best sense of the word, the one who held the home together and created a family for a fine strong America. I swallowed this garbage right down the line.

One of the things that made me change was that the magazine didn't give me the man to meet at the door. I got a drunk and a gambler and a guy who loved to show me the lipstick on his handkerchiefs—and it wasn't my lipstick. So I thought, How in the hell am I going to be an American housewife if I don't have the guy?

Also I was not the same person I had been when I married him. I realized that I had grown. I could take care of

BACK HOME FOR KEEPS

The great day's coming! You'll be in his arms, in his heart, in his home. You'll laugh, you'll love, you'll live . . . when he's back home for keeps.

Back home for keeps, too, very soon we hope, you'll find America's favorite silverware . . . the Community that brides have been telling themselves they'll have when the war is won. You'll see it at your jeweler's . . . each pattern in the finest silverware tradition (if it's Community, it's *correct!*). Each fork, each spoon, is overlaid with an extra layer of solid silver at hard-wear points. Picture them on your table, your table-for-two! Wait for *lifetime* Community . . . it's the silverware you'll want *for keeps.*

Community

THE FINEST SILVERPLATE

*Coronation

If it's Community. *it's correct*

FREE! *If you'd like a full color reproduction of this painting, without advertising, write* COMMUNITY. *Dept. M-6, Oneida, N. Y.*

®REG. U. S. PAT. OFF.   COPYRIGHT 1945. ONEIDA LTD.

SPEED THE DAY ★ **BUY WAR BONDS!**

myself. I did not need to go from my father's house to my husband's house. My husband did not care for my independence. He had left a shrinking violet and come home to a very strong oak tree. This did not make him very happy. I had a friend who was at the University of Southern California in the psychology department, and she gave me a long lecture. She said I had to let my husband feel as though he were still the boss. He was the leader, the strong man, and if I wanted to keep a happy marriage I must defer to him.

But my husband was a gambler, and an alcoholic, and I realized that I could not live with him. I told him, "Unless you can change, I do not need you. I would like to live with you, but I do not have to, because I have a teaching credential, I can go out and make a living." This came as a jolt to him, but it didn't change him. He was a compulsive gambler, and I don't think he was able to stop, so finally I left him. It was not an overnight decision. I had

gone ahead and fulfilled the American dream. I had tried it for seven years. I had two children. But I knew there were options open to me that I had never realized were open to me before, and the war had brought this change about in me.

I saw the same thing happening to friends of mine—a new wave of independence. I think the seeds of my liberation and many other women's started with the war. The first intimation I had that it was taking place came when I was invited to a friend's house for Sunday dinner and I heard his mother and grandmother talk about which drill would bite into a piece of metal at the factory. One said, "I always use such and such with a number two." My God, this was Sunday dinner in Middle America, and to hear, instead of a discussion of the church service, a conversation about how to sharpen tools—it was a marvelous thing. I remember thinking that these women would never again be the same.

SHIRLEY HACKETT

When our husbands returned we were deliriously happy they had come home and in one piece. Not all of them did. But you were torn, because you were so used to living an independent life and no one was there to say "You do it this way." The moment your husband stepped in the door, though, all that changed. That was what happened to me.

When my husband returned to the States, I didn't know exactly what day he would be arriving home. I was anxious about his coming back, because I had supported myself and taken care of myself while he was away. I thought, He doesn't know how much I've changed. I can't be the girl he married, because I'm not that way anymore. So I invited this older woman I knew to come over and talk. She was very smart and down to earth, and I felt I could listen to her. Unfortunately my husband arrived the very night she had come over to talk. She left immediately, of course, but as soon as she'd gone the first question my husband asked was, "Why did you ask her to be here?" That set me off. I felt guilty immediately and didn't really tell him the truth, that I was just frightened. I didn't know how to act. From then on, I decided, in order to get along with this man, I had to step back and bury my feelings, because I didn't want to cause any antagonism. I was so grateful that he was back that I wanted to please him and do what he wanted me to do.

I remember, though, that immediately we began having discussions about handling the checkbook. I was paying the bills and he informed me right away that that wasn't woman's work, that he would do it. "I'm home now," he would say. I can remember that expression being repeated the first few weeks. "Why do you want to do that? I'm back!" It infuriated me because I had been balancing the checkbook for four years,

and all of a sudden I didn't know how to do anything. I tried a few times to talk with him, but he seemed to feel that I was insulting him, that I was not trusting him to be a provider and make a home for us. So I dropped the subject.

Perhaps if women had spoken up more then we would have avoided many divorces that started happening in the fifties. In my own circle I can't remember one couple that's still married. But all of us went right back into the syndrome with which we were brought up—the quiet wife. The man's the boss, and you do what he says, even though you've been on your own for several years. I remember changing tires on cars, taking care of the motor myself, yet he treated me as if I were insane to think that I could do these things. I think back now and ask myself why I didn't speak up, why I didn't say, "I want to do my share. I want to have a real partnership." But I didn't. I reverted to the role of housewife and mother until several years later when I started asserting myself and had trouble in my marriage.

BARBARA DE NIKE

I think that the war changed all of us, particularly those in my age group. After the war was over I wanted to block it out. I didn't want to see war movies. I didn't want to read books about the war. I felt that it was something I just wanted to put behind me and forget

about. I wanted to get back to as normal a family life as I could.

When my husband came back from the Navy, he had a difficult time adjusting to our daughter and realizing that she was a person and part of our family. She was fifteen months old when we started living together again, and it became clear to me how much of her early development he had missed, and the effect that it had on him. When my son was a little baby he was extremely interested in every phase of his development. Of course he missed all that with her. She was at the stage where she was trying desperately to get her spoon from the cereal dish to her mouth, and landing it on her ear. To me this was progress, because she could hold a spoon and she could make a reasonable attempt to use it. But he got very impatient with her over little things like that, and I realized how much he had missed.

When my husband returned, he had a sense of having taken part in a big adventure, which, of course, I didn't share. I think that it was very difficult for him to come back and try to take on the responsibilities of a family and the everyday problems of living. Also he did not go back to the job that he'd had before the war, but tried several jobs before he found something that was suitable. So it was still a very unsettling time for us.

We both found it difficult trying to decide what to do with our lives. I think my husband really had lost a sense of direction and a sense of anything like planning a career. It was quite a while before he really got that back. It took us several years actually before we began to feel as if we had control of our lives again.

GEORGE PEABODY

I had been very active before my injury. I especially liked to ice-skate and hike, and when I was wounded I made the statement that if I lost one of my legs I'd kill myself. That's how important walking was to me. Though I did lose the use of the muscles of my right leg, I'm still walking. That's because of a lot of skilled surgery and determination. But being crippled required me to make a difficult psychological adjustment.

After I was wounded I was in the sick-bay tent on the beachhead at Iwo Jima, then in the sick bay of an attack cargo ship, where I was immobilized in a body cast from toes to shoulders and taken to Guam. From Guam, we flew to the Johnson Islands, and then to Hawaii. I was at the Aiea Heights Hospital of Hawaii, in traction, for about twelve weeks. Once again immobilized in a body cast, I was flown to the Oak Knoll Hospital in Oakland, where my wife came to visit me. That was the beginning of the improvement in my self-image. The impact of her joy at seeing me and my joy at seeing her overcame the feelings of fear that I had about being crippled. Whatever fear I had was washed away with a tremendous flow of gratitude in seeing my wife again and seeing her looking at me, seeing she was glad to see me, too.

From there I was taken to the San

Diego Veterans Administration Hospital, and relatives were coming from everywhere to visit me. No one was shocked, nobody was horrified—even though I was down to ninety-seven pounds. They were just glad to see me and happy to know that I was back and alive. Earlier, I had been reported as missing in action, which had scared the family pretty badly for a while.

After I came home from the hospital an incident occurred which proved to me that I still was emotionally disturbed by my injury, that my self-esteem had been badly affected. I had been on crutches for a considerable period of time, making visits back and forth from the hospital to home. My wife would come to Long Beach to get me and bring me home so our two kids and I could get acquainted after my being gone so long. Really I was an intruder in the house, that's what it amounted to, and not a very fun intruder either. Well, on one occasion we had to go and get some gasoline while I was on crutches. We pulled into a gas station which was near the house, and the young fellow who was the service attendant called my wife by her first name. And there I was crippled and on crutches. I got out of the car with every intention of beating him to death with my crutches because he called my wife Pat instead of Mrs. Peabody.

So, my being crippled was getting under my skin, but it was a difficult experience for her to have to go through, too. Somehow I managed not to strike the fellow and got back into the car again. I really was ashamed of myself; but I was learning about morale and discomfort and things that I'd never given much thought to before.

When I finally did come home to stay, the readjustment was difficult for all of us. I came home very much the "sergeant" in the Marine Corps. Everybody had to do everything I said and do it now, not just for convenience but because it was supposed to be done now, that's what had been expected of me for two years. You did what you were told, because you were a United States marine; that went for your wife and your children too. It was a very uncomfortable situation for my family, having this marine intruder come into the house. And then, being disabled, I had to be waited on quite a bit; so the combination of the do-it-now attitude and needing to be waited on was very difficult for an undisciplined young wife to swallow along with caring for our two children. And it was difficult for the children because sometimes I was unnecessarily violent with them for their age when they weren't responsive to my demands. The violence was not necessarily physical but vocal; and sudden surges of anger occasionally caused me to jerk them or act in ways toward them that a father normally wouldn't.

Fortunately, Lockheed and the laws of the land both were in agreement that anyone who came home from the armed forces was to be reestablished on his old job. And fortunately I had those five years at Lockheed in the way of seniority before I went into the Marines, which gave me a very secure position. Such security helped me provide for my family and was very important in my opinion. Not to be able to provide for my family is the most hopeless situation that ever could face me. I must be a provider.

So I applied to Lockheed for reemployment, and they said, "Come on in whenever you're ready." I went in on crutches; and they found I could continue to do work I had done prior to entering the armed forces, except I wasn't able to move around out in the factory as much as I had before. So they appointed me as tool-planning checker—in other words, an inspector of the work that other tool planners were doing; so I didn't have to leave the desk very much. This was a prestigious position for me because I was looking over other people's work, and it increased my self-esteem. Then, as time went by, I wasn't really satisfied with that. I wanted to get into the shop more, so I found myself more and more on crutches out in the shop. It wasn't very much longer before I became involved in the development of new procedures and techniques for manufacturing parts. These new techniques caused a certain amount of stir in the shop, and some members of management were interested. Pretty soon I began leading management into the shop. I was back and forth on my crutches, becoming very active again, except now it's the crutch-type athlete. Lockheed, the U.S. government, labor unions, all were supporting my ability to be progressive and productive; and my wife and family still needed me to provide for them. I didn't have any serious readjustment problems once I got back on the job.

·13·

THE LEGACY OF WORLD WAR II: IMAGE OF A NEW NATION

We came out of the war the only country that wasn't
destroyed. That put us in the number-one position in the
world. We were the most prosperous nation in the world, and
the people took advantage of it.

—Henry Fiering

When the war was over we felt really good about ourselves.
We had saved the world from an evil that was
unspeakable. . . . We were a God-sanctioned invincible holy
power, and it was our destiny to prove that we were the
children of God and that our way was the right way for the
world. . . . Good times were going to go on and on;
everything was going to get better. It was
just a wonderful happy ending.

—Laura Briggs

Although the United States was spared the massive destruction of
lives and property that occurred in the homelands of other
countries, the nation and the American people were still profoundly
changed by World War II. Most nations emerged from the war poorer
and weaker than when they entered it—their economies shattered,
their industrial plants destroyed. Among the major powers only the

236 • THE HOMEFRONT

United States—never bombed, never invaded—emerged from the war stronger than before.

A modern Rip Van Winkle who dozed off to sleep in 1939 and awoke in 1945 would hardly have believed that the six years of America's mobilization for war could have so altered the character of life in this country. In both foreign and domestic affairs, the nation witnessed the end of an old order and the beginning of a new age.

The economic and social forces generated by the nation's response to war brought the Great Depression to a resounding end, completing the recovery that the New Deal of the thirties had begun. The tremendous production achieved by industry, labor and agriculture reaffirmed people's faith in capitalism and American political and social institutions. At the same time, however, a vast array of developments in demography, social mobility, race relations, large-scale organization, the status of women, family structure, science and technology either transformed aspects of society or carried the promise of transforming change. The war years in America uprooted millions of Americans and transported them to a new age.

Wartime spending—$186 billion in federal expenditures for war production alone—brought full employment and booming prosperity to the nation. The widespread prosperity refurbished the middle class and added millions of people to its ranks. A postwar depression would have reversed these developments, but the pent-up demand of returning veterans and civilian workers, along with astute reconversion policies of the federal government, fueled a strong postwar boom. Millions eager to purchase a new home, a new car, modern appliances and other goods of the mass-production/mass-consumption society now had the means to do so. Affluence was so pervasive that most people did not see that minorities and working women had a limited share of the postwar prosperity. No one could have envisioned that the economic recovery of World War II would carry forward with only minor setbacks for forty years until the great recession of the early 1980s.

The wartime economy accelerated the prewar trend of bigness in business, labor, agriculture and government. Large corporations, awarded about eighty percent of the federal-government defense contracts, entered the postwar era with the capital, technology, production capacity and organizational skills to dominate the market at home and abroad. Labor, particularly the Congress of Industrial Organizations (CIO) that had organized unskilled workers in the nation's major industries, benefited from the labor shortages and expansion of the work force during the war. After the war, fifteen million union members effectively pursued their interests in both the economic and political arenas. The family farm remained the most common economic unit in agriculture after the war, but the high cost of land, livestock and machinery assured the continuing development of large-scale corporate farming. Finally, the federal government continued to exert a major influence over the economy despite the rapid dismantling of the mammoth wartime agencies. Big government and huge federal budgets were here to stay. The postwar economy, highly complex and interrelated with world resources and markets, was the strongest in the world.

The mobilization of people for the military and the homefront war-production effort had uprooted millions of Americans. In 1945, fifteen million Americans were living somewhere other than where they had been on December 7, 1941. People migrated from country to city, from South to North, above all from East to West. The result was an extraordinary redistribution of the population. When the war was over, many were eager to return to the familiar surroundings of their home communities; but others, attracted to the opportunities and lifestyles of a new locality, never went back to their former homes. Both groups found that something was lost and something gained in the postwar society, and disillusionment was the partner of great expectations.

The war had also altered the status of blacks and other minorities by lowering social and economic barriers to their advancement. The notable exception to this development, of course, were the Japanese Americans who were subjected to relocation and internment. Minority and civil-rights groups were proud of their wartime accomplishments and were determined to keep and expand these gains after the war. Many whites were equally determined to maintain segregation and discrimination. The most notable victories for minorities came not at the grass-roots level, but from the federal government. President Harry S. Truman led the way in 1948 by ordering the desegregation of the armed forces and a ban on discrimination in federal employment. The Supreme Court broadened the assault on second-class citizenship in 1954 by striking down the "separate but equal" doctrine, thus inaugurating the slow but measured desegregation of public schools. The civil-rights movement that emerged in the sixties was impelled in part by the frustration among blacks that the expectations raised by the war remained unfulfilled.

Women who had worked in defense industries or who had lived alone while their servicemen husbands away were another group whose expectations and self-image were altered by their wartime experiences. Many were unprepared for the abrupt change in their lives that occurred with the coming of peace. The swift closing of many war industries literally left millions of women unemployed overnight. Their efforts to continue their employment in nontraditional jobs were largely unsuccessful, although some returned to work in defense industries during the Korean War of the 1950s. Women employed ouside the home after the war usually had to settle for low wages for working on the assembly line or as cook, dishwasher, waitress or secretary. Many became full-time homemakers, with the intent of being happy wives and mothers, only later to have their marriages end in divorce, often on their initiative. No one knows how many marriages were terminated because the wife's expectation of life had been altered by her experiences of wartime, but the divorce rate skyrocketed to a historic high in 1946, setting a record that stood until the 1970s. The women who seemed to have profited most from their wartime economic independence may also have been the most determined to retain their independence after the war. Indeed, some may have passed on their liberation from an unequal union and from traditional pursuits to their daughters and granddaughters.

Finally, America's mobilization and involvement in World War II transformed the nation's foreign and defense policies. In foreign affairs, the United States embarked upon an international course of unparalleled dimension and scope. Isolationism was firmly relegated to the past. The country joined the United Nations and provided that international organization a permanent home as well. American soldiers joined in the Allied occupation of Germany and presided alone over the reconstruction of defeated Japan. Economic and military aid flowed to both Europe and Asia shortly after the war, followed by formal alliances. The breakdown of wartime cooperation with the Soviet Union gave an anti-Communist character to U.S. foreign policy, spawning the Cold War between the two countries. The Cold War in turn necessitated the buildup of the nation's armed forces, including the development of nuclear weapons and the planes and missiles to deliver them. Paradoxically, as America's military might increased, the nation's security decreased in the face of new technology and weaponry.

The many complexities and paradoxes of postwar life have encouraged Americans to look back wistfully upon the World War II years. Life seemed much simpler then, and it was. The war itself presented a contrast between good and evil that left few doubts about the righteousness of America's cause. Many of the wartime generation miss the love of country and the national unity that flourished during World War II. They remember when America's triumph over its enemies was unconditional and conclusive. They still consider those years our country's finest hour. This nostalgic view of the past, mixing reality with illusion, influences both national life and the life of individuals and becomes, in its own way, a legacy of World War II.

JAMES COVERT

My mother had a grocery store, and during the late Depression I remember so many of the people in the neighborhood would come in and receive credit. In fact, she had a little box where she kept a list of their charges. People would pay when they could, but it was always a big chore to get them to do it.

When the war started and people began to work, they actually plunked down money on the counter—hundreds of dollars, it seemed. I remember Saturday nights when my mother would count all the money and take it to the bank. I was fascinated seeing all that currency, the wads of money that would be going to the bank.

For the first time we began to have money. My mother had a great fear of a renewed depression, and she didn't trust banks anymore. She thought if they failed once they might fail again. So she would take silver dollars and put them in little packages, and we would use them for doorstops in our house. Silver dollars were better than paper money in case things got bad again. By 1945 we had a thousand dol-

lars in one box as a doorstop in our house, where five years before we were completely impoverished.

While there wasn't that much to spend the money on during the war, it still changed our lifestyle and, more important, our outlook. You sensed that prosperity was coming. You started to think you could do things. We used to go out to a restaurant now and then, where we would never do that before the war. We hardly ever went to picture shows during the Depression; now I did all the time. There was a feeling toward the end of the war that we were moving into a new age of prosperity. Affluence was already in people's minds, and there was a belief that the war would really end on a positive note. My mother saved enough money to buy a modest home. That was the first home we ever bought.

Yet other changes were also taking place. My mother had a neighborhood grocery store, but by the end of the war these Mom-and-Pop stores couldn't compete with the big supermarkets and the chain stores. People had cars and they began to go outside the neighborhood to shop. Society became larger, more impersonal. My mother actually had to leave and find a different kind of employment. For maybe ten years our life was working in a little grocery store, but by 1946 our little grocery store was gone and with it that sense of closeness we had experienced during the war.

WILLIAM PEFLEY

When I first went into the navy yard I made a dollar an hour. At the end of the war I was making two-seventy-five an hour as a progressman, which seemed like more money than I had ever heard of. I couldn't believe my good fortune.

From the minute the war broke out, I would buy a bond at payday. I felt that by saving the money through the government I wouldn't spend it, and at the same time they would have my money to use for the war effort. When the war ended I had accumulated enough to make a down payment on a home.

Without the war I feel like I'd probably be back where I started from, working a few months a year, still struggling to make a living. So the war did bring on a better life as far as I was concerned. Working in the navy yard I gained a lot of skill in production. After the war I started building houses and used all that knowledge I had learned building ships. The building industry turned out very well for me. After all the hardships of the Depression, the war completely turned my life around.

ROGER MONTGOMERY

I think that one of the important things that came out of World War II was the arrival of the working class at a new status level in this society. I don't think the people I worked with in the plant in Elyria, Ohio, realized how much their lives were about to change. Most of the people that I worked with lived in rented houses and close to slum con-

ditions. By the fifties almost everybody in that kind of social world expected that they would live in a suburban house—one that they owned themselves. The war integrated into the mainstream a whole chunk of society that had been living on the edge.

Everything that happened during the war had something to do with that transformation—the fact that Appalachian hillbillies served in the Army and that Boston slum kids worked in the war factories and made enough money to give them the down payment for a new house. It was an enormous social change, but it was for white people, not black.

HENRY FIERING

We came out of the war the only country that wasn't destroyed. That put us in the number-one position in the world. We were the most prosperous nation in the world, and the people took advantage of it.

By the end of the war labor was well entrenched. The most important segments of American industry were organized. And they were organized for good. There was nothing that could dislodge the unions from the shops. Nothing. There was no power strong enough for that. So they had to be dealt with.

Moreover, the conversion period was not as traumatic as everybody was afraid it was going to be. The companies were eager to get on peacetime production, so they did it with a minimum of layoffs and dislocations.

The workers felt they were in a good bargaining position, so they went after some more things. From that time on, we saw the kinds of modern contracts we see today: continual improvement in wages, fringe benefits like holidays, vacation, medical plans, dental plans, all sorts of things that provided more security for people.

One of the effects of this improved standard of living was to change the thinking of people. During the Depression people were radicalized. They were convinced of the need for social change, that the system as it was wasn't good enough. But with increased economic security people began to think more moderately. They developed a stake in the country. They had something they owned which they hadn't before, and the radical ideas which they had embraced during the Depression suddenly became very alien to them. Because of their new position in society, they wanted stability, not change. They had brought about just as much change as they needed at that time. They were content to leave it at that.

For myself, though, the war determined the course of my life. It confirmed my commitment to the trade-union movement. If it had not been for the war, my life might certainly have taken other turns. I might have gone back to school. I had hopes at one time of being an engineer, but during the war I didn't even think about that. Life was interesting, it was exciting, and I was in the middle of it.

WILLIAM MULCAHY

One of the major changes that the war brought about was a rise in hopes and expectations of young fellows like myself. Before the war I was running a factory for a rectifying company. I was working six full days and I took work home on Sundays, and for this I was earning twelve dollars and fifty cents a week. It was a scrape-by job with very little to look forward to.

The war allowed me to enter a whole new strata that I hadn't met before—middle management. This introduced me, and many other men, to the techniques of supervising people so that they were happy in their jobs. It also gave us an opportunity for mobility and financial improvement.

Prior to the war American industry was composed very heavily of small family-oriented and medium-sized businesses. The demand during the war for immense quantities of material, capital investment, and plant facilities changed the whole complexion of our industrial structure. The major cor-porations emerged as the driving force because they were the only ones ca-pable of gearing up to produce the incredible amount of materials that were necessary. So today, when a big job needs to be done, there is now a big company available to do it. That may be one of the prime changes that the war wrought in the economic structure of this country.

Another major impact of the war was on the electronics industry, which bur-geoned after the war. I think there were two reasons for this. First, the development of speed assembly techniques allowed us to manufacture more electronic equipment at lower cost, which allowed more people to buy them and consequently put more people to work making products like television and stereos that were unheard of in 1941. Second, we began to develop techniques for miniaturization which enabled us to make portable many of the electronic devices which were not available to the consumer before because they were just too big.

JOHN GROVE

The war changed my life quite drastically. Where I was working, at Shell, I was so beaten down that I wouldn't even call myself a scientist. I just said I was a scientific worker. I didn't think I had any ability to do anything, really.

Then, all of a sudden, I was thrown into the Manhattan District and found I had real abilities. It definitely changed my life, even though it was indeed difficult to find a job after the war when the project was ended. There just weren't that many scientific jobs available. In fact, at one point I had to start all over again completely and work myself back up. But by now I knew I had the ability. So it's conceivable that had there not been a war I would have just decayed in the job I was working in.

Of course, the war had a great deal of impact on this country too. Most of the soldiers had gone through a depression, as children or teenagers, and then they went through a war and they were further deprived. When they came back, they wanted it all. I saw this in southern California and in the Bay Area—people, veterans especially, moving out to the suburbs to find a home for twenty dollars down and pay the rest of your life, then going into debt right away trying to get everything they could: cars, refrigerators, all the good things in life. What I saw then was a materialistic attitude which I had never seen before in Americans. I could see it very strongly. After all those years of having nothing, or very little, you couldn't blame them.

SHIRLEY HACKETT

After the men came home from the war, they all seemed to have great goals in mind. They wanted to get ahead, have material things. It was very strong. I got the feeling with my own husband that he felt as if he had lost time during the war and now he had to make up for it. He was determined to succeed and devoted the better part of his life to it. It seemed to him that the more money he could make, the better off we were going to be. He seemed to forget completely about anything else. All of the men were that way. It was "How much money are you making this week, Joe? I got this deal this week. I'm getting my wife a mink coat, a diamond ring." Material things seemed to be all that counted after the war.

BARBARA DE NIKE

During the war a sense of patriotism, a sense that we're all in this together, made having to do without material things more bearable. But once the war was over, the material things became all-important. We wanted houses, we wanted new cars, we wanted refrigerators. I think the postwar boom was brought on by a reaction to all the years that you had to do without so many things. You just wanted things.

LARRY MANTELL

I am sometimes critical of my children because they don't have the same values that I do.

When I was a kid, if twice a year during the summer I got to go to a baseball game (it cost a quarter to sit in the bleachers), that was an exciting event in my life. When my son was growing up, I already owned a box at Dodger Stadium between home and first base. For my son to sit there was no big deal.

Because of the Depression and the war, we developed certain values that are hard to come by today. It's hard for us to retain and perpetuate those old values. Probably each generation could say that. It's easy to look back thirty years and say what was right and wrong.

We had less options and less decisions then. But the war brought options and affluence. That affluence has created a different lifestyle for my children, which has made it harder to maintain the old values.

DON CONDREN

There was very little mobility where I grew up in Texas. Once in a while somebody would move to another town. But I used to go down the street in Amarillo and I'd know almost everybody I'd see, even though it was a town of several thousand people. They'd all been there forever.

During the service I was in California, Texas, Florida, England. When I went to aircraft-mechanic school in Burbank I enjoyed California, and I remembered it when I was looking for a job after I graduated from the University of Colorado. North American Aviation came to Denver to interview prospective engineers, and they hired me, so my wife and I packed up and moved to Los Angeles.

There were similar changes in my hometown. A munitions plant was built there during the war and brought strangers into town. There was also an air force base that did the same. A lot of people who came to work in the munitions plant or who were stationed at the base liked what they found in Amarillo. After the war they stayed there, or they came back as I did to California.

But increased mobility has had a negative side, too. I think we suffered a great deal in terms of loss of community—in that you no longer know your neighbors that well, or care about them, and therefore you don't have those standards imposed on you by the community. Nobody's going to vandalize the community that he's part of and feels pride in and knows the people personally he's vandalizing.

I don't think loss of community is due entirely to the war, but the war accelerated things like mobility that cause it. People move to a new place, they don't have roots, they're not as-sociated with any particular thing. I remember the church we used to go to on Tuesday nights in Amarillo. It was Tuesday-night singing. People who didn't enjoy preaching and praying would still go to the singing on Tuesday nights. They'd sing religious songs, but there would be quartets and duets; it was basically a glee club. It was a community activity, and there was a lot of closeness and togetherness and the community pride that goes with it. That's not so easy to find today.

VERNON SIETMANN

After the war the farmer was definitely changed. Maybe his son had been in some foreign country or he'd been in other parts of the United States, and he brought back with him new ideas, things he had seen and things he wanted to do. I think it made a definite difference in the outlook of the farmer.

The war also made the small town and small community more a part of the world. We learned what was hap-pening elsewhere, our interests changed and we became more a part of the nation than we had in the years past.

At the same time the family farm was threatened a little bit as the commercial operations began to move in. It didn't end the family farm completely, but it did start a movement in that direction.

DON JOHNSON

One of the biggest impacts the war had was to create a much more mobile society. As a result we have people who are not tied into the community structure in the same way they were before.

They don't have the same sense of obligation to each other, or to the community. They don't feel personally responsible when they know something needs to change. This allows us, when there is a problem, to let some-body else solve it.

Somehow, as a society, we have never gone back to the prewar values of fam-ily, friends, church and community. There seems to be more of "I need to get mine; you've got yours. Or if you didn't get yours, that's your problem. Don't question my actions, I'll do what I please."

I believe all of this is a result of the dislocations of the war years and it is a problem that we, as a society, must give some attention to.

VIRGINIA RASMUSSEN

I think the war caused a definite root-lessness in our society. We would marry servicemen and follow them from one camp to another, and suddenly all of our roots were gone. We didn't have the security we had grown up with any-more. The relationships we made with others were temporary relationships. You didn't lean on them the way you did when we were children: Mom, Dad, the girl down the block.

Growing up I had all this security at home in Indiana. Then after the war, when my husband started his work in California, I was adrift. Suddenly I had nobody to turn to. He was employed all day and I was home alone with the baby. We lived in a basement because that's all we could afford, and I didn't know anybody. All of that was very un-settling for me, and I was terribly homesick. When you get yourself into that kind of emotional state, you begin to pick and find fault, which I did until I realized what was happening.

One thing that has evolved from that experience is that I have learned that I can take care of myself. I don't have to lean on any other individual any-more. It took a long, painful road to prove that to myself. But it was a mat-ter of survival. I could never have coped otherwise.

Still I miss what we had as children. One of the regrets I had when I was raising my own was that, because of the divorce, I was never able to give them that same kind of life. I used to call it "my light in the window." When we were kids in Indiana, we would drive along the street at night, and the liv-ing-room curtains of the homes would be open and you could see the whole family sitting there, playing a game to-gether, or listening to the radio and laughing. I always wanted that for my family and never completely achieved it. And I feel I've done a disservice to my children because I was not able to supply that for them. I think that over-whelms the fact that I gained inde-pendence.

GEORGE PEABODY

I think World War II destroyed the American home as we knew it prior to the war. I think it destroyed our understanding of how important self-esteem is to a child, and how a child develops the very best kind of self-esteem from having a parent at home, not merely from peer acceptance.

Before the war, I provided everything that my family needed in the way of income and sustenance. My wife provided what the home needed in the way of comfort, cleanliness, child instruction, moral support and encouragement. She had visions of what the children should grow up to be. She was "the boss" at home, and she was there running it all the time. As far as I'm concerned, being a successful wife, homemaker and mother is a more difficult career than sales, trades or management.

Since World War II, most of the women who have the capacity to be career wives, homemakers and mothers have defected to careers as breadwinners. During World War II women started taking jobs to support the war; and we're all locked into that trend. Now, man and wife both have to work as breadwinners in order to provide just the necessities, or a little comfort beyond the necessities. So we haven't a mother at home doing all the things important to the family. She is losing her skills as wife, homemaker and mother. Consequently there is a loss of sufficient personal relationships between parents and children, and the children in many families have grown up without the full self-esteem they might otherwise have had, the measure and type of self-esteem necessary to make constructive, intelligent and honest decisions.

BARBARA NOREK

Before the war there was never a divorce in our family. There just wasn't. Since the war, I have only one sister and one cousin who have stayed married. I'm from a very large family, too, and they're all marrying and divorcing, and it seems as if there isn't any end to it.

I feel that I was a casualty of the war. I lost stability at home. I lost my companionship with my father when I truly needed it. I was exposed to too much, too soon. I wasn't ready to handle the type of ego that was thrown at me with all the exposure to men. I really think it affected my life as I grew older. I never was able to handle the fact that when you get older you're not beautiful anymore, you don't have all this attention. And going through three marriages proved that.

WINONA ESPINOSA

If the war hadn't come along I would have been a homemaker. I guess I wouldn't have ever budged out of that shell. This way I got to try something different. I learned from that experience that if I really wanted to do something enough, there were ways to accomplish it.

The end of the war was a real setback for women. We all sank back into our shells. The fellows came back home and everybody made babies. Women got into this homey-type thing and just stayed at home with their families. There's nothing wrong with that. I love being a family lady. But we never thought beyond that. It was as if we'd forgotten everything we'd learned through the war years. We just stayed in the house and didn't do anything until the sixties, really. It was our children who had to open up our eyes and our minds to these possibilities again.

FRANKIE COOPER

After the war fashions changed drastically, you were supposed to become a feminine person. We laid aside our slacks, our checkered shirts, and we went in for ostrich feathers, ruffles, high-heeled shoes. All this was part of the propaganda in magazines and newspapers to put a woman back in her "rightful place" in the home. Go back now, forget all you've learned, be feminine. Go home and make your bread, raise your children. Forget you had them in a nursery and you were out there in pants.

Like a lot of women, I responded to the articles and the newspapers and the pressures from my family as well. I did what I thought was right. I went home. And I did all the things that I had been feeling guilty about not doing during the war. My husband would have been happy if I had gone back to the kind of girl I was when he married me— a little homebody there on the farm, in the kitchen, straining the milk. But I wasn't that person anymore. I tried it for three years, but it just didn't work out. All at once I took a good look at myself, and I said no. No, you're just not going to do it. You're not going back where you started from. From here on in, you're your own person; you can do anything you want to. You're the same person you were in 1942. So I thought it was time then that we looked at ourselves, but my husband was satisfied. He was content to remain on the farm, but I wasn't. We argued constantly about it and became further and further apart. Finally our marriage ended.

After my divorce I moved to Cincinnati and began to look for work. General Electric was building their big jet-engine plant in Evandale. I saw an ad in the paper, "certified welders wanted." They would not interview anyone without an application, so I mailed in an application. I received a reply asking me to come for an interview. When I met the personnel manager he said there had been a mistake. They thought I was a man, because they had assumed my name was Frank. I said, "What about my qualifications?" And he agreed that I was highly qualified. I said, "Well, we're going to talk about this, because I really need a job." Finally he said, "I will go out in the plant and check with the men I've already hired. If you are acceptable to them and if they will work with you, I'll hire you." When he came back he said, "I asked the men and the men said they would rather not work with a woman." I said, "Is it your policy to check with employees on someone you want to hire? Is this your policy?"

I continued to hunt for a job, but I could not find one where I could use the skills I had acquired. Finally, after three months of looking, I ended up washing dishes in a kitchen to feed my daughter. In a greasy little restaurant, a horrible place. I was making about three dollars a day. At the shipyards I was making a dollar-fifty an hour.

It took a while, but eventually I got a job setting fuses for ninety-millimeter guns. Still it was a woman's job at woman's pay. Then I found another job at RCA assembling television tubes. I'd become interested in unions during the war, and I ran for president of the union at RCA, and I won. I've been involved in labor work ever since. I know that what happened to me during the war gave me the confidence to pursue this, to keep looking for a better way of life. Being far away from home, having to learn a lot of different things, different ways than I was used to, I just had to learn to depend on me. My experiences during World War II changed my whole life. I know it's terrible to say that about a war, but I can't remember anything about it that wasn't good for me.

RACHEL WRAY

During the war I think the values of many women changed. They became more independent and self sufficient. When I was growing up my mother was always home with the children and my father came home when he got ready. He did what he wanted to do; my mother didn't. In my mind I said then, That's not the life for me. I've always worked, and in raising my two daughters I felt that they had to have a career. I felt that getting married just wasn't enough.

I suppose that's why they both are so independent. My older daughter makes her husband feel inadequate because she changes her own oil in her car. She can change the spark plugs if she decides to. My younger daughter has gone so far as to change the doors on her refrigerator to make it right- or left-handed. They both say they don't know any other way, because that's the way their mother was. I think that's the result of what I learned in the war.

SYBIL LEWIS

Had it not been for the war I don't think blacks would be in the position they are now. The war and defense work gave black people opportunities to work on jobs they never had before. It gave them opportunity to do things they had never experienced before. They made more money and began to experience a different lifestyle. Their expectations changed. Money will do that. You could sense that they would no longer be satisfied with the way they had lived before.

When I got my first paycheck, I'd never seen that much money before, not even in the bank, because I'd never been in a bank too much. I don't recall exactly what it was in the aircraft plant, but it was more than three hundred dollars a month, and later, in the ship-yard, it was even more. To be able to buy what you wanted, your clothing and shoes, all this was just a different way of life.

When I first got my paycheck I bought everything that I thought I had ever wanted, but in particular I bought shoes. I wore a large size as a child and I could never be fitted properly for shoes. The woman I worked for in Oklahoma wore beautiful shoes, and I remember thinking then that when I got a chance to make some money I was going to buy shoes first. So my first paycheck I bought mostly shoes. And it felt very good. To be honest, today I still buy more shoes than anything else.

Other experiences I had during the war were important, too, like having to rivet with a white farm girl from Arkansas and both of us having to relate to each other in ways that we had never experienced before. Although we had our differences we both learned to work together and talk together. We learned that despite our hostilities and resentments we could open up to each other and get along. As I look back now I feel that experience was meaningful to me and meaningful to her. She learned that Negroes were people, too, and I saw her as a person also, and we both gained from it.

I also saw in California that black women were working in many jobs that I had never seen in the South, not only defense work but working in nice hotels as waitresses, working in the post office, doing clerical work. So I realized there were a lot of things women could do besides housework. I saw black people accepted in the school system and accepted in other kinds of jobs that they had not been accepted in before. It's too bad it took a war to motivate people to move here to want to make more of their lives, but if it had not been for the war offering better jobs and opportunities, some people would have never left the South. They would have had nothing to move for.

After I graduated from college I returned to California and started applying for civil-service jobs. Had it not been for the war I probably would have ended up a schoolteacher in rural Oklahoma, but the impact of the war changed my life, gave me an opportunity to leave my small town and discover there was another way of life. It financed my college education and opened my eyes to opportunities I could take advantage of when the war was over.

ALEXANDER J. ALLEN

I'd say World War II was a watershed for blacks. Up to that point the doors to industrial and economic opportunity were largely closed. Under the pressures of the war, the pressures of governmental policy, the pressures of world opinion, the pressures of blacks themselves and their allies, all of this began to change. You get a new beginning in a sense. After World War II people began to relate to each other in a different way.

Prior to the war it was believed, particularly by whites, that it was impossible for blacks and whites to work together, or to live in the same neighborhoods, or to use the same public facilities. We used to have an expression during that period—"You learn what you live." Preaching, teaching, is not too effective, but if you actually live it, then you learn. So, our objective was not to get a chance to preach at people so much as it was to influence policy—policy decisions that resulted in people being thrown together on a peer basis, so that out of that experience their attitudes would change, and they usually did.

After the war was over, then some of the earlier divisions in our society began to be felt again. The old rules for minorities began to apply: last hired, first fired. That meant a disproportionate loss for blacks. But there certainly were some lasting benefits that came out of the experience. The war forced the federal government to take a stronger position with reference to discrimination, and things began to change as a result. There was also a tremendous attitudinal change that grew out of the war. There had been a new experience for blacks, and many weren't willing to go back to the way it was before. That laid the basis for change later on. I think that *Brown v. Board of Education*, the 1954 Supreme Court case that began the dismantling of the segregated school system in this country, was a logical and perhaps predictable outgrowth of the trends started during the war.

JOHN ABBOTT

I would say that being a conscientious objector during World War II was probably the most formative experience of my life. I don't think the war changed who I was, but it accentuated certain of my characteristics, particularly my willingness to fight for my beliefs. Even though I was pretty naïve and inexperienced at the start, I found that I had principles, that I was capable, and that after I'd had a few strokes with the bat I could do pretty well for myself.

After the war I continued to fight for what I believed. Because I was a conscientious objector and had served more than a year and a day in jail, I was classified a felon. And being a felon meant that I had automatically lost my civil rights. I couldn't vote, I couldn't serve on a jury, and I didn't have the right to live where I wanted without registering with the police. Even though I had served my time, paid the penalty for violating the federal law, I was still considered a felon. And I thought, Why should I pay taxes in a country where I can't vote for my own representative? What kind of citizen was I? Why should I be deprived of my civil rights for refusing to kill people?

So, with the help of the American Civil Liberties Union, I went to the Supreme Court twice and the Superior Court once and won landmark decisions which changed the rights of felons, not just conscientious objectors, but all felons so they could be first-class citizens again and regain their civil rights. All that grew out of my experiences in the war.

For myself, and that's the only person I can talk for, I can say that the stand I took against war was right for me. It was a lot of hell, but I would do it again today.

ROGER MONTGOMERY

One change that certainly came out of the war was the way in which we viewed ourselves as a country. America was now incredibly powerful, the most powerful country in the world. The world was now the central stage on which we, as a collectivity, played out our lives.

It seems to me that the world I grew up in was very much circumscribed. The universe we lived in was the U.S., from the Atlantic to the Pacific, and that was our economy. Before the war most of life was lived in reference to what was in the U.S. After the war we lived in the context of an international political economy.

For me, personally, my experience during the war had a tremendous impact on shaping the way I think about the world. The steelworkers' union with which I was involved was a Communist-dominated local. My contact with the members left me with an openness and a sympathy and some understanding of Marxism. I would say that my general way of looking at the world is Marxist in major dimensions. And I think it was the exposure at that time

that got me started. I learned a little bit of sidewalk, or union-level, Marxism, and that's been a kind of base for my thinking about things ever since.

The war and the homefront atmosphere made that possible. I don't think I ever would have felt I could maintain my connections with my moderately liberal family and the world I'd been brought up with and spend hours and hours learning about Marxism, except for that popular-front, war-induced sense that they were part of my world. During most of my life, we've had the sense that there are two world views, the American world view and then the Marxist world view, which is very foreign.

In the fifties Marxists went underground. If they existed they didn't talk to you. But during the war it was no threat to talk to a Marxist.

I always depended on the easy acquaintance with Marxist ideas that I got in that period to be open to thinking about things. Marxism is both a politics and a way of thinking. As I grow older I think I'm more on that side than I was forty years ago.

ADELE ERENBERG

World War II made me love this country, because there was a spirit of love in America which has never been here since and probably will never be back in my lifetime. I had a respect for my country and fellow citizens, and for my leaders. I thought the country had great promise, and I was really happy that I was living in a period of history when I could play a part.

The quality of life during that time was probably higher than it has ever been. People ate better then under rationing than they do now on food stamps. It is no great sacrifice to eat a piece of bread without butter. American people are so spoiled about their standard of living. We don't even know what sacrifice is. Nobody went into a gas station and hit each other with fists when we had gas rationing the way they did a few years ago when we had a gas shortage. We didn't have the violence in everyday life that we have now. People were future-oriented. You had a sense of purpose, a sense of moving with the country. People don't have that hope today.

I feel about that period a little like you feel about your first love when you lose it. No matter how many loves you have afterwards, they're never quite the same. That's how I feel about this country during World War II. I don't know if we could ever recapture that spirit.

LAURA BRIGGS

The war made many changes in our town. I think the most important is that aspirations changed. People suddenly had the idea "Hey, I can reach that. I can have that. I can do that. I could even send my kid to college if I wanted to." These were things very few townspeople had thought about before.

The war made us aware that there was a larger world outside of Jerome, Idaho. Of course, for me the turning point was when we were in California those few months. I knew that someday I would return and change the lifestyle my family had lived for generations, change it for myself and for my children. But I think everyone had more hope, more expectations for a better quality of life.

When the war was over we felt really good about ourselves. We had saved the world from an evil that was unspeakable. We had something no other country had. We were a God-sanctioned invincible holy power, and it was our destiny to prove that we were the children of God and that our way was the right way for the world. I think all of us felt that way. We were so innocent and naïve. We believed everything good about ourselves. Life was going to be glorious from now on, because we deserved it. Good times were going to go on and on; everything was going to get better. It was just a wonderful happy ending.